# Narrative in the Age of the Genome

Explorations in Science and Literature

Series Editors:

John Holmes, Anton Kirchhofer and Janine Rogers

Explorations in Science and Literature considers the significance of literature from within a scientific worldview and brings the insights of literary study to bear on current science. Ranging across scientific disciplines, literary concepts, and different times and cultures, volumes in this series will show how literature and science, including medicine and technology, are intricately connected, and how they are indispensable to one another in building up our understanding of ourselves and of the world around us.

**Published titles**

*Biofictions*, Josie Gill
*Imagining Solar Energy*, Greg Lynall
*The Diseased Brain and the Failing Mind*, Martina Zimmermann

**Forthcoming titles**

*Fictions of Prevention*, Benedetta Liorsi

# Narrative in the Age of the Genome

*Genetic Worlds*

Lara Choksey

BLOOMSBURY ACADEMIC
LONDON • NEW YORK • OXFORD • NEW DELHI • SYDNEY

BLOOMSBURY ACADEMIC
Bloomsbury Publishing Plc
50 Bedford Square, London, WC1B 3DP, UK
1385 Broadway, New York, NY 10018, USA
29 Earlsfort Terrace, Dublin 2, Ireland

BLOOMSBURY, BLOOMSBURY ACADEMIC and the Diana logo are
trademarks of Bloomsbury Publishing Plc

First published in Great Britain 2021
This paperback edition published in 2022

Copyright © Lara Choksey, 2021

Lara Choksey has asserted her right under the Copyright, Designs and
Patents Act, 1988, to be identified as Author of this work.

For legal purposes the Acknowledgements on p. ix–xi constitute an extension of
this copyright page.

Cover design by Namkwan Cho
Cover image: 'Crawling Around' by Alex Zwetsloot

This work is published open access subject to a Creative Commons Attribution-Non Commercial-No Derivatives 3.0 licence (CC BY-NC-ND 3.0, https://creativecommons.org/licenses/by-nc-nd/3.0/). You may re-use, distribute, and reproduce this work in any medium for non-commercial purposes, provided you give attribution to the copyright holder and the publisher and provide a link to the Creative Commons licence.

Bloomsbury Publishing Plc does not have any control over, or responsibility for, any third-party websites referred to or in this book. All internet addresses given in this book were correct at the time of going to press. The author and publisher regret any inconvenience caused if addresses have changed or sites have ceased to exist, but can accept no responsibility for any such changes.

A catalogue record for this book is available from the British Library.

A catalog record for this book is available from the Library of Congress.

ISBN: HB: 978-1-3501-0254-5
PB: 978-1-3502-1384-5
ePDF: 978-1-3501-0255-2
eBook: 978-1-3501-0256-9

Series: Explorations in Science and Literature

Typeset by Deanta Global Publishing Services, Chennai, India

To find out more about our authors and books visit www.bloomsbury.com and
sign up for our newsletters.

*For Yannik, Soli, and Llus.*

# Contents

| | | |
|---|---|---|
| Acknowledgements | | ix |
| Series preface | | xii |
| Introduction | | 1 |
| 1 | Deindustrialization and the selfish gene | 21 |
| | Gene and strike | 26 |
| | Overpopulation and whiteness in *The Memoirs of a Survivor* | 34 |
| | Brackets and choice: Samuel Delany's *Trouble on Triton* | 41 |
| 2 | Cultivating dreamworlds | 55 |
| | Mutual aid | 57 |
| | Cultivating humans | 60 |
| | The Fifth Problem in *Roadside Picnic* | 63 |
| | Genogeography and Kir Bulychev's 'Another's Memory' | 74 |
| 3 | Memoir and the laboratory | 83 |
| | Metaphors of the Human Genome Project | 89 |
| | Welfare, profit and ethics: The Vitruvian Man | 93 |
| | *Never Let Me Go* and the end of development | 99 |
| | *Gattaca* and algorithmic governmentality | 111 |
| 4 | Speculative ancestry | 119 |
| | Ancestry-making | 122 |
| | Genre, genetics and genealogy | 125 |
| | Henrietta Lacks and stolen flesh | 127 |
| | Reparation, romance and kinlessness | 130 |
| | Leaving: Saidiya Hartman's *Lose Your Mother* | 135 |
| | Staying: Yaa Gyasi's *Homegoing* | 143 |
| 5 | Toxic infrastructure | 149 |
| | Chernobyl and the postgenomic condition | 152 |
| | Adaptation, improvisation and epigenetics | 156 |

Mutation and fragmentation in *Chernobyl Prayer* 162
　　Transitional characterization in the Southern Reach trilogy 172

Disappearance, community, characterization, genre and scale 189

Works cited 195
Index 206

# Acknowledgements

These acknowledgements begin chronologically, but – in cahoots with the ramshackle flights of time that this book attempts to describe – quickly revert to paroxysms of memory. I'll start by thanking the Arts and Humanities Research Council, the Wolfson Foundation, Warwick University's Institute of Advanced Study and the Wellcome Trust for funding the research and writing that make up this book. Thank you for making it all possible.

I'd like to express profound gratitude for the intellectual generosity of the *Explorations in Science and Literature* series editors, John Holmes, Janine Rogers and Anton Kirchhofer, for their careful early comments and thrilling ideas about what form this book might take. Thanks also to anonymous reviewers who have helped shape it into the form it has, and to David Avital, Ben Doyle and Lucy Brown at Bloomsbury, and Mohammed Raffi at Deanta, for their editorial excellence. The assistance of the archives teams at the University of East Anglia, the Harry Ransom Center, and the Wellcome Collection was invaluable. Thanks especially to Bridget Gillies at UEA for all her help with the Whitehorn letters, and to Christine Green for two delightful stays in Norwich.

Presenting some of this material at conferences and symposia over the last couple of years has benefitted this work tremendously. Thank you to Ros Williams, Clare Hanson and those who attended my *Genetic States: Policy, Fiction, Nation* workshop in 2018, and to all the participants in Clare Barker's *Global Genetic Fictions* and *Biocolonialism* symposia in 2019. It has been a privilege to become part of the dazzlingly interdisciplinary community of the British Society of Literature and Science, and thanks also to Martin Willis, Keir Waddington and the ScienceHumanities crew at Cardiff. A huge shout-out to the students on *Introduction to Alternative Lifeworlds* at Warwick in 2017–18, in part and by no means least for the impromptu Tarkovsky fan club. Clare Hanson: thank you for being a fierce and generous interlocutor, and for sharing this extraordinary space in which we find ourselves.

A chance encounter with one Richard Williams at Protima Dutta's Ballygunge Bengali lessons in 2012 led to a PhD proposal, so thanks to Richard for laying it all out over momos and for his friendship since.

Much of the methodological heavy lifting of this book was worked out at the Department of English and Comparative Literary Studies at the University of Warwick under the supervision of Stephen Shapiro and Graeme Macdonald. I thank them both for the many, many things I have learned from them, and all the encouragement and inspiration that they have given over the last six years. Thanks also to Nick Lawrence, Pablo Mukherjee, Neil Lazarus, Daniel Katz and Michael Gardiner for being exceptional colleagues. My time at Warwick was made happy and warm by Aditya Sarkar, Sourit Bhattacharya, Arunima Bhattacharya, Tania Ganitsky, Erik Urbeita, Jenny Lander, Michael O'Neill, Demet İntepe, Angus Love, Natasha Bondre, Roxanne Douglas, Katja Laug, Jack McGowan, Joseph Shafer, Rochelle Sibley, Simon Turner, Florence Sunnen, George Ttoouli, Mara Duer and Dino Jakušić.

To brilliant teachers who keep the faith: Lizzie Beesley, Denis Flannery, Naveen Kishore, Ravindra Kumar, Partho Sarothi Ray, AbdouMaliq Simone, Gayatri Chakravorty Spivak and Simon Swift. You are all inspirations.

The Global Warwickshire Collective has been a source of shared strength over the last two years. Meleisa Ono-George, Leon Sealey-Huggins, Nathaniel and Jerome Prescod, Jerome Lammy, Cherelle Harding, Skecia Mardenborough and Danni Ebanks-Ingram have pooled together passion and care in a hostile environment. Nathaniel Adam Tobias C—, you are a sibling. Thank you for everything you do and everything you are.

This project has roots in Kolkata. To those who made the city my home: Noshir Mehta, Deena Ardeshir, Khursheed Ardeshir-Vatcha, Darius, Indira, Zafia, and Farhad Anklesaria, Arup Sen, Rahul Dhankhani, and Nasreen Bibi and her family. By extension, Saurja Sen and Romola Sanyal, and my beloved Kentucky family, Ave Lawyer and John Campbell.

For much of the writing up of this book, I have been deeply fortunate to work alongside colleagues at the Wellcome Centre for Cultures and Environments of Health and the Department of English and Film at the University of Exeter. For extending wisdom, friendship, hospitality and solidarity, I thank Abe Foley, Andrea Wallace, Angelique Richardson, Arthur Rose, Astrid Schrader, Chris Campbell, Debra Ramsey, Dora Vargha, Florian Stadtler, Fred Cooper, Gabriella Giannachi, Ian Cook, Jana Funke, Jessie Stanier, Kate Montague, Kate Wallis, Katie Natanel, Katrina Wyatt, Kazuki Yamada, Kelechi Anucha, Luna Dolezal, Malcolm Richards, Mark Jackson, Mark Steven, Martin Moore, Melanie Shaw, Michael Flexer, Nicola Thomas, Peter Riley, Ranita Chatterjee, Robin Durie, Sam North, and Treasa De Loughry. It has been a joy to work on the Index of Evidence with Steven Hinchliffe, Mike Michael, Gill Partington and Laura Salisbury, a project whose ideas and impressions contour some of the arguments here. Branwyn Poleykett, Charlotte Jones and Veronica Heney model the kind of academic sisterhood I hope to take with me wherever I go, and thank you all for being wonderful readers.

Josie Gill, Elena D'Orso, Mengia Tschalaer, Jhipo Hong, Manoj Dias-Abey, Pier Luc Dupont Picard, Ashley Vanstone, Bridget Anderson, Madhu Krishnan, Grant Cook, Kenny Cummins and the Peck family – Rhiannon, Ash, Gracie and Claudie: thank you for making Bristol even more magical. The Taylor family, the Sanders family and the O'Donovan family have all offered raucous welcomes and resting places over the years. Thank you to each and every one of you. To Toby Lyons, Malveen, Hardeep and Jeeva Jandu, and Anna Horsley. To Patricia, Frank, Kaspar and Lucas Joshi, to my parents, Munchi and Ursha Choksey, to my siblings – Ysanne, Jonathan and Richard – and to Soonoo G, I love you all without end.

And the final four, the champions, my personal punk band, the chosen folks without whom I'd have been lost: Kelly O'Donovan, Sophie Sanders, Sophie Taylor and Sophie Thorne.

This research has been funded by the Wellcome Trust [Grant number: 203109/Z/16/Z]. Thank you to Wellcome for making this book open access. Huge thanks also to Alex Zwetsloot for his generous permission to use his prize-winning image, 'Crawling Around,' for the cover of this book. It shows a microscopy of dynamic skeletons, the tissues built by cells that allow them to change shape and move around.

# Series preface

In spite of the myth of the 'Two Cultures', science and literature have always been shaped by one another. Many of our most powerful scientific concepts, from natural selection to artificial intelligence, from germ theory to chaos theory, have been formed through the careful – and sometimes careless – use of written language. Poets, novelists, playwrights and journalists have taken up scientific ideas, medical research and new technologies, exploring them, reworking them, at times distorting or misjudging them, but always shaping profoundly the wider culture's understanding of what they mean. This intimate and productive relationship between literature and science generated a steady stream of insightful scholarship and commentary throughout the twentieth century and has grown into a substantial field of study in its own right since the turn of the millennium. Where the idea of 'Two Cultures' does still have a hold, however, is in academic disciplines themselves. In schools and universities, we study science and arts subjects in different classrooms, taught by different people with different expectations. Literature and science studies has, so far, been largely a sub-discipline of literature, with only rare contributions from or addressed to scientific experts. In a world of ever-increasing specialization, failure to communicate across these disciplinary divides risks failing to appreciate the contribution that the study of literature can make to our understanding of science, medicine and technology, the uses that science makes of images, narratives and fictions, and the insights that scientists can bring to bear on literature and on culture at large.

Explorations in Science and Literature aims to speak across this divide. It has a particular mandate to bring the insights of literary study to bear on science itself; to consider the significance of literature from a scientific point of view; and to explore the role of literature within the history of science. The books therefore examine the complex interrelations between science and literature in cross-disciplinary ways. They are written equally for scholars and students of literature and for scientists and science students, but also for historians and sociologists of science, as well as general readers interested in science and its place in culture and society. By showing how each field can be enhanced by a knowledge of the others, we hope to enrich scientific as well as literary research, and to cultivate a new cross-disciplinary approach to fundamental questions in both fields.

The series will encompass topics from across the physical, biological and social sciences, medicine and technology, wherever literature can inform our understanding of the science, its origins and its implications. It will also include books on literary forms and techniques that are informed by science, as well as studies that consider how science itself has been articulated. Along with literature in the broad sense of written texts, books in the series will also consider other cultural forms including drama, film, television, and other arts and media.

John Holmes, Anton Kirchhofer<br>and Janine Rogers

# Introduction

The genome has destroyed humanity. If the double helix is an icon of the modern age, then the genome is one of the last grand narratives of modernity. This book is about a period of science that took place over two decades, one that may not yet have ended (only entering a different phase), but which contains the ingredients for the destruction of its primary reference subject: the modern concept of the human. The genome is the last in a set of descriptions about biological life that privilege the individual organism as the primary unit of evolutionary history, the genome as the primary unit of individual life, and the gene as the primary unit of the genome: the age of biological atomism. This has given way to the age of complexity, which means more than just saying that things are more complicated than genes. At a moment when the chasm between information, meaning-making and truth-telling seems to grow ever wider, understanding complex systems as 'networks of multiple interacting causes that cannot be individually distinguished' means 'dancing with them', rather than seeking universal solutions (Poli 2017, 181). Nonetheless, the quest for cause, effect and solutions is an older and hardier logic, alloy in the wheels of the stories we tell about the worlds we inhabit, about ourselves, our power, what we value and our logics of valuation, how we communicate – with each other and with nonhuman entities – and how the worlds we inhabit also inhabit us.

The genome was one such story. It promised a blueprint that would tell us about biological complexity, and why human worlds seem so deeply complex in comparison to nonhuman ones: a code that could tell us not only what makes us human but how humanity is made and remade. Sequencing the human genome was to open up uncharted territory in the realm of human health and scientific understanding. These aims gave way to other questions when results of sequencing did not offer the answers molecular biologists had assumed they would find. Humans express about 2 per cent of their entire genome, and what molecular biologists had long dismissed as 'junk DNA' is in fact instrumental to the ongoing expression and silencing (methylation) of genetic material. The story of the genome was inconclusive, and this lack of conclusion has introduced a whole new set of questions around the ways organisms are more like ecosystems than individual actors, constantly interrupted and contested and consumed by – and cohabiting with – others (Margulis and Sagan 2003). Ed Yong calls this the 'long waltz' of the holobiont (2016) – me, plus my bacteria, fungi, viruses and more – creatures living in community with others, communicating across dimensions of matter, remaking ecological lifeworlds anew, in complicated and sometimes dangerous ways, and in the process undermining modern notions of liberty located in the individual.

Molecular biology has entered the so-called postgenomic era, but what exactly this shift means and to whom it matters is under considerable negotiation. Before investigating new metaphors of self and society introduced by what Jenny Reardon has called 'the postgenomic condition' (2017), this book looks back over the era of the genome – the narratives it produced and was produced by, its neologisms and homonyms, analogies and metaphorical infrastructure. Reading the era of the genome through literary and cultural imaginaries is a way of anticipating and countering some of the repetitions of what has come after it – the recapitulations that tread familiar ground – as well as attending to imaginaries that fall outside, resist or outright refuse the reduction of life to molecular text. The idea of the genome has transformed horizons of self, health, wealth, labour and identity, while also depending on older constructions of human experience without necessarily declaring these as partial or suspect.

Artefact of neoliberal globalism, relic of late capitalism, cultural phenomenon of Faustian proportions, the massive cult power of genomics – practices of sequencing the whole genome – dominated the life sciences over the 1980s and 1990s. The dates of the Human Genome Project's conception correspond to the transformation of capital flows from the late 1970s and early 1980s, with industrial production outsourced from Western Europe and the United States to South Asia, South East Asia, Latin America and Africa, and finance capitalism becoming a new globalized mode of deregulated exchange. As Reardon notes, these reconfigured relations meant new forms of governance, 'reconfiguring who people were and who could legitimately represent them'; amid these transformations, genomics offered 'powerful new practices for differentiating among human beings' (2017, 72). This capitalism of finance flows needed new target subjects, whose function in this regime began to encompass not only labouring and consumption but also donating information via digitalized data collection. Genomic information became a prototype for this regime after the landmark 1980 ruling of *Diamond vs Chakrabarty* in the United States, which legalized the patenting of engineered biological matter. This opened the door for the wholesale commercialization of genomic information, and the United States set a new global standard for private biotechnological companies seeking to cash in on technologies of cloning, sequencing and editing biological material.

Encountering oneself as a string of code means not just thinking about what makes us human, but confronting ourselves as human beings in code: an encounter akin to Jacques Lacan's account of the mirror stage, seeing the self reflected back at oneself for the first time, when a relation is established between organism and environment (2001). In the genomic situation, this moment of self-recognition is mediated by an apparatus of political and economic interests – the substitution of bodily appearance with a collection of letters. Kaushik Sunder Rajan has argued that in this novel biopolitical arrangement, 'the life sciences are overdetermined by the capitalist political economic structures in which they emerge' (2006, 6): not caused by them, but made into a context – an environment – for the perpetuation and prolongation of capitalist modes of production. In this regime, he adds, 'life becomes the explicit centre of political calculation' (79). This in itself might not be seen as something new; what is crucial for the era of genomics is the scale at which political calculations of biomatter can be made into surplus value by new technologies of data capture. The individual is on the precipice of disappearing into caches of comparative data, which in turn shift 'the grammar of life towards a future tense' (Rajan 2006, 14). That is, a conception of life as something that can be mapped, calculated, predicted, engineered and rearranged either for the benefit of individuals who can afford to invest in their own futures, and/or the futures of their offspring.

Does the messiness of matter go away with the advent of datafied and predictive futures? Eugene Thacker places biological exchange in the era of the genome alongside other forms of exchange – political, cultural and economic – while acknowledging that unlike these three other spheres, the stuff of biology is messier, wetter and less congruous than more obviously divisible units of power, signs and value (2005). More than this: it is unevenly overlayed, shaped by and constitutive of all three realms. Genomics relies on the messiness of materiality, partly to keep uncertainty locked into its speculative forms of value-making, and partly because of its connection to older practices of what might also be termed biotechnology – livestock, breeding and agriculture (2005, 19). For Thacker, genomics is not purely informational, but is based on a contradiction: 'that biology is information, and that information is both immaterial and material' (2005, 21). It is in this contradiction that the basis of genomics' epistemological onslaught to capitalist modernity lies. In a nutshell, because it cannot be contained to the realm of unit-thinking. The reliance of biological thinking on metaphors from other realms – on biological stuff being like value, like signs, like power, while never completely reducible to these things – ends up undoing the logic of unit-thinking. It becomes impossible to 'think' the body 'in' space, restricted to specific fields of action, parts becoming relevant at different points in chronological time. Systems biology has come closest to getting at this, but bodies are not networked either. Knowledge about the operations of life itself are at best, partial; hence, learning how to dance with them, rather than reducing them to value, signs or power relations, is vital.

In this unwieldy kaleidoscope of possible meanings, where technology breaks biomatter down into component parts and tries to make sense of them, narrative is both a strategy of containment and a way of dancing with complexity. As Clare Hanson puts it, 'From the outset genetics has been entangled with meanings which extend far beyond the biological' (2020, 19). Genomics has done new things to processes of signification, 'allowing us to grammatically conceive of life in certain ways, not in terms of an Aristotelian poeisis, but rather as those whose futures can we can calculate in terms of certain disease events happening' (Rajan 2006, 14). This marks a departure from the imaginative field of evolutionary theory in the nineteenth century, which, to follow Gillian Beer, moved between two elements: growth (as experience) and transformation, which fuelled nineteenth-century preoccupations with *märchen* (folklore), fairy-tale and myth (Beer 2010, 97). Genomics is largely uninterested in growth, and appropriates transformation into either genomic diagnosis (i.e. deleterious transformations that might be visible in the genome) or genomic futurism (i.e. the editing or eradication or insertion of elements that might facilitate better, longer and more productive lives). To sell itself, genomics has relied on repurposing words that carry a degree of stability and recognisability for its own logic, and which taken together convey a metaphorical field of pattern – code to signify configurations of genes, pair to signify the arrangement of nucleotides, sequence to signify the order of pairs. It also relies on forms of juxtaposition and contrast, and constructs molecular temporalities (the time taken for certain genetic processes to occur) to insist on the necessity of speed in its experimental operations. Maps and tracking devices proliferate, while molecular worlds are translated into sequences of signs.

For Rajan, this amounts to a take-over of the grammar of life: no less than the biomedicalization of ontology, and the reduction of poiesis (as transformation or making) to the level of the molecular. But is this takeover as total as it looks? This is one of the biggest questions of this book: how is language involved in an ongoing negotiation over the status of the human, and how does the messiness of what genomics does not account for – other histories, other forms of inheritance, other modes of being – interrupt and destabilize the seemingly implacable logic of cause and effect bound up in the idea of a molecular script? Mike Fortun is more optimistic about the possibility of resistance in language: 'language, which allows us to invent concepts that are a little off the chart, is one of the few things that can keep up with the inventions of genomicists' (2008, 29). Rather than submitting to a version of life determined by code, narrative in the age of the genome involves complex compositions of power negotiations, semiotic events and value fluctuations, which are attached to a range of interests and relations, mechanisms and localities.

Such negotiations intensify the relationship between speculation and narrative. Fabrizio Terranova offers an expansive understanding of 'the force of narration as a way to tell stories which can make "possibles" exist' (in Pihet 2017, 66–7). This is more than reducing aesthetics to narrative; it is to use fabulation to 'create autonomous objects . . . no longer connected via a whole string of attachments', which confound the presuppositions of storytelling within established literary genealogies (67). For Didier Debaise, this sense of fabulation nourishes a form of speculative philosophy that departs from post-Kantian idealism, which involves 'thinking beyond a purely human perspective or condition, taking into account the importance and irreducibility of abstractions, freeing the imagination from any exclusive ties to representations, intensifying the sense of possibles . . . without losing the pragmatic sense of experience' (in Pihet 2017, 68). Narrating genomics necessitates this mode of speculation in forms of representation already beyond the human as finite individual, and the ethical dilemmas of body-as-code exceed what legal frameworks have been able to imagine, let alone legislate.

Narrative in the age of the genome is concerned as much with what falls outside the calculable, statistical and algorithmic as it is with tracing the ways that genomics offered a prototype for the rearticulation of humans at the beginning of the twenty-first century as producer-consumers of data in the Global North or as peripheral and precarious manufacturers of technologies for interpreting these data in the Global South. Critiques that foreground the operations of racialization as a condition of capitalist production have articulated this difference as one constituted by racial capitalism (Robinson 1983). Hortense Spillers differentiates between flesh and body, and between 'captive and liberated subject-positions' (1987, 67). The ideology of genomics has been complicit in economies of flesh, 'that zero degree of social conceptualisation that does not escape concealment under the brush of discourse, or the reflexes of iconography'

(67). This is an economy of marks made data, constituting crimes against bodily matter. Flesh produces an idea of the body as a productive agent, a unit of possible liberation, around which a host of practices can be organized. In Lars Schmeink's words, 'health is no longer a necessity for survival in a social group that depends on it, but rather a lifestyle choice, the body becoming a work of art or a demonstration of scientific possibilities' (2016, 147). Keeping hold of the racialized distinction between these forms of labour is key: genomics has facilitated the consolidation of these two groups in technologies of algorithmic governmentality, where information of the flesh generates narratives of the body, which fuels production, which needs more information to keep up with the speed of innovation.

Narrative also attends to what Beer describes compellingly as 'the *chanciness* of consequences, the phantasmagoric outflaring of need and dread into acts which confirm their own predictions', out of which 'determining patterns' might be resisted, and new stories made (2010, 202). This extends to moving about and playing around with evidentiary objects. By de-emphasizing some influences, and ramping up others – or by arranging them without any obvious order or logic, layering different strands of documentation together, or through strategies of withholding and distracting – narrative might deliver what Beer calls 'communal insights' (163). Not universal ones, but those formed through mismatching, cobbling together, where it is not truth or transparency that matters as much as some kind of temporary consensus over why a particular narrative might make sense at a particular time, in a certain place. If the genome has been purported to be a transparent ledger of existence, then narrative in the age of the genome attends to the sedimentations and unmarked burial grounds of forgotten evidence – the way it emerges in unexpected places, or when genomic proof cannot do the kind of cultural work it promises to do.

Central to this is the question of repair. As Evelyn Fox Keller notes, the shift from genetics to genomics in the 1970s was facilitated and motivated by the concept of genetic disease. It is this powerful concept – that disease events might be located in the genome and mitigated against – that 'represents an ideological expansion of molecular biology far beyond its technical successes' (1992, 293). The concept of genetic disease propelled genomics into the era of neoliberalism as the key to disease-free futures, which could be speculated on through both technological innovation and bioeconomic investment: the era of biocapital proper. Genetic disease 'created the climate' for the Human Genome Project: the massive, multinational effort of sequencing – in Keller's careful formulation – 'what has come to be called "the human genome"' (293): a reference genome made up of aggregated data from several people, all falling under the Caucasian ethnic grouping, the majority of whom were male. The focus in molecular biology turned from the question of how genes mould certain traits or characteristics (physiological, behavioural), to genes that code for particular diseases. As Keller notes, 'good health' becomes attached to a normative reference genome, and deviations from this standard point to varying states of 'unhealth' or abnormality (295). Despite the elusive nature of the genomic norm, health futures are organized around the affective power of abnormality – the topos of deviations in need of repair – even when treatment might not be readily available.

Precision genomics – the tailoring of treatments to personal genomic data – has been granted a great deal of space, particularly in the corporate healthcare sector that targets private health consumers. It is the realm of a deeply rarefied market, trading on drug trials and gene therapies (replacing mutant genes with functioning ones) at the frontier of possible cures. Putting to one side the question of the varying efficacy of these trials and therapies, a bigger question emerges: whose futures are being privileged, and at what cost? Hilary Rose and Steven Rose discuss a rejuvenated transhumanism for a new millennium in genomic idealism characterized by entrepreneurs and big business, marked by 'the possessive individualism of the neoliberal economy, where the mantra is choice and the consumer is king or queen' (2012, 156). In such an economy, who benefits, who pays, and who is left out? There are questions around the ethnic diversity of biobanks, as well as the slow take-up of classed dimensions of health, and often 'appropriate representation has been left to the good conscience of the researchers' (Rose and Rose, 279). While the cost of whole genome sequencing has reduced dramatically since 2001 (from millions of dollars to one or two thousand, depending on the company), this is the equivalent of cracking the door open. Inside is a vast market promising possible cures at competitive prices that patient-consumer might wander around indefinitely, possibly at huge personal, economic and psychic cost. This route to healthcare is still in the process of establishing the realm in which it operates, and this uncertainty is partly generated by a 'collect now, ask questions later' approach to data gathering. As in other examples of Big Data, Big Genomics needs the scientific narratives to catch up with the information, so that it can be made into evidence (Prainsack 2017).

The composition of scientific narrative is a point of departure for this book – what narratives make data meaningful in the age of the genome? And how can narrative redirect flows of interest and information towards imagining a different set of correspondences between biology and society, attending to the imbrication of one in the other at the level of empiricism, and taking risks with new metaphorical infrastructure? As Reardon reminds us, 'making genomic data valuable is a very hard problem' (2016, 122). The manifold challenges of knowing life in what Reardon calls 'the midst of a growing sea of genomic data' involve transforming plots and experimenting with genre for the sake of sense-making (Reardon 2016, 122) – that is, it involves the work of interpretation and poiesis, within and outside the laboratory.

The relation between signification and valorization is one reason for positing molecular biology as the necessarily rarefied sphere in which liberal humanism has destroyed its own condition of possibility. This is because the limitations of genetic approximations matched with the grandiosity of genomic utopianism reveal a gaping hole in capitalism's speculative operations. Capitalism has not been able to perform the conjuring trick of making biomatter 'appear as the results of its own realization', nor to transfigure living processes into 'the result of its existence' (Marx, in McLellan 1971, 126). As much as it wants to, capital has not been able, consistently and completely, to 'create its own prerequisites' and to impose 'its own reality' when it comes to living processes (Marx, in McLellan, 126). The totality of organic life has always remained outside the creation of surplus value, escaping its reduction to dead labour, because capitalist modes of production have been unable to close the gap between labour power and living processes. The persistent illegibility of organicity means that living processes that expand temporal parameters of individual existence are never fully calculable as biopower. Their messiness – not only their spatial specificities but the *plurality* of relationality in their spatio-temporal configurations – has proved irreducible to the play of value, power, and signs. This messiness has pushed back at capitalism's ambition to annihilate multiplicity in favour of mass reproduction (even when this reproduction is given multiple and niche forms). It has been up to narrative to stage this irreducibility, often in spite of its own tendencies towards reduction.

This irreducibility is not banked in recourses to ecological romanticism, but in attending to weird forms that escape valorization. For theorists operating within and alongside Marxian critique, the weirdness of living processes has offered a site of critical experimentation that stands against capitalism's attempts to portray its productive rationalism as natural rather than historical: Charles Sanders Peirce's Interpretant (1867), Henri Bergson's *élan vital* (1907), Walter Benjamin's aura (1935), Georges Bataille's excess energy (1949), and Gilles Deleuze and Félix Guattari's rhizome (1980). These interventions are epistemological in as much as they intervene in rhythms of relation between (organic) process and (socio-economic) production. These figures hold off living processes from complete subsumption into raw material, because their signification cannot be fully processed by capitalism's metaphorical and machinic infrastructure. While accelerated operations of techno-scientific industrial complexes throughout the twentieth and into the twenty-first centuries have obscured this reality, the era of the postgenomic has shown up massive and irresolvable lacunae in biogenetic explanations of life and its processes. The tendency has been to try to lasso these lacunae back to the lexicon of unit-thinking, but this logic has run out of steam. In this situation, the weirdness of these processes takes form in narrative via resistance to and transformation of capitalism's *a priori* reductionism, contesting the ontological stability of its most valuable source of capital: living bodies.

The contest over genomic narratives has not been restricted to a science-culture war. There is a history of conflict within the life sciences around the appropriation of genetics into pernicious hierarchies of human and species, and this often rehearses resistance in the eighteenth and nineteenth centuries to biological accounts of supremacy. The 1960s and 1970s saw a flourishing of a radical science movement. In Anglo American biology, this was directed against the biologization of a patriarchal, heteronormative, militarized and white-dominated society espoused by theories of sociobiology and the selfish gene. A group of Marxist biologists – led by Stephen Jay Gould, Richard Lewontin and Richard Levins, along with feminist scientists like Rita Arditti, Ruth Hubbard, Ethel Tobach and Ruth Bleier – pushed back at forms of science that privileged both male practitioners and viewpoints that seemed to underscore masculinist essentialism (Rose and Rose, 290). These interventions were set against the ways that genetics was being used to naturalize social inequities in ways reminiscent of late-nineteenth-century co-options of evolutionary theory. The issue here was to argue against the flattening of social life into liberal universalism at the cost of recognizing and attending to historical inequalities. At stake for the US-based antagonists to sociobiology was a battle over 'what would constitute a liberal American society' (Perez 2013, 105). The arguments against sociobiology – partly due to its localization in elite universities in the United States – formed part of the globalized narrative around genetic reductionism and its possible evils as the decade went on, as genomics became constituted as a new global standard in biological research.

More recent examples of challenge include interventions from the non-profit Centre for Genetics and Society, located in the belly of the beast – Berkeley, California, next to Silicon Valley. University College London's recent public reckoning with its infrastructure of eugenics – its buildings and laboratories named after Francis Galton and Karl Pearson, and its hosting of an under-the-radar annual eugenics conference until as recently as 2017 – has galvanized discussions around the central role of British science in the development of a pseudoscience that for a long time has been primarily associated with Nazism (Bressey et al. 2020). This is particularly loaded in a context of austerity policies in the UK since 2010, which have acted as a form of everyday, bureaucratized eugenics through cuts to health, education, welfare and housing.

How to sustain this backlash against the classed, racialized, gendered and ableist fault lines of genomics, amid the eugenic forms of neglect that the COVID-19 pandemic has exposed in the United States and the United Kingdom? Angela Saini notes the continuation of racist stereotyping in health research against a backdrop of disproportionate death rates of Black, Asian, Hispanic and minority ethnic peoples: 'time and again, I have seen health researchers erroneously invoke social categories as though they are biological ones' (2020, 1605). She speculates that part of the reason for the continued reintroduction of race as a biological reality rather than social category into explanatory frameworks for health is because of the drive towards 'personalised medicine so precise that every person's biological profile is perfectly understood'; in lieu of the necessary data to do this, 'researchers instead turn to social categories as proxies' (1605). That is, the drive towards increasing individuation in health results in further entrenching racialized inequities, bound also, inevitably, to those of gender, class and disability.

Precision medicine offers projected models of life experience that move at pace towards what Steve Fuller has called the emergence of 'Humanity 2.0': 'the mind-body problem', he writes, 'is increasingly operationalized, if not outright replaced, by those who . . . would continue to anchor humanity in our carbon-based bodies or those who . . . would leverage humanity into more durable silicon-based containers' (2011, 3). If the rhetoric of Silicon Valley transhumanism cannot yet be matched by technology, these visions nonetheless shape the kinds of dreamworlds that feel possible, even while their horizons remain at a distance. These futures function as orbs dangled in front of consumers' visions, while resistance towards the encroaching digitalization of everyday life – and the organization of datalogics around particular types of consumer – is restricted, counter-intuitively, to the same platforms that source data (documentaries on streaming services, social media campaigns, digital communications and the digital archives of street-level protests). While the space for speech seems to have expanded exponentially, the challenge of mounting a coherent, sustained and strategic collective resistance to digital co-option is fragmented across a multiplicity of sites.

Nikolas Rose puts it this way: 'If our medical "imaginary" – our image of what healthcare should be – is "all about me" it may well have serious consequences for my willingness to pay for, let alone care about, the health of others who are not related to me – not just others in my town or country, but others in far away and distant places' (2013, 351). Despite the caution, Rose emphasizes here the imaginative power of caring about others' health, not in an abstract way, but in ways that might intervene in the corporate instrumentalization of genomics into an ideology of ostensibly private decision making. This is also a significant point of departure for this book – how narrative does not just register or represent, but can form structures of care that move past models of (atomized) individual and (ethnonational) population to collective aims for health.

The machinery of eugenics still determines genomic futures. Depoliticized accounts of climate change (Sealey-Huggins 2018), uncritical arguments about overpopulation in the so-called Global South, and the hardy postwar ideology of meritocracy as a route to longer and better lives (Hanson 2013) all illuminate an infrastructure of colonial-capitalism that has not yet been dismantled. Genomics' privileging of certain kinds of human over others is a reflex of a long history of eugenic thinking – the use of biological heredity to improve society via the breeding in of 'good' and the breeding out of 'bad' stock. This history of prevention and promotion has fallen along familiar lines of identification – class, race and ability – and also involves policing the reproductive rights of women (Richardson 2003). The sweeping popularity of eugenics across the political spectrum in the late nineteenth and early twentieth centuries is a history with which Anglo American biology at large has yet to reckon fully (Kevles 1985; Mazumdar 1991). Indeed, much contemporary scholarship around the early years of eugenics dates back to the scaling up of genomics. The bogey men of eugenics have long ceased to be caricatures of Nazi scientists; eugenics offered a scientific justification for centuries of imperial domination, enslavement, genocide and settler colonialism, while also anticipating the economic power of this hierarchy of human life in post-colonial globalism.

Narrative in the age of the genome engages and grapples with some of the life sciences' most intractable imaginaries: survival of the fittest, human supremacy, resource scarcity and genetic norms. This requires a supple toolkit of rhetorical strategies, and often this means blurring the borders of mimesis (repetition/representation) and poiesis (transformation/making). This book moves between these two methodological registers: the empirical and analogical. The ways that genomics is represented in form, plot, character and intertextuality (as evidence), and the ways that narrative intervenes in discourses of heredity through the plotting and arrangement of space, time, metaphor and architecture (as epistemological field).

This involves a certain promiscuity when it comes to genre. Many of the texts in this book are huddled under the expansive umbrella of speculative fiction (sf). Joan Slonczewsky and Michael Levy note that in the new millennium, there is an enduring fascination with biotechnology as both a plot and anxiety of sf, which 'also leaves us fearful of biological warfare, and wondering how our moral traditions of the past millennia will survive the technological challenges of this one' (2003, 185). In *Liminal Lives* (2003), Susan Merrill Squier argues that speculative fiction offers a space for registering anxieties and ideas around biotechnology, as well as a space to imagine alternative uses, and to foreground alternative epistemologies: 'Fiction gives us access to the biomedical imaginary: the zone in which experiments are carried out in narrative, and the psychic investments of biomedicine are articulated' (17). But getting too mired in boundaries of genre can dissipate the more radical interventions of sf when it comes to form, metaphor and plot – knowing 'one set of things as fictional and another as factual' (Squier, 20). Sf not only represents fact in fiction but also tilts the metaphorical infrastructure of realism. When a character in realist fiction is sad and the sky pours with rain, we know that the ordinary rules of non-correlation between human and natural worlds privileged in realism are being temporarily suspended for the sake of pathetic fallacy: the exaggeration of affect via the orchestration of the external world to mirror a character's internal world. But in sf, the correlation between emotion and weather could be – and quite often is – made literal.

At the same time, 'realist' accounts of science often rely on the more radical temporalities and topographies of sf to set out their programmes and to institute their legacy. As Mieke Bal has argued, identifying a piece of fiction as a realist representation of a given lifeworld is a fallacy, and even a misunderstanding of fiction itself. Description does not interrupt narrative by reminding the reader of a text's grounding in a reality external to it, but is rather a 'motor of narrative': rain and sadness, weather and affect. Reading from description to description, 'the reader complies with, falls for, and perhaps incidentally, resists, the novel's appeal to her to construct the imaginary but coherent-enough world in which the recounted events can happen' (Bal 2007, 572). This book reads the various declarations, impositions and blurrings of genre in gauging what Fortun calls the 'affective register' of scientific developments (2016).

If the modern myth of liberal humanism has relied on a construction of individual time as chronological and has sequestered 'the environment' as a context in which this individual develops, then one of the interventions narrative makes is in its representation of time. While genomics needs patient-consumers to invest in a certain idea of chronology in order to sell tests, drugs and therapies – and to sustain the horizon of a disease-free future – its technologies have also made the destruction of this ordering of time inevitable. When individuals disappear into databases, they are broken up into component parts, becoming disaggregated in a massive storehouse of genomic data. While they can also be fairly easily retrieved, concerns around this involve the misuse of data in insurance and employment decisions. On one hand, genomics promises a certain kind of continuity for the self in genealogical time. Dorothy Nelkin and M. Susan Lindee describe DNA as 'a relic, a piece of the person that contains the full self', as well as offering a portal to 'lost biological connections': quests for genetic roots, for example, 'suggest that to find one's biological parents is to find one's essence, and that without this essence a person can never be complete, whole, fulfilled' (1995, 69). Narrative in the age of the genome offers routes to the past, where gaps in family history might be filled in, where the genetic can move to the limits of the known world and become a tool of ancestry-making. But as well as big reveals, it also de-sediments normative constructions of relatedness and kinship: who or what shapes our feelings of belonging, what allegiances and tribalisms accompany this, and how to forge solidarity with worlds that do not resemble our own?

In the era of the genome, memoirs organized around genomic figurations of essence, heredity and belonging were incorporated into a museum of the species. At the turn of the twenty-first century, Matt Ridley described the genome as 'an autobiography of a species in twenty-three chapters', twenty-three numbering the pairs of chromosomes that make up human DNA (1999). The genome was imagined as an archive of *Homo sapiens*, a normative subject constructed through technologies of sequencing and mean calculations of a composite reference genome. But what is omitted from archives – or what never make it in – is just as significant to investigating the narration of humanity in code. The HGP's construction of this composite reference genome out of Anglo American genomes from people 'of European ancestry' was a demonstrably supremacist gesture, even as the HGP's protagonists insisted on the indefensibility of race as a genetic reality. In a discussion of decolonial aesthesis and museums, Rolando Vázquez Melken argues,

> What happens in the museum is the constitution of a normative subject. A public that belongs to the cultural archive of whiteness attends the museum in order

to acquire the power and entitlement of the normative subject, yet for others the museum gives no possibility of any such identification and entitlement. (In Wevers 2019, 2)

Imagined as an autobiography in a museum of the species, the genome becomes part of an assemblage of racializing techniques that further legitimize the description of human value in biological terms. These techniques are necessarily complicit in adding to the formation and reproduction of a normative public within 'the cultural archive of whiteness'. This is insistently linked to the emergence of the bourgeois public sphere and the creation of national character through bric-a-brac of traits and tendencies that the rise of the novel-form and biography in the eighteenth century transformed into mass culture.

At the tail end of European modernity, the genome becomes a resource of self-cultivation, collapsing narratives of self and species into the molecular. For Paul Gilroy, this biologization of culture – the extraction of difference into statistical pre-emptions – marks a convergence of nature and culture, to which the power of race is central:

> The messy complexity of social life is thereby recast as a Manichean fantasy in which bodies are only ordered and predictable units that obey the rules of a deep cultural biology scripted nowadays in the inaccessible interiority of the genome. (2004, 6)

To critique the construction of a normative human subject within a reference code is also to contest the hegemonic arbitration of humanity within the terms of racial supremacy. Inscriptions of race and ethnicity as geographic and phenotypic realities become placeholders for civilisation as an iteration of human sovereignty and for the work of encompassing natural and cultural spheres into the long-term project of human progress. I situate this critique within a plurality of 'alternatives to the legal conception of personhood that dominates our world', which seek to depart from 'a delimited notion of personhood as property', in Alexander Weheliye's words (2014, 81). Figured as a museum of the species, we might rethink how to inhabit this museum – to follow Vázquez, is it 'an instrument for the curator', and is this curator an individual or a community, a collective, an assembly? Decolonial interventions in the genome-as-museum would mean 'turning the museum into an instrument, so that the museum can be inhabited, resignified, made to speak about what goes beyond its enframing, and what is has been designed to silence' (in Wevers 2019, 10).

As much as it organizes health futures around individual chronology as a way of plotting of liberal personhood in orderly and ordered time, investment in genomics also banks on 'a time out of joint', the juxtapositions of past and present for the sake of transhuman futures, at great speed. As Fortun has argued, the triangulation of speed – what he calls 'the haste function' (2008, 105) – ethnonationalism and corporate investment is one of genomics' more disturbing trends. Iceland's deCODE project sought to construct a mythological Icelandic heritage out of the imaginary of an isolated, centuries-old population; gathering donors for its database of Icelandic genomes, the project's leaders deployed rhetoric which – in Fortun's words – 'pushed the incongruous inconsistencies of a time out of joint to their limit, reterritorializing an eleventh-century sword in the territorial battles of twentieth century biosciences, where the opposition is not so much unarmed or unprepared, but unplugged' (73). This is an extraordinary collocation of weaponry, drawing together premodern and late capitalist tools of colonization, conveying the *longue durée* of violence in which the biosciences are situated, however much this history is denied or played down with protests of scientific objectivity.

Fortun also identifies two intersecting possibilities for resistance here: first, vigilance over the appropriation of imaginary communities in techno-capitalist means for neo-eugenic ends; and second, plugging in to the technologies that facilitate the large-scale application of these technologies to imaginary populations. Thacker argues, 'Sociobiology today is arguably not so much a school or scientific discipline as it is a way of managing the social as a collectivity' (2005, 311). Biosciences in the twenty-first century are complicit in the datafication of the everyday, part of an increasingly globalized toolbox for managing and tracking the mass movements of people caused by warfare, economic deprivation, climate change, land dispossession and resource extraction. The spaces for social cooperation are not increasing, but quickly shrinking, while biotechnology – as part of a wider apparatus of personalized tech mediated increasingly through one or two devices (Reardon 2016) – upholds a mythology of bourgeois individualism. The work of resisting and transforming this state of affairs begins, then, by plugging into its conceits, feints, lures and networks; that is, its metaphorical infrastructure.

A final note about worlds before turning to an overview of the chapters. If the texts here can be grouped into a genre – that is, if they share a common trait – it is the genre of unsatisfactory conclusions. There are plot holes, worm holes and loose ends. Some worlds come fully constructed; others start to move and transform through mechanisms of space-time that are left unexplained. Characters fall out of stories and into other ones that we never get to read. Genetic lineages are blurred, erased or lost. Moments of self-development are sequestered in parentheses, while human trajectories are infiltrated by nonhuman ecosystems. Throughout, there is a stitching together of modern ruptures between 'Man' and 'Nature', those categories which have made possible what Jason Moore calls the Capitalocene, 'the way of organising the relations between humans and the rest of nature' that characterizes modern history since the 1400s (Moore and Patel 2018; Moore 2013). Narrative in the age of the genome reckons with the limits of atomized accounts of being in the world – at the level of gene, genome, organism, group and species – and reconstitutes forms of meaning-making that have constituted a logic of segregation: of humans from nature, from other humans, and from other forms and accounts of life itself.

World-building in these texts is never a complete or total endeavour, and is unmoored from the co-option of survival metaphors into measurements of relative fitness. It is more akin to what AbdouMaliq Simone has described as an ongoing working-out of scale in fragile and temporary collectivities, among those who live between different dimensions of time, proximities and interdependency, where characters 'find themselves simultaneously in many space-times' (2018, 55). This is a confounding of chronology made possible – even accelerated – by the social power of the genome, and its displacements of evolutionary history in segments of extracted code; with these displacements, the genome also unseats its claims to universality and its promises of utopias free from glitches in the code. Simply put, how can these be guaranteed, or controlled, or implemented, amid the vast rhythms that make up collective life? Plots without end engender a refusal to inhabit the body in terms that subject it to its ongoing capture and annihilation, even as its potential is capitalized on in the name of the futures of those who have not yet been born (the impossible, 'real' subjects of precision genomics, who never will be born).

The book's five chapters are arranged more or less chronologically, and according to scalar units of calculation: genes and families in the 1970s, groups and communities in the 1980s, data bodies in the 1990s, ancestral lineage in the 2000s and ecosystems in the 2010s. Chapter 1, 'Deindustrialization and the Selfish Gene', considers the genome as a prototype for a new kind of subject under neoliberal globalism, via new techniques of isolating and cloning parts of the genome. I situate E. O. Wilson's sociobiological applications of genetics to behaviour and Richard Dawkins's concept of genes as competitive and selective agents driven to perpetuate themselves in perpetuity in a wider ideological battleground between the end of the post-war consensus around welfare and the role of the state. Reading Dawkins's *The Selfish Gene* (1976) as an argument against trade unionism, I go on to readings of Doris Lessing's *The Memoirs of a*

*Survivor* (1974) and Samuel Delany's *Trouble on Triton* (1976) through questions of whiteness and decolonization, eugenics, data profiling and queer kinship, and the emergence of genetic engineering as a tool of neoliberal self-fashioning.

Chapter 2, 'Cultivating Dreamworlds', moves away from Anglo American biology to consider genomics in the Soviet Union, contextualizing its fractious status in a longer history of Russian biology as primarily a domain of agricultural cultivation, rather than individual heredity. The chapter considers what I call the cultivation metaphor in Russian anarchist theories of mutual aid and Soviet agricultural policy, and in Soviet imaginaries of the New Man and the masses under Stalin. While officially banned from 1948, genetics was crucial for the Soviet Union's clandestine biological warfare programmes, and this is the context through which I read Arkady and Boris Strugatsky's *Roadside Picnic* (1972). By the late 1970s, a fusion of Soviet environmentalism and Western biotechnology mirrored a crisis of national cohesion as the Soviet Union moved towards its final years, its various crimes against its own peoples obscured and silenced, as Kir Bulychev's story about genetic cloning in a ramshackle government laboratory at Moscow's periphery, 'Another's Memory' (1985), shows.

Chapter 3, 'Memoir and the Laboratory', considers popular imaginaries of the genome in the decade when it reached global superstardom through the Human Genome Project and its utopian promises to revolutionize healthcare: the 1990s, a period rich in blockbuster science fiction and poised for new cultural objects of paranoia in the wake of the end of the Soviet Union. I consider how popular memoirs published by some of the HGP's key players transformed the genome into a cultural object that could give humanity the answers it sought about its place in the world and, more pertinently, account for its creaturely supremacy. Memoir becomes a space of experimentation akin to a laboratory, where new narratives for human progress are tested out. As I go on to argue in readings of Kazuo Ishiguro's *Never Let Me Go* (2005) and Andrew Niccols's *Gattaca* (1997), questions about possible abuses of genomic science were worked through in speculative fiction during and after the genome project, in which the spectre of eugenics loomed large. Alongside this, anxieties about the disappearance of character as a reliable site of development in the wake of sequencing technologies – where the individual is reduced to body part or aggregated sections of code – were registered by a crisis of narrative: how could the story of the human continue to be told when it was disappearing into vast genomic databases?

Chapter 4, 'Speculative Ancestry', contests the idea that bioengineering was a phenomenon novel to the late twentieth century, arguing instead that the history of colonial-capitalist modernity has been premised on trait thinking and on splitting humans from their sense of developing through time, and into component parts of relative productivity: the logic of humanizing Europe through the dehumanization of millions of African peoples through the transatlantic slave trade and the system of plantation enslavement through which the cross-continental industrial development of Europe and America was made possible. For this reason, new technologies of genetic ancestry testing that emerged in the early 2000s were doing a different kind of cultural work among African American communities, attached to a precedent of discontinuous lineage, a *longue durée* of genealogy in the wake of obscured family histories, and held the promise of repairing the long-term damage done by stolen time. I read Saidiya Hartman's *Lose Your Mother: A Journey Along the Atlantic Slave Route* (2006) and Yaa Gyasi's *Homegoing* (2016) within the uncertainties that accompany this promise, considering how they foreground trajectories of non-biological kinship and ancestry-making in their reckoning with annihilated and occluded genealogies.

The final chapter, 'Toxic Infrastructure', reads the rupture to the idea of the genome as a transparent ledger of life at the end of the Human Genome Project through peripheral narratives of global shock. The postgenomic era has once more brought the question of environmental influences on genetic expression to the fore, with 'the environment' classed variously as molecular, lifestyle factors, exposure to pollution and epidemiology (disease). I introduce some of the key debates of the postgenomic era through narratives of two environmental catastrophes, global in scale and reach: the Chernobyl nuclear power plant explosion of 1986 in Svetlana Alexievich's *Chernobyl Prayer* (1997) and Jeff VanderMeer's fictional biological cataclysm in his Southern Reach trilogy, *Annihilation, Authority,* and *Acceptance* (2014). I read both as postgenomic accounts of the vast complexity of biological relationships, which coincide with anxieties around the illegibility of data, alongside its misuse or disappearance. The postgenomic era's central problem is not the gathering of data, but making this data legible while old certainties about the immutability of DNA – and the relative stability of the genome across life spans – start to break down. In both these texts, this coincides with a problem of genre: what new stories does the postgenomic yield about lifeworlds, what new characters does it introduce – or indeed, how does it change forms of characterization – and can these stories be told in an age of planetary crisis?

Finally, a note on this book's global methodology, which understands the global as a world-system reproduced through the ongoing production of core, semi-periphery and periphery, both within and across national borders

(Wallerstein 2006). This resists the wholesale application of categories of Global North and Global South in an era of rapid urbanization, at a time when megacities, rather than nations, are fast becoming the go-to units of calculation for international health and finance organizations. To borrow from Wallerstein, the methodology assumes that disaggregated phenomena of politics, culture, economics, structure (and, here, science) are imaginative constructs rather than reliable descriptions of the multiple ways worlds are experienced, lived, made and remade anew (2006, x). This is not just an argument for thinking with and in complexity; it brings into relief the various levels in which an episteme functions – in this case, the ontology of 'natural' processes. While genomics has certainly been a technology of globalization – part of the empirical standardization of organic life across the world – its influence is neither total, nor reducible to silos of social organization. For this reason, it has been vital to include alternative epistemologies and practices around genomics and human biology in my discussions of Soviet biology and African American ancestry testing. This book is not just about the globalization of genomics, but also about its differentiated cultural values and political relevance, which intersect and come into conflict with assertions and conceptions of where what is called human life sits in a wider panoply of living and non-living beings.

This book is also informed by a history of feminist critique that has challenged biological determinisms, particularly those in Black feminist scholarship, a site of critical enquiry that has long resisted the reduction of women's lives to vessels for the reproduction of labour power to sustain a liberal humanist order organised around whiteness, as in the work of Dorothy Roberts, Alondra Nelson, Hortense Spillers, Joy James, Ruha Benjamin and Sylvia Wynter. The era of postgenomics has seen a new wave of feminist perspectives that caution against the instrumentalization of a branch of biology that could still be a compelling alternative to genetic reductionism – epigenetics – into new molecular essentialisms of environmental influence, a topic that Sarah Richardson, Hilary Rose, Evelyn Fox Keller, Ruth Müller, Susan Merrill Squier, Wendy Wheeler, Catherine Malabou and Clare Hanson have tackled in different ways and through a range of disciplinary perspectives: sociology, literary criticism, aesthetics, philosophy, the history of biology and political economy.

At this critical juncture in theories and technologies of life itself, there is a danger of falling back into older ways of framing life that privilege not only 'the human' as the centre of biological inquiry – the life-form to which other forms are compared – but also particular types of human. Instead, the life sciences and beyond can (and, in some instances, are poised to) transform the epistemological field of their experimental practices, objects of analysis and tools of measurement. As Sophia Roosth and Astrid Schrader argue, feminist interventions in the construction of scientific knowledge emphasize the political urgency of 'thinking across or beyond' the critical and empirical, the semiotic and the material, as this practice 'invites us to write and think against neat distinctions between theories and things, between matter and method, and to query the analytic constructs we have inherited' (2012, 2). This is the challenge that this book takes up in its querying of the place and status of the genome, and the way that its terms of reference ended up doing the kind of transformative cultural work suggested by Roosth and Schrader, while not in the way that its key players may have hoped for or imagined. The idea of the genome as a reliable or total description of life itself has collapsed into something far more radical, which threatens the terms of its own logic.

As the development of novel gene editing technologies via CRISPR-Cas 9 and investment in their possible future uses happens at pace, it remains vital to emphasize the regionalism of genomics: its emergence out of a particular moment of Anglo American biology, its *a priori* commitment to a certain concept of DNA's social power, and allied to this, a certain idea of what human freedom looks like. This book is situated in a large body of existing scholarship on the co-option of genomics into narratives of national, ethnic and group belonging, a phenomenon that has extended across the world, from nineteenth-century imperial biology into twenty-first-century descriptions of humanity's future, creating centres, peripheries and enclaves in its wake.

1

# Deindustrialization and the selfish gene

In the early 1970s, twenty years after Francis Crick and James Watson published the structure of DNA in the shape of a double helix, molecular biology was in its golden era. The double helix offered a new poetics in the form of a string of alternating letters programming each cell of a living body, and forming whole ecosystems: the foundation of life itself. But the lure of reading life as text also introduced questions of what reading meant at the level of biological process. What is reading what, and how? And what matters outside the code? The elegance of the double helix and the neat linearity of the Central Dogma – that DNA is immutable, isolated and all-powerful in forming proteins – left some big questions unanswered: what, exactly, do genes code for, and how does genetic programming relate to development, behaviour and biological difference? While molecular biology dined out on poetic form throughout the 1950s and 1960s through a global mushrooming of laboratories and research programmes, narrative was chomping at the bit: what did all of this mean for the multiplicity of human experience?

The crisis of Anglo American hegemony during the early 1970s is a significant context for how the genome became a prototype for a new kind of subject in the late twentieth century. The development of genomic sequencing techniques by Fred Sanger during this decade marked a watershed moment for possibilities of reading the genome. Post-war alliances were being placed under pressure by geopolitical uncertainty, and the balance of power seemed to be turning against Anglo America. Keynesian economics was about to give way to neoliberalism, but, for a moment, alternatives seemed possible. In this uncertainty, a new articulation of freedom emerged, which swept up the radical propositions of the 1960s into an ideology of limitless choice based on an idea of the individual as an endlessly malleable entity. At the same time, a different kind of governance would be required – not a radical break from liberalism, but rather a different set of operations, in which this individual would be broken down into component parts formed of desires, movements, labour, but – most importantly – remain trackable. This new subject was born out of data, a hyperextension of an eighteenth-century statistical imaginary, now reduced to molecular form. Sequencing practices offered a prototype for the imaginative formation of a neoliberal subject, and the transition from the state discipline of individuals, to the corporate control of data.

If, as Evelyn Fox Keller has argued, the twentieth century was 'the century of the gene' (2000), then in the 1970s the gene transformed from icon to economic unit. The idea of genetic material propagating itself through evolutionary history as the primary unit of natural selection, positioned processes of genetic heredity as antithetical to welfare, planned societies and collective action on behalf of a commons or community. Genes were anthropomorphized into competitive entities driven towards moving themselves through time, with bodies as vessels for genetic material. The story of the gene's bent towards self-perpetuation derived part of its immense cultural power from the transformation of global politics during this decade, and a conservative backlash against post-war decolonial and anti-capitalist movements, as well as Black Power, the Civil Rights movement, second-wave feminism and Stonewall. These were social and political movements which, in different ways, were responding to a long history of deterministic explanations for social and global inequalities – that is, to such inequalities being described as natural (and increasingly across the course of the nineteenth and twentieth centuries, as biological), rather than social. This is part of a longer history of liberal humanism, which has been premised on the exemption of enslaved, colonized and indigenous peoples (Lowe 2015) – what Sylvia Wynter calls 'Man 2': the Western bourgeois male subject (2003). The strategy of this backlash was not to insist on the biological case for white male supremacy, but to code the survival practices of whiteness as the biological status quo.

Evolutionary theory has long relied on economics for its metaphors. Darwin's theory of natural selection drew on Thomas Malthus's 1798 essay on resource scarcity and natural checks to population growth, and Adam Smith's invisible hand – individual actions out of which good social outcomes emerge. Ian Hacking describes this reduction in the context of the emergence of the statistical imagination during the eighteenth and nineteenth centuries and the 'counting' of human behaviour: 'Data about averages and dispersions engendered the idea of normal people, and led to new kinds of social engineering, new ways to modify undesirable classes' (1990, 9–10). Foucault's concept of biopower is that it derives from practices of tracking birth rates, death rates, biological disabilities and environmental effects, a form of power that 'deals with the population, with the population as a political problem, as a problem that is at once scientific and political, as a biological problem and as power's problem' (Foucault 2003, 245). It engenders disciplinary infrastructure that creates arbitrary boundaries in human experience: racial difference, sexual difference, gendered difference and differences of ability. Phenomena are translated into discrete units of observed characteristics as the coordinates for social organization, obscuring sociopolitical change not determined from the top down, and not accounting for biological events that appear as non-genetic inherited changes.

Updating evolutionary theory at a time of increasingly computational laboratory practices meant adapting its metaphors. At this crisis point, the collapse of social arguments into biological absolutes was enfolded into a tug-of-war between free market capitalism and state-oriented welfare liberalism. Military metaphors were central to this, as new forms of governmental security emerged to monitor and surveil, rather than to discipline and punish, as Gilles Deleuze argues in 'Postscript on the Societies of Control' (1992). Achille Mbembe theorizes this as a new geography of resource extraction correlated to 'an unprecedented form of governmentality that consists in the management of multitudes':

> The extraction and looting of natural resources by war machines goes hand in hand with brutal attempts to immobilise and spatially fix whole categories of people or, paradoxically, to unleash them, to force them to scatter over broad areas no longer contained by the boundaries of a territorial state. (2003, 34)

Mbembe distinguishes this from techniques of policing and discipline in 'the colonial *commandement*', which have been replaced by 'technologies of destruction that have become more tactile, more anatomical and sensorial, in a context in which the choice is between life and death' (2003, 34). This chapter is organized around the role that the genomic imaginary played in this transition from discipline and punish to military surveillance, first through the metaphor of overpopulation in Doris Lessing's *The Memoirs of a Survivor* (1974), and then in Samuel Delany's *Trouble on Triton* (1976), where the prophylaxis of endless choice for white-collar consumers becomes a technique of population-level control.

In this new regime of governmentality, to which the gathering of data is central, genes as discrete segments of information offer the material basis for tools of necropolitical governance, in which – following Mbembe – 'weapons are deployed in the interest of maximum destruction of persons and the creation of *death-worlds*' (2003, 40). This focus on data organized around the disaggregation of human bodies into units of information effectively eradicates the need for a landscape external to it, whether this landscape is characterized as the human bodies that house this data, or the ecologies those bodies inhabit. Under the aegis of both the Modern Synthesis and the Central Dogma, molecular biology made developmental biology largely peripheral to its concerns; that is, the question of whether or not adaptive demands of and upon an organism's environment play a part in selective evolution (Huneman and Walsh 2017). If it does not – and this was by no means a consensus – then what did that say or deny about the power of human agency (individual, collective) to transform these conditions of existence and social organization? The exclusion of development, itself a narrative bound in particular kinds of exclusion, accelerated the emergence of 'new and unique forms of social existence in which vast populations are subjected to conditions of life conferring upon them the status of the *living dead*' (Mbembe 2003, 40). Narrating the self in the era of the genome bracketed plural, non-chronological and environmental accounts of development; the individual does not develop across all kinds of intersecting temporalities. Rather, it is divided into a-temporal genetic units of code that determine a rigid chronology, which is itself reliant on a strictly genetic account of lineage. The only time that matters is the time of reproduction, when an inheritance is passed on.

In 1973, the evolutionary biologists John Maynard Smith and George Price published a paper in *Nature* called 'The Logic of Animal Conflict'. In it, they present an argument for why conflicts between animals of the same species tend to take the form of limited war: battles that involve both sides using 'inefficient weapons or ritualized tactics that seldom cause serious injury to either contestant' (1973, 15). Why, if natural selection means that individual organisms are constantly engaged in struggles to ensure the promotion of their own genes for subsequent generations, wouldn't natural selection have fitted animals with 'maximally effective weapons and fighting styles for a "total war"' (15)? Why do snakes wrestle rather than kill, or deer hold back from 'foul blows', or antelope 'kneel down to fight' (15)? The question Maynard Smith and Price ask in 'The Logic of Animal Conflict' is an extraordinary one: in essence, why don't animals of the same species kill each other, if the primary purpose of natural selection is the promotion of individual germ-lines? Why is nature not in a state of total war?

Their answer is that selection needs to promote a range of responses in order to give individuals the best chance of surviving, even if this sometimes means retreat. Applying game theory to evolutionary models did two things: it offered a way of calculating the probability of certain kinds of behaviour, and accounted for these behaviours by describing them as genetic. There are selective advantages for a range of possible responses to a given conflict, and these responses correspond to genes. Game theory characterizes behaviour as essentially competitive, and suggests that this behaviour can be more or less reduced to genetics; this held the further implication that it was sealed in the code of the double helix, impermeable to external influences, and that strategies (and subject positions) of mouse, hawk and bully were therefore fixed as calculable probabilities.

Lessing and Delany imagine new forms of social organization after moments of crisis, and with them, formations of subjectivity that grapple with the ideology of natural selection. These texts are deeply concerned with the relation between infrastructure and lineage, and particularly in how socio-economic forms can transform inheritance. The city is a key site in these negotiations: for Lessing, a version of London after an unspecified disaster, and for Delany, the planet Triton, where every social possibility is permissible, but which has transformed material history into endless surfaces. In Lessing, the more radical possibilities of this new iteration of London are still embedded in the muscle memory of modern categories of who deserves more or less care. The subjects that are marked for survival, and those who head off into uncertain futures, are divided across a failing post-war consensus between the working, middle and governing classes – and these are racialized divisions. The emancipatory rhetoric of second-wave feminism collapses into the centring of white female leadership as a strategy of gender equality, in lieu of a functional welfare state accessible to all. Informal markets emerge to supplement the diminishment of state welfare, and this is also racialized. In Delany's *Triton*, the city Tethys is divided into the unlicensed and licensed sectors, which the novel's protagonist Bron moves between in a misguided search for inspiration or reproduction. A war serves as background noise, while Bron tries to find a sense of purpose and place in a society where taking on any identity – in theory – is possible.

Both Lessing and Delany's novels probe the conceptual gap between programme and junk: what is predetermined, and what is incidental or waste material. These narratives are marked by a troubling of chronology, through the unpredictable and uneven vacillation between memory – as monologue, sequestered within parentheses, or behind walls – and action. This vacillation forms subjects who seem to move without restriction through new lifeworlds, but who are simultaneously bound to typological constraints of selfhood and identification: forms that do not change, despite the crisis, and where heredity figures as the transmission of sociobiological memes.

In these novels, biology is a site for possible transformation, but is tied into processes of social reproduction which render disputes around labour and social organization redundant. Genetics becomes an alibi for social norms. Cities in these texts are spaces for producing what will later become the algorithmic subject of late capitalism, pieced together by bioinformatics, in which the genomic provides a conceptual and technological keystone for the disaggregation of subjects into component genetic parts. This new subject is not confined within a disciplinary regime, but rather a biopolitical regime of security and personalized health (Foucault 2003; Novas and Rose 2005) that serves as an alibi for necropolitical governance.

In making some of their key claims for general audiences, evolutionary biologists in the 1970s frequently turned to economic and political metaphors to set out their arguments. In what follows, I consider how Richard Dawkins and E. O. Wilson use narrative, character and metaphor in their respective imaginaries of human potential, and the limits of agency when it comes to biological programming. It is partly through their books that the gene transformed from an icon of heredity to a unit of evolutionary currency that might be exchanged or taken out of circulation. Surveillance is key to this: the genome is above all an object that is made visible through techniques of mapping. As I go on to explore, the cities in Lessing and Delany are sites of ambivalent and mysterious forms of surveillance: no one is ever really sure if they are being watched, but everyone acts as if they are.

While the global megacity appeared as a new geographical site for a multitude of probabilistic mappings that took populations as their units of calculation, the idea of the genome was imagined as a site of competition, genes jostling for space and recognition, while also acting as control mechanisms. It is in this decade that it becomes possible for the genome to become imagined as akin to what Stephen Shapiro describes as a pre-emptive networked response system for 'the control of danger by recourse to a mathematically-enabled knowability' (2018, 56). These imaginaries do not need an opposition between individual and collective; crucial, instead, is the aggregation of data, and the creation of signifying, mass narratives about what that data might mean at the level of population. Lessing and Delany depict this disjointed process of aggregation and signification as in flux, and inescapable.

## Gene and strike

In his preface to the 1989 edition of *The Selfish Gene*, a startling detail about the composition of its first two chapters jumps off the page: Dawkins recounts writing them amid power cuts and blackouts during the 1972 coal miners' strike. The strike spanned six weeks, from early January to late February, with high-risk areas going without electricity for nine hours a day (Johnson 1972). Unable to do laboratory work, Dawkins drafted the chapters that would become 'Why are people?' and 'The replicators'. The strike was over a pay dispute between the National Union of Mineworkers (NUM) and Edward Heath's Conservative government. A state of emergency was declared one month in, on 9 February. The strike was successful: the Wilberforce Inquiry – which was begun and ended in one week during the strike – recommended a pay increase of 27 per cent. Further strikes happened in 1973 and 1974. When the blackouts ended, Dawkins went back to the lab, coming back to the book while on sabbatical in 1975.

This is not a small biographical detail, given that these chapters put forward an argument about the relationship between labour power, genetic programming, and automation that casts the human worker as a computer carrying out instructions from a programme at a distance, a collection of data that is expressed at different points, and the body as a conduit for code. Dawkins's side note situates his claims explicitly in the ideological conflicts of British deindustrialization: the transition from industrial capitalism, factory and mine, to finance capitalism and office spaces connected to a network of transnational, and increasingly digitalized, monetary flows.

The 1972 strike was the first in a decade of strikes that broke the post-war 'stalemate' between the British working and middle classes (Worsthorne 1959, 421), a stalemate characterized by what Jim Phillips calls the almost-universally 'grudging attitudes to the postwar economic, social and political "settlement"' (for either going too far or not far enough) (Phillips 2006, 202). The 1972 strike had a profound effect on British domestic politics, undermining Heath's government, and 'sharpen[ing] social conflict', after pit closures in the 1960s (Phillips, 187). Phillips argues that Margaret Thatcher's description of the strike as 'a victory for violence' served to legitimize her own attacks on organized labour the following decade (187). The government had responded with strategies of strike breaking, arrests and police violence at the picket lines. Michael McGahey, the Scottish miners' president, decried a 'fundamental working-class bias in the laws used to control pickets' (Phillips, 188), foreclosing the end of Heath's tenure, at a time when he was pushing for entrance into the European Economic Community (EEC). But from the perspective of British industrial history, the 1972 strike registered both the devastation of pit closures during the 1960s for miners, and foreshadowed mass deindustrialization during Thatcher's rule.

At the outset of *The Selfish Gene*, Dawkins declares that he is making a case for generosity, given that at the level of genes, nature is programmed to be selfish. Organisms are nothing but 'survival machines' – conglomerations of competing genes – and societies are, at most, constellations of individual survival machines. These machines encounter other survival machines in their milieu as competitors, unless directly related or in some kind of biological kinship relation. Another survival machine 'is something that gets in the way, or something that can be exploited' (66). It is important to cultivate generosity and altruism, Dawkins argues, because care for non-biological kin is not part of the evolutionary story. Only behaviours that advance the propagation of one's own genetic material matter, 'because we are all born selfish' (3). Evolution does not work at the level of the group or species – contra Vero Cooper Wynne-Edwards, Konrad Lorenz, Robert Ardrey, Irenäus Eibl-Eibesfeldt. It works, for Dawkins, on the individual.

This reads as a treatise against collective forms of organization, positing them as antithetical to biological interests. For Dawkins, appealing to the natural equality of all peoples flies in the face of the laws of natural selection, which favours selfishness as a vessel for genes to travel through time as long as they can. The early caveats in the book about the importance of cultivating generosity and altruism (just because genes are selfish, it does not mean that humans have to be) are nonetheless bound up in a refutation of class struggle as a means of social change.

Writing a popular science book for a mass audience, Dawkins uses easy-to-grasp metaphors to describe biological processes, and he has a particular fascination with machines. The processes of the body should be understood as mechanisms akin those that motivate sewing machines, looms, automatic bottling factories, or hay baling; and in many of these artificial machines, 'timing is achieved by that brilliant invention, the cam' (48). A mechanism which the classicist Andrew Wilson dates back to the third century, and also described in the Arabic scholar al-Jazari's *The Book of Knowledge of Ingenious Mechanical Devices* (1206), the cam works by transforming rotating motion into linear motion. It is a way of regulating the timing of mechanical devices, and – as Dawkins intimates – was fundamental to some of the technologies that enabled the industrial revolution. He also mentions the punched card invented by Herman Hollerith in the early 1900s: a piece of card with holes punched into it that signify particular configurations of data, like those used in music boxes or automatic pianos (a punched card features in the opening credits to the first season of *Westworld* (2016–), a show whose plot is organized around technologies of automata and predestination).

For Dawkins, these earlier technologies of automation are not the best fit for analogizing biological processes. 'Survival machines', he writes, 'seemed to have bypassed the cam and the punched card altogether' (48). Instead, biological mobility involves uses a timing apparatus that 'has more in common with an electronic computer' (48). In this swift switch of analogies, Dawkins outlines the tension between two modes of capitalist production – industrial and finance – and distinguishes two modes of socio-economic governance: liberal and neoliberal. The former assumes what Hardt and Negri call a 'scarcity economy' (2009): that is, the impossibility of sharing resources due to their shortage, and with this, the division of public and private spheres based on a capitalist account of property. The latter operates precisely by obliterating the borders between public and private. Dawkins goes on to proscribe neoliberal governance through the metaphor of a genetic control system, distinct from the laissez-faire free market model of classic liberalism proposed in Wilson's account of sociobiology.

In the first chapter of *The Selfish Gene*, Dawkins notes the 'great intuitive appeal' of group-selection theory, while dismissing belief in it as being akin to the naïve and untutored idealism of undergraduate zoology students 'indoctrinated by misinformation in school textbooks' (8). On the following page, after citing Ardrey's 1970 book *The Social Contract* and its promotion of 'animal righteousness' in contrast to human self-annihilation at the level of species, comes this revealing speculation:

> Perhaps one reason for the great appeal of the group-selection theory is that it is more thoroughly in tune with the moral and political ideals that most of us share. We may frequently behave selfishly as individuals, but in our more idealistic moments we honour and admire those who put the welfare of others first. We get a bit muddled over how widely we want to interpret the word 'other', though. Often altruism within a group goes with selfishness between groups. This is the basis of trade unionism. At another level the nation is a major beneficiary of our altruistic self-sacrifice, and young men are expected to die as individuals for the greater glory of their country as a whole. Moreover, they are encouraged to kill other individuals about whom nothing is known except that they belong to a different nation. (Curiously, peace-time appeals for individuals to make some small sacrifice in the rate at which they increase their standard of living seem to be less effective than war-time appeals for individuals to lay down their lives.) (9)

If this sounds like a confusing conflation of social groups – union, nation, army – then it is worth staying with the confusion. Dawkins is playing on the substitution of biological process for social lifeworld in the movement between anthropological and biological descriptions of living processes. While making a case against unionism as a form of altruism that, paradoxically, requires displaying selfishness towards another group (here, the middle classes), he also makes a case against the evolutionary purpose of war, which impedes individuals promoting their own gene lines. In both cases, either a kind of extended individualism bolsters the barricades, or is put to one side for the sake of another group identification: the nation. In describing the particular form of control that genes represent – neither police nor paramilitary, but forms of distant command – Dawkins describes a new kind of governance. Genes are not a disciplinary system, having very little to do with checks and regulations, but more like a control system. 'Sealed off from the outside world', genes are akin to 'computer programmers', he writes (47). Bodies carry out their programmes 'without the help of the master' (47), and mothers are machines 'propagating copies of the genes' (123).

Another context is important here. As the strike took place, Heath was in the process of campaigning for Britain's access to the EEC – later subsumed into the European Union. The combination of the collapse of the Bretton Woods monetary system and the oil crisis had led to Heath's attempts to create a domestic 'demand' economy, leading to inflation and the attendant need to limit wage growth (Bancroft). He went about the latter without consulting the Trades Union Congress, and this was, in part, what had led to industrial action (Bancroft). EEC membership would offer the government legal grounds for limiting unofficial strikes and inter-union disputes (Phillips, 191). The decentring of the nation in favour of a European regionalism based on economic integration accentuated the antagonism between working-class and middle-class interests. But if, according to Dawkins, it was individual interests, and not national ones, that were of primary biological significance, then accession to a system that promoted such interests made greater evolutionary sense. Group selection – at the level of union or nation – runs contrary to selective advantages.

Finally, Dawkins's arguments are embedded in colonial imaginaries and a racialized, Malthusian discourse of overpopulation. For Dawkins, genes represent a form of control that extends across vast distances to determine the mechanisms of the survival machines they encompass, a description of imperial governance via globalized computation. In a later chapter, 'Family Planning', he lists a number of natural checks on population numbers: famine, plague, war, 'or, if we are lucky, birth control' (111). The preceding paragraph is about population increase in Latin America: the site of peripheral profligacy is no longer the slums of England's cities, as it was for Thomas Malthus whose rhetoric on 'natural checks' he imitates; rather, it is the Global South, where 'if the population continued to increase at the present rate, it would take less than 500 years to reach the point where the people, packed in a standing position, formed a solid human carpet over the whole area of the continent' (111). Genes want to reproduce, and the survival machines that carry out their programmes are designed to do just this. Hence, to deal with this drive towards selfishness, birth control measures in areas of the world where there is high population growth would be a form of generosity towards the rest of the world, ensuring a fairer distribution of resources. That these measures and natural checks are situated in the periphery and semi-periphery implies that for Dawkins, core sites have managed to facilitate equilibrium between social control and biological programming.

One year earlier, the American evolutionary biologist Edward O. Wilson had published his book *Sociobiology* (1975). This was a much longer argument for the genetic basis of behaviour, and how selection acts to promote lineages of certain characters: hunters, home-keepers, carers and so on. For Wilson, certain behavioural traits have been stabilized via selection, and derive from genes. Without giving a definition of what he means by behaviour, he argues for the genetic predisposition of certain social actors to particular kinds of behaviour, and his examples traverse the categories of social organization that were under so much pressure at the time he was writing: gender, ideology, sexuality, labour, race, ability. Racialized and classed hierarchies and divisions of labour have selective advantages, and (it would follow) a genetic basis. Women are 'predisposed to be more intimately sociable and less physically venturesome' (133). Anarchist forms of sociality are 'biologically impossible' (208). While there may be some negotiation at the level of phenotype, these negotiations are always centred on the selection of individual lineages.

For Wilson, ethics should be loosed from the hold of philosophy and handed over to biologists. There is no such thing as 'ethical intuitionism' – an inherent understanding of the difference between right and wrong, formalized by logic. Pitching himself against Enlightenment thinkers – Locke, Rousseau and Kant – he contests John Rawls's theory of 'justice as fairness', arguing that the intuitionist position 'relies on the emotive judgement of the brain as though that organ must be treated as a black box' (287). Rather, it is 'the true, biological joy of warfare' that gets closest to a universal principle of human relations, through which 'the spread of genes has always been paramount importance' (298). For him, it is the biological tendency towards violence, rather than justice, that has led to the evolution of the human species in its current form. In the last few pages, Wilson extends this to a plea against 'planned societies', his arguments registering laissez-faire liberalism:

> If the planned society – the creation of which seems inevitable in the coming century – were to deliberately steer its members past those stresses and conflicts that once gave the destructive phenotypes their Darwinian edge, the other phenotypes might dwindle with them. In this, the ultimate genetic sense, social control would rob man of his humanity. (300)

This is not just an argument about economic libertarianism, but also a defence of warfare as a means of ensuring human freedom. For Wilson, the state does not and should not need to intercede in social relations, because biology's natural rhythms of selection and destruction ensure that certain phenotypes retain their 'Darwinian edge' (meaning, here, the process of selection). Hence, biology is not only a justification for certain kinds of governance (or retreat of the state); it also becomes tied to spatial metaphors for human societies.

These arguments caused considerable outcry among scientists and non-scientists alike, whose main line of argument was that first, evolution is more complex and multilayered than natural selection operating on the individual (organism or gene), and second, that reducing social experience to biological inheritance tends towards justifications of the status quo (Allen et al., 1975). A group of prominent Marxist biologists resisted Wilson's co-option of sociology and anthropology, including Richard Lewontin and Stephen Jay Gould, identifying sociobiology as a broader harnessing of Darwin to conservative rhetoric about the genetic basis for social organization and cultural practices. For these critics, this only reflected the author's world view. The so-called sociobiology debate erupted across the pages of the *New York Review of Books* in letters dating from 1975 to 1978, resulting in the publication of an essay collection with contributions from some of the key responders (mostly critical), and including rebuttals from some of the anthropologists Wilson had cited to back up his theory. These commentators argued that there was a lack of scientific justification for 'the spurious promise of reducing such disparate fields as economics, government, and psychology to a biological science' (Gould et al. 1979). They denounced Wilson's view of behaviour and social structure as 'organs' of genetic programming, describing Wilson as one of 'the long parade of biological determinists whose work has served to buttress the institutions by exonerating them from responsibility for social problems' (Allen et al., 1975).

Planned and laissez-faire societies are not in opposition, but mark an oscillation between different moments of liberalism, which organize themselves around the question of warfare and economic power, tending to privilege territorialization. It was Dawkins who anticipated what was on the horizon: the large-scale expansion of neoliberalism, and the disappearance of individuals into conglomerations of genes, premising selection at the level of molecular replicators (genes), not organism. In *The Selfish Gene*, he posits a model of governance that leap-frogs the reinstating of classic liberalism as a counter to post-war Keynesianism, and a new modality of state power, analogous to the mechanisms of genetic governance, or at least how these mechanisms appear to him. While, for Wilson, the genetic basis for behaviour implied the inefficacy of state regulation – an argument for the evolutionary explanation for free market economics – for Dawkins, the fundamentally selfish activity of genes constitutes a need for security, given that individuals are only survival machines for hosting swarms of selfish genes. As Clare Hanson argues, while this might resemble theoretical feints of poststructuralism and postmodernism,

> Neo-Darwinism offers a decisive picture of human nature and history, a Lyotardian 'grand narrative' backed by the epistemological authority of science. The category of the human may have been decentred but in place of our traditional self-conception, neo-Darwinism tells us that much of our behaviour stems from dispositions which evolved in the ancestral past. (2020, 9)

The curious paradox Hanson outlines above informs the readings of Lessing and Delany that follow: humans at some point made history, but this history is now embedded in genetic programme. This grand narrative formed the ideological basis for the Human Genome Project over the following two decades, as Chapter 3 explores.

Reading Wilson and Dawkins together shows an intermingling of liberal and neoliberal ideologies in the new sociobiological determinism of the 1970s, with Wilson advocating a laissez-faire approach akin to classic liberalism, and Dawkins – in a neoliberal bent – suggesting the incorporation of state control (militaristic, institutional) as a way of managing the inherent selfishness of gene promotion, and likening this form of control to a satellite system of militarized surveillance. When Dawkins says that he is 'not advocating a morality based on evolution', but rather describing 'how things have evolved', he is also making a case for the kinds of interventions that would enable a certain kind of individual flourishing to persist, and one located in particular regions of the world (2). That is, a racialized narrative of overpopulation, which continues to centre Western bourgeois man as the individual whose propagation matters most. I turn now to the metaphor of overpopulation in Lessing's *The Memoirs of a Survivor*, a narrative that challenges the perpetuation of this subject at a time of social disintegration. Lessing also anticipates the disappearance of an idea of the developing human through the collapse of public and private, and in the mechanisms of a control system for tracking, rather than disciplining. Characters remain trapped in imperial spatializations that are based on logics of surveillance, and racialized topographies are key to this.

## Overpopulation and whiteness in *The Memoirs of a Survivor*

Lessing's *The Memoirs of a Survivor* (1974) depicts racialized inequities that are sustained and reproduced through socio-economic collapse, in imaginaries of overpopulation, anti-unionism and the role of white feminism in nourishing the liberal public sphere. It asks what might happen when the historical basis for the privileges of whiteness is threatened by the emergence of postcolonial counter-histories after the disintegration of empire, when the home country has begun to disintegrate. *Memoirs* unfolds in the *longue durée* of racial capitalism. The novel reconstructs how whiteness functions in the broader field of necropolitical power wielded in the name of nation and empire, and explores how white feminism is entangled with neocolonial forms of population control. The reconstitution of imperial hierarchies takes place through a rupture in women's alliances across racialized faultlines: white female leadership enables the sociobiological establishment of neocolonial white supremacy.

The novel takes place at a point of national crisis in a city of a former imperial centre: unnamed, but recognizably London. A disaster has struck the city. Resources are short, electricity supplies are unstable, public transport infrastructure has broken down, and people travel by foot. The narrator is an unnamed middle-aged white woman, who takes in a twelve-year-old girl, Emily. Emily and the narrator exist in uneasy and uneven sorority, while Emily gets on better with Hugo, the narrator's cat. The narrative's back-and-forth, fragmented composition reflects how the seams of social organization are becoming unstitched, held together by a feeble nostalgia for a disintegrating past. Emily meets the younger June Ryan, from a large Irish–Catholic family, and, later, Gerald, the leader of a pseudo-anarchist children's commune. These two characters are key to the way that the crisis gets worked out through Emily's position in relation to both of them, in terms of re-establishing the conditions for whiteness within a reformulation of public and private spheres.

The space of the city is critical to this. Most of the novel takes place within the narrator's flat, a single unit in a development 'built by private money' (6). From here, she looks out over the activity on the street below, watching groups of people migrate out, in search of survival. As a group of young people are leaving, they sing 'We shall not be moved', a Civil Rights song, and 'Down by the Riverside', a Black spiritual. The Rhodesian Bush War was ongoing at the time of *Memoirs*' publication, and the narrator likens an old hotel to an African township outside a mine where the Black workers live: Rhodesia's mining slums, out of which emerged a series of strikes in the 1930s that would eventually lead to the independence movement. The history of empire is held in the degeneration and depopulation of the city:

> [B]y that time, with so many people gone from the city, the families who lived in these blocks were not all the class for whom the buildings had been put up. Just as, for years, all through the eroding streets of the poor, empty houses had been taken over by squatters settling in families or groups of families – that for a long time it had been impossible to say, 'this is a working-class area, this is homogeneous' – so, too, in these great buildings once tenanted only by the well-to-do, by the professional and business people, were now families or clans of poor people. (6)

While the crisis seems to have transcended class boundaries, living space remains segregated. 'Squatter' holds the implication of homelessness and trespassing, and 'clan' implies a tribal identity, pre-urban: etymologically, from Old Irish 'cland' and Scottish Gaelic 'clann' (offspring, family). It also signifies a group identity, the migration of an entire genetic cluster, and holds the threat of possible invasion – group selection, not individual diversity. These words draw a racialized border between the narrator and the newcomers with regard to class and place of origin. She is the neutral not-clan, the not-squatter, the permanent resident, the settled, singular. 'They' are the multiple, the pagan, the destitute, the migrants. While social organization has changed as a result of this unknown crisis, the stratification of social hierarchy based on owning private property remains.

The names of the people living on the ground floor of the building along with the narrator are the Whites, the Smiths, the Joneses, Miss Foster, Miss Baxter: Anglophone names. They are not multiples, but 'self-contained units', one or two people per flat, and the narrator barely sees or talks to anyone on her floor (113). Compare this to the Indian family from Kenya, the Mehtas, and the Irish–Polish family, the Ryans, who live upstairs. These families are described in the language of sprawl, not in a proper place, always in motion. The Mehta children – appearing as a group, a multiple – are playing in the street, outside. To the narrator, they appear as a uniform group of 'dark-skinned boys and girls, all dazzling white shirts, crisp pink and blue dresses, white teeth, gleaming hair' (15). She breaks them down into details that appear to her – implicitly setting up a contrast of their pale clothes and white teeth with the darkness of their skin, how they appear en masse. To her, they are a mass of contrasts of colour, simply appearing. She never speaks directly to them; their communication is restricted to a nod and smile. She accesses Mr Mehta's informal economy upstairs, which she compares to a street market, 'through an irregular gap in the wall' (116), hidden behind a heap of things. The Mehtas are narrated through an orientalized veil of excess and irregularity that exists simultaneously with the ordered white world below where the narrator has come from, supposedly part of this territory but split off from it.

If the Mehtas have carved out a space of informality to supplement their exclusion from state provision, then the Ryans are narrated through their exhaustion of welfare resources. Mr Ryan is a violent and alcoholic Irishman, Mrs Ryan a Polish refugee; both are Catholics. Catholicism here is implicitly placed in opposition to the Anglican whiteness of the narrator and Emily, and also serves as a signifier of uncontrolled reproduction and the profligacy of the poor, straining the resources of the state. The parents are usually drunk, the eleven children will not stay in school, and their fifteen-year-old daughter gets pregnant (118–19). They do not hold the same social position of whiteness – coded white Anglican British – as the residents of the ground floor, and it is always from this position that we see these characters. In her description of the Ryans, the narrator remarks, without intended irony:

> It often happens that a single case takes wing out of its anonymity and represents others; in our city alone there were thousands of 'Ryans' of all kinds, colours, nations, unknown except to their neighbours and to the authorities, and these people in due time found themselves in prison, Borstal, remand homes, and so on. (118)

The Ryans are made to stand in for all types of non-white groups, representative of a mass of the unemployed, unknown and dissolute, who cause social problems that neighbours and authorities have either to take on or solve. This mass is multicultural; to draw on Judith Butler's critique of multiculturalism, they are presupposed by the narrator as 'already constituted communities, already established subjects' (Butler 2009, 31–2). The narrator's description has no insight or interest in the Ryans except as a social ill, a general degeneracy; they could be any number of non-white communities, described as 'communities not quite recognised as such, subjects who are living, but not yet regarded as "lives"' (Butler, 32).

The narrator's description of the Ryans articulates a neo-Malthusian anxiety around the 'over' breeding of the urban poor, racialized as non-white and classed as the sub-proletariat. Malthus's arguments in his *Essay on the Principle of Population* (1798) set the stage for Francis Galton's later theorization of eugenics. Malthus depicts poverty as a natural category of certain kinds of human, the poor characterized, in Philippa Levine's words, as 'fecund beyond their limited resources and unconcerned at bringing weak or poor stock into the world' (2010, 51). Similarly, the British welfare state needed to create undeserving subjects in order to define the limits of its action: this is the long history of the sensibility of 'enough is enough'. Virginia Noble (2008) and Michael Lambert (2017) have written on the construction of the 'problem family' as an object of exclusion, not through provision and in legislation of the welfare state, but rather through street-level decisions made by welfare officers about who would and would not be eligible for benefits – and that this street-level decision making became policy, rather than the other way round. Lambert argues that the problem family was not just a discursive category but also a 'very real and material product of the operational structures of the welfare state to condition access to benefits based on the performance of gendered norms' (2017, 246). These negotiations often took the form of 'unspoken, unseen, and unheard agreements which underpinned the governance of society' (246), carried out by street-level bureaucrats – welfare officers and social workers.

The novel is split between the transformation of public space outside the flat, and remnants of the past on the inside. Another space opens up in the walls, a kind of double world of disused rooms littered with broken and destroyed commodities of empire. The rooms on the other side of the wall function as a historical imprint and as an explanation for these social divisions. There, empire is reconstructed. One room is described as an eighteenth-century salon of the 'French, Second Empire', a rich and formal room, scattered with old wood furniture upholstered in silk, now laid to waste, in disorder, full of piles of rubbish. Another looks like the scene of a recent battle:

> The place looked as if savages had been in it; as if soldiers had bivouacked there. The chairs and sofas had been deliberately slashed and jabbed with bayonets or knives, stuffing was spewing out everywhere, brocade curtains had been ripped off the brass rods and left in heaps. The room might have been used as a butcher's shop. (40)

Savages and soldiers are characters in a scene of colonial invasion. The semicolon between the two groups is important: it suggests a relation of equivalence between savage and soldier, making it unclear which side committed violence. The scene describes a disembodied destructive force, an invisible tearing apart of an established order. There are two different historical moments suspended together here: the violence of colonial invasion and the spoils of imperial wealth. Confrontations between savages and soldiers happen at frontiers of invasion, and here the frontier is the salon brought into existence by a European project of wealth accumulation through territorial acquisition. The space behind the wall compresses these two moments, whereas in chronological time they are divided into discrete units of historical record (or left out entirely). Imperial trauma has become part of the cultural backdrop.

Figures of militarized liberalism that defend borders mark the transition between liberal and neoliberal forms of control. The narrative sets up pairs of pre- and post-crisis authority figures: the narrator, confined to the walls of her apartment, and Emily, able to move between spheres but unable to escape her own socialization; Professor White, the white patriarch 'placed high in administrative circles' (MS 56), who patrols the borders of his territory (the block of flats) like a sergeant, and Gerald, post-crisis white male vanguard who oversees a network of subordinates on the streets and in squats, upholding racial and sexual norms of imperialism for the sake of maintaining the network. The difference is that in this new order, it does not matter who comes and goes, as long as whiteness retains its position.

This eugenic legacy goes back to Galton, whose ideas set up a framework for biologizing race as a technology for improving the white race through selective breeding, rather than only as a justification of imperialism. In *Hereditary Genius* (1869), Galton instrumentalized Charles Darwin's arguments about biological heredity in *The Origin of Species* to posit it as the cause for innate inequalities between humans, and to imagine class as a subcategory of race. Galton argues that intellectual ability is inherited through parents, and that a 'high reputation is a pretty accurate test of high ability' (11). For him, hereditary superiority surfaces through social rank, and he speculates that 'it would be quite practicable to produce a highly gifted race of men by judicious marriages during several consecutive generations' (11). He ranks Black Africans below white Europeans in terms of natural ability, and argues that the ablest race in history was the ancient Greeks: '[T]he average intellectual standard of the Negro race is some two grades below our own' (307). Levine argues that Galton's link between race and natural ability was 'fostered in a climate suffused with notions of European imperial superiority, bolstered by a growingly confident scientific establishment' (6). His invention of a science of good (eu-) origins (-genes) to bolster his phylogenetic ranking of human capacity became, in the twentieth century, inextricably linked to genetic theory; a biological justification for social organization which placed European man – whiteness – at the top of the tree.

What is important about drawing Galton into a reading of *Memoirs* is his justification of eugenic partnerships on the basis of reproducing 'good stock'. Gerald and Emily seek to improve society through their partnership, adopting a different set of governing techniques. In Gerald and Emily's living space, there is 'no furniture at all, but there were curtains, and shutters were scrubbed and whole, and mats and mattresses were rolled and stood along the walls'; the communal rooms of middle-class domestic organization are gone – dining room, sitting room (128). There is only a 'long room for eating, with trestles and benches, everything scrubbed bare'; apart from this, 'each room was self-sufficient as a workroom or as a home' (128). The function of objects – mattress, table – are not fixed, but used according to need, and belongings are distributed among the community. This sparse space is stripped of the commodities laid to waste on the other side of the narrator's wall, the rolled-up mattresses acting as ramparts against the walls, where the past might lurk, and private ownership has been overturned in favour of communal property.

Even here, Emily tells the narrator, "'It is impossible not to have a pecking order. No matter how you try not to,'" as the narrator watches the way the nameless children react when they see Emily: 'This was how people respond to Authority' (129). Emily is the reluctant leader in this new society, run through controls which function 'like a self-deforming cast that will continuously change from one moment to the other' (Deleuze, 5). Emily's complaint about a pecking order is not a Hobbesian observation about the necessity of government to suppress the natural human tendency to violence, but rather an acknowledgement that while she and Gerald have attempted to repress the memory of the old world, she has nonetheless risen to the top of governing the new one, and not by accident.

This control society is an extension of the disciplinary one, not a radical break with it, and follows the same protocols of racialization and sexual socialization. Emily is prepared to reproduce whiteness by choosing Gerald, the rational, enlightened benefactor, as a sexual partner. Instead of resisting the old world, Emily is also socialized into it; behind the wall, she becomes white. The scene of trying on the white dress shows her trying on various kinds of social possibilities for inhabiting the place of a white female leader; most often the dress is a bride's dress, connoting marriage; then a young girl's dress for purity and innocence;

then a transparent night-dress to signify sexual availability and beyond this, fertility; then an evening dress to connote her mastery of polite society. There is no real Emily to be seen here, either in the trying on or in the assumption of various positions; she slips between roles, invisible to the narrator, who has forgotten 'the hidden person in the young creature [...] the self which instructs, chooses experience – and protects' (57). The narrator's forgetting is not a sign of senility or being elderly; rather, she is only able to conceive this 'self' in an abstract sense, as an ideal, while in the real world, 'Emily' moves between archetypes. This schizophrenic subjectivity facilitates the development of this new society of control.

Emily's role is to move between public and private realms in the constitution of a new sphere for economic growth that remains organized around the promotion of British, Anglican and white subjects. This role produces a rupture along lines of class and racialization between June and Emily. Their alliance is challenged and eventually annihilated by the difference in value assigned to their bodies in this reconstituted economy of whiteness. Irish–Polish Catholic June is described as smaller, younger, in awe of Emily, in love with Gerald. Emily adopts her like a child, looking after her like a benefactor, but refusing any kind of equal relationship. When June becomes a competitor for Emily's position after a sexual encounter with Gerald, Emily knows that this marks a break in her relationship with her; she seems frustrated by the protocols that demand this break. But she also knows that he has to 'make the rounds' of female bodies within his network (142), tracking and incorporating, a constant modulation, accumulating data and resources. June, on the other hand, comes back from her sexual experience with Gerald traumatized. The word 'raped' is not used, but June's growth has stunted, falling apart after a premature sexual relationship. She eventually disappears with another group, out of the city and out of the events of the novel, becoming invisible and untrackable the only resistance made available to her character.

*Memoirs* tells a story about how eugenic ideology foreclosed the collective social contract that formed the basis of the post-war consensus. The eugenic underpinnings of welfare restrict the transformative potential of post-war social movements and mass migration, and identity politics are de-politicized into individual characteristics that represent potential (Emily), profligacy (June), authority (Gerald), colonial nationalism (Professor White), colonial nostalgia (the narrator) and informality (the Mehtas). What's key is the reinstitution of whiteness as the governing order of a world in crisis. By privileging the white female leader as the only character moving through a developmental trajectory, the narrative effectively annuls any sense of autonomy or collective freedom that this trajectory has been assumed to afford (the invisible hand is of no use if there is only one person being guided by it). The novel's primary violence is the reflex of heteronormativity, which is organized around the perpetuation of white lineages. In *Trouble on Triton*, Delany explores a similar crisis of developmentalism where an endless choice of identifications collapses the difference between inner and outer worlds and the attending distinctions between social organization and subjective cohesion. Rather than adopting some of the more radical implications of this collapse of the bourgeois private sphere, the novel's protagonist lives between full expressions and parenthesis – what is expressed, and what is suppressed or forced back – in order to mitigate his alienation from an idea of what individual development should look and feel like.

## Brackets and choice: Samuel Delany's *Trouble on Triton*

*Trouble on Triton* is an experiment in queer narratology, set on a planet where heteronormative framings of kinship, identity and social organization are no longer relevant, but which is still reliant on biological categories of identity. These categories sustain a biomedical industrial complex of biosocial reconfiguration, where self-identification is inexorably tied to state surveillance. The narrative follows the unfailingly unreliable Bron Helstrom, a cisgender heterosexual white man from Mars establishing himself as an expert in 'metalogics' after a traumatic career as a prostitute. Bron's gaze makes what Guy Davidson calls the 'panacean possibilities of Tritonian society' peripheral – even grotesque – in his 'devotion to masculine bravery' (2008, 106). This devotion leads him to undergo gender transition, via surgery and hormones, to become the perfect woman – the kind of woman whom, he imagines, will be the 'counterpart of his deluded macho self-image' (Davidson 2008, 106). His friend Sam, once a small blond cocktail waitress who has now transitioned into a tall, Black male government agent living across multiple co-ops in various kinds of intimate configurations, tries to indicate a more plural and capacious set of practices around sexuality, intimacy and care to Bron. Nonetheless, for much of the text Bron is driven to assert his dominance over the novel's female characters as a way of securing his own sense of inhabiting a coherent and congruous identity. Both Sam and Bron are caught in a bigger story: Triton's endless war, and its correspondingly endless capturing of its citizens' data. Identity politics are co-opted into military datalogics, and any opportunities for its protagonist's personal development – held up to surface of the text – disappear into the novel's cipher-like composition, which circles its subjects rather than trying to figure them out.

On Triton, no one is really watching, but the government holds everyone's data. The novel takes place in chronological time, but Bron's narrative is repeatedly undercut by parentheses and monologues, which constantly take him out of his voice, marking the edges of what he wants to be and think and do.[1] His thoughts form a series of undulating interruptions, marked by a frenetic going-towards whatever it is that is currently the object of interest or desire. He constantly attempts to categorize his experiences, to place these in some kind of order, setting up a distance between actions and impressions, while taking any opportunity he can to reminisce – often at length – about his past. This place between parenthesis and expressed or direct narrative mimics the description of the activation and silencing of genes, described at length by another scientific rationalist.

This correlation between narrative form and Bron's ongoing attempts to make himself make sense on Triton anticipates forms of alienation under data capitalism, wherein labour is no longer a site around which to organize. The novel charts the sublimation of collective resistance into forms of bioengineering that evacuate identity politics from history, reducing identity from political community to individual choice. In the context of his own choice to transition, 'hungering for a settledness that *girl* and *woman* had never given me', Eli Clare describes 'trying to wrench my transformation away from the medical-industrial complex', while knowing that 'in truth, the people who control transition technology are all embedded in the white Western system of medicine, trained to identify and repair body-mid trouble' (2017, 179). What Clare describes here is not just the imbrication of individual decision-making and private profit, but also the way in which collective movements become reduced to chemical compounds, Big Pharma profits, and the ideology of 'cure' (2017, 179). For Clare, this tension is not resolvable, and instead, he allows 'choices and politics [to] jostle against each other' (2017, 181). Bron is ultimately unable to do this, seeking instead a point of resolution, and relying on all kinds of parenthetical gestures to streamline his individuation across all his internal contradictions and interpersonal dead-ends. He remains cordoned off from messier versions of reality and relationality, and punctuated by hormones and genes.

---

[1] The pronouns used for Bron here follow Delany's in the text: 'he/him' until gender transition, then 'she/her'.

The novel begins in Tethys, a city on the planet Triton, a planet involved in an interplanetary conflict between Earth and Mars. For much of the novel, the war is background noise. Five million people are killed in a single explosion on a planet we never see. In Tethys, distractions from interplanetary terrors are the way characters get through their days, and Bron's passages through spaces of the text are marked by a meandering waywardness. He moves from the men's co-op he lives in – the Serpent's House – to his white-collar office, then pursues the text's white rabbit, performance artist The Spike, through the dark streets, narrow alleys, and miscellaneous dwellings of Tethys's unlicensed sector ('the u-l'). Many people have moved to Triton because there are freedoms and benefits there which, on Earth, would be restrained and restricted. People on Triton are tracked but not disciplined. The war is prompting redundancies, and Triton's civil rights problems roughly resemble Earth's: Miriamne, Bron's temporary Black female co-worker, is fired by Bron because he sees her as a sexual competitor for The Spike's attention, and because she has no sexual interest in him. Bron goes on an undercover mission to Outer Mongolia, more or less accidentally, gets interrogated and tortured by soldiers on Earth, and is eventually rejected by The Spike. Arriving back on Triton, he becomes an accidental war hero – arriving in the right place at the right time to save some of his friends from being blown up. Experiencing PTSD but unable to name or talk about it, Bron's fixation on finding a mate heightens, while the 'horrors of war' become central to his performance of masculinity. His hope is that by transitioning, he will be able to preserve the species by encouraging reproduction of his own genes; in a logic reminiscent of Wilson, Maynard Smith, Price and Dawkins, he sees those genes that programme heroism and aggression as an evolutionary route to species survival.

Bron thinks he still lives in a world governed by statistics. Davidson notes *Triton*'s appearance at a moment of economic stagnation in the West, which 'necessitated significant changes in the organisation of capital', from the mass production lines of Fordism to the flexible forms of accumulation in post-Fordism, 'in which economies of scope supplant economies of scale, resulting in a seemingly unrestrained proliferation of 'niche' consumer options' (2008, 101). *Triton*'s narrative is constructed through the difference between understanding the self as a statistical object – a type, a tendency – with its implication of being part of a developmental story about human potential, and the dissolution of this subject into any number of possible identifications, and with this, the dissolution of a developmental narrative. There is an excess of possibility on Triton, where citizens have all number and manner of self-transformations at their disposal and, it seems, without bearing huge financial costs. In this world, identifications of gender and race become 'surfaces' (Chan, 190), 'aligned with the more obviously cosmetic, and ever more easily rearranged, significations of identity such as dress and adornment' (Davidson, 106). While what Davidson calls Triton's 'statistical imaginary' provides an anchor for Bron's sense of self-coherence, offering possible answers to his problems and a platform on which he might unravel his dishevelled psyche, the psychological (reduced to a spectrum of types) is only another space for shoring up the consumption of every available experience.

On Triton, genetic engineering is one of the technologies of these transformations, while metalogics forms the basis of an economy running on informational descriptions of reality. Genes are a pathway to different expressions of human experience. Bron spends lots of time trying to see himself clearly in a reflection, describing his body in parts – hair, eyebrow, body-type. Early on, sitting in front of one of the 'ego-booster booths' at the transport station which gather information from the civilians who use them for 'the Government Information Retention Program', he takes in this disjointed impression – 'his face . . . distraught. One eyebrow . . . rumpled', the leather collar, 'the irregular coloured web for his chest' – and thinks, 'I haven't really looked at my final person. I – ' (7). This 'I – ' marks the interruption of Bron's ability – which underlies the whole text – to locate a sense of self developing through time. While *Triton* is, as Davidson argues, 'preoccupied with the classification of people in terms of types' – and therefore, with an informational gaze – the text also points to the instability and incompleteness of these optics in envisioning a free self. As Bron tries to find an ending by any means possible (which really means staying connected to a nostalgic sense of what masculinity 'means' for and to the species), the text's form holds him in a 'continuous unending searching and questioning', to borrow from Kathy Acker in her 1996 preface to the novel (xii). This searching and questioning is an ongoing offer of possible freedom that Bron never takes up, which seems to elude him, but which in fact he spends much of his time running from.

Readings of the novel have been organized around the question of whether Triton is a postmodern utopia ('a utopia of difference' – Pearson 2009) or – in Edward Chan's words – a 'heterotopian narrative'. The former – in Wendy Gay Pearson's words – 'succumbs to an impoverished view of difference' that restricts interpretation to 'the meagre axes along which Western epistemologies are able to think about and name it' (2009, 465). Chan reads *Triton* as 'a book about surfaces' formed by 'micrological details', a heterotopian narrative that questions the epistemologies that found the basis of utopian imaginings, and 'hits us over the head with the shock of what we imagine as social difference' (2001, 182). While typology is the 'manifest level' of the book – the subject that its characters talk about and struggle with – it is through the manipulation of bodily surface that Delany tackles the problem of social identity (190). Pearson notes that Triton's cultural critique depends on 'a heterotopian dismantling of the apparent naturalness of the social ordering predominant at the time it was written' (2009, 464). This dismantling comes through anticipating the weaponization of postmodern identity politics into neoliberal military regimes, and the generation of antipathy through what might be termed an excess of meaning. Biological accounts of ontology – as well as the kinds of gaps they leave for understanding and reconciling being in the world – are central to this weaponization.

Bron is caught between sociobiology and the selfish gene, between the liberal developmentalism of progressive evolution, and the neoliberal extraction and rearrangement of biological information. His conversations with The Spike are organized on this axis. The Spike tells him early on, "'You seem to have making a family down as an economic right denied you which you envy, rather than an admirable but difficult economic undertaking'" (112), one option among many – and, for her, bound up in the language of commerce, money, profit and risk. The family is no longer the primary unit of bourgeois participation; accessing this sphere is made possible by learning how to perform participation and to convince others that this is culture. All that really matters is exchange. The Spike is the perfect conduit for neoliberal contradictions: the peace-promoting performer, outside the formal sector, whose activities are funded by military security budgets. Her name is Gene, connoting origin, a word charged in this text with references to a medical industrial complex of transitional technologies, and biological renderings of identity: Gene as a segment of code, floating in the air, telling stories to individual listeners, programming from a distance, and something to be deciphered. Bron cannot understand her. She seems always to be very far away from him, and he does not learn how to read her.

The Spike's performances are also integral to military campaigns. When Bron meets her on Earth as part of a travelling diplomatic mission, they hear a young woman in the background say that "'no one is fighting [the war] with soldiers'" (150). The Spike's theatre company is on tour as "'part of an exchange programme between warring worlds so that all cultural context isn't cut off'" (154), she tells Bron. Perpetual war can go on for as long as cultural exchange – reduced to de-politicized appearances across warzones – is facilitated, while destruction takes place offstage. This regime highlights again the emphasis on security, rather than discipline, as the primary means of ensuring this form of freedom. On another planet, Lux, five million civilians are killed without comment, and these are not counted as losses. What matters instead is the representation of the full gamut of human experience on Triton, for which only a few people need to remain alive. Bron's early sexual harassment and unfair dismissal of his Black female colleague Miriamne does not only not matter to the movement of his own plot; it does not register as a problem to him, because race and gender have been reduced to opt-in/opt-out identities without specific histories. His hatred/adulation of Sam and his hatred/dismissal of Miriamne are viscerally anti-Black, and his ultimate inability to parenthesize either of them is one of the text's small victories against white supremacy.

Anticipating current discussions around the generation of data through online tracking systems, and the recent classification of Big Data as a potential military weapon, Bron considers the feat of getting people to give up information that could be used against them through the ego-boosting booths dotted around the city. He compares this to 'mak[ing] Dachau or Auschwitz a paying tourist attraction before the War was over' (5), making a point about how to make civilians buy in to the securitization of civil society – with its invisible guards and fences – and their own oppression. This is the only war story available; it is the only one that produces a reaction from those he tells it to, getting 'a number of laughs' (5). Bron's real experience of war begins at a border guard station, and ends over lunch with colleagues back at the office.

Genetics comes more explicitly into the narrative when Bron decides to transition. It functions as a vocabulary of misdirection and obfuscation, a conceptual toolkit for adhering to sociobiological reductionism. Bron is looking to save the species by becoming the perfect woman, while his transition counsellor, Brian, gives a genetic account of sexual difference. A chromosomal rearrangement and some hormones cannot 'make' Bron a woman, and Brian explains the process of sex change in technical terms. Her explanation to Bron parallels Bron's explanation of metalogics to Miriamne at the beginning of the novel. These are performative expositions, which place science as the primary arbitration of truth. This is the 'reality' of the gender-sex relation that Bron is asked to accept, the genome as a complex, quasi-computational system that technology can hack into and try to rewrite, but which he cannot supplement. This means accepting that some things might never be whole, or fully cured. Brian emphasizes the biological as a site of unknowns in a nihilistic key – "'life enclosed between two great parentheses of nonbeing and straited on either side by inevitable suffering'" (225) – and that improvement or even development goes against this logic. All you can do is follow the data, track the algorithms and hope for the best. To follow Clare, this exposes an ideology of cure that espouses the normal or natural as averages, 'the most common and best states of being for body-minds' (2017, 173). Here, genetics works in the same way as the ego-boosting booths: a way of examining one's reflection in parts and choosing what to pick out, while also a forming a molecular prison.

These violent parentheses of nonbeing structure Bron's own narrative, a way of coping with categories of social space that he is 'unable to reorder to his satisfaction' (Pearson, 464). Parentheses do not just mark the difference between speech and non-speech, but arrange Bron's experience of space and time into a hierarchy of meaning. The arbitrariness of this ordering of detail into higher and lesser importance in Bron's stream of consciousness indicates the way that Bron is unable to correlate observation and embodiment, the former often breaking up the latter between brackets and subclauses, before resolving into an action. This bracketing makes it possible for him, as a subject, to move through the spaces of the text:

> He smiled at the pink pavement. (The frown still hung inside, worrying at muscles which had already set their expression for the crowd; there was no crowd . . .). At the corner, he turned toward the unlicensed sector. (8)

The parentheses follow the plotting of space; as Bron moves through the city, he crams incidental or passing details – a frown formed through the experience at the ego-boosting booth – into non-essential grammatical space. This is about appearing in public, and appearing to be a coherent individual capable of public 'expression'; that is, of following a programme arbitrated by the pressure of the crowd, even when this crowd is absent. These parenthetical gestures delineate what Bron considers to be important and significant, but also what is necessary to express in order to appear in public. They become a way for him to hold the contradictions between the body's reactions and the world in which it operates – '(for the crowd; there was no crowd.)' Muscle memory prepares itself for realities that do not exist, but which Bron has nonetheless been socialized to expect, preparations and expectations which Bron is then compelled to silence in order to deal with them. This play between expression and silencing is rendered in the vocabulary of being responsive, and of reacting appropriately.

Parenthesizing seems to be a social phenomenon on Triton:

> The underpass was lit either side with cadaverous green light-strips. Bron entered. Those afraid of the u-l gave their claustrophobic fear of violence here (since statistics said you just wouldn't find it inside) as their excuse.

This is a space lit by the colour of decaying bodies, between formal and informal sectors of the city, where death happens out of sight. The fears of those living in the planned area of the city of its informal parallel world are projected onto this non-space. Here, statistics are subordinated into parentheses, because they do not offer evidence for this fear. What is highlighted instead is the parallel between 'claustrophobic fear' and the green-lit underpass, connected through a sense of compression and hiddenness, as if fear has become part of the infrastructure of the city. Parentheses in both these cases are used to exclude details about the city that are not relevant to the unfolding of narrative, but which nonetheless point to other possibilities that are not part of consensus reality – muscles prepared to face a non-existent crowd with a frown, and statistics that show that there is no evidence to fear the unlicensed sector.

The repeated use of parenthesis is an example of genomic form. Brian ascribes a grammatical form to the genome when describing the expression and silencing of genes, where certain details are emphasized and others bracketed off. Similarly, Bron's subjectivity is dominated by differentiating between what is relevant and irrelevant to his stream of consciousness, and to his sense of being in the world. He cannot exist fully in his voice, going into constant asides, making details incidental. At the same time, these subordinated details are awkwardly arranged. He is arranged into formal and informal spaces of awareness and observation.

There is a disjunction here between the temporality of the body, and the socialized time that it follows. Bron's constant bracketing is a way of streamlining the messiness of being; he regulates the constant flow of information and its accompanying interpretations that the city activates and silences as a way of staying within his sense of himself. In her theorization of the erotohistoriographical – which she defines as 'a politics of unpredictable, deeply embodied pleasures that counters the logic of development' – Elizabeth Freeman notes that 'bourgeois liberal entities from nations to individuals are defined within a narrow chronopolitics of development at once racialized, gendered, and sexualised' (2005, 58, 57). Bron's attempts to adhere to what he considers to be the official timeline of Triton is the imposition of his own chronopolitics of development, resulting in chronic and undiagnosed anxiety. The bracketed information flows unevenly into the narrative space of the text, gesturing both to the way that information needs to be managed between unregulated and formal activities, and how this regulation does not follow divisions of public and private spheres. In both the quotes above, the public – as 'crowd' and 'statistics' – is relegated to parentheses, becoming incidental to the passage of the individual through the city.

Bron's anxious parenthesizing for the sake of this narrow chronopolitics manifests as an identity crisis. After transition, she returns to the clinic, concerned that she does not '"feel like a woman ... all the time, every minute, a complete and whole woman'", but only remembers when she thinks about it, or when "'some guy makes a pass at me'" (249–50). Brian's response is another misdirection, but an instructive one: genes cannot be isolated and made to account for experience, because "'any string of nucleotides they might isolate is really only a section of a very complicated interface, both internal and external'" (250). Ontology escapes genetic grammar, because it is also contingent on the kinds of environmental conditions that determine the usefulness and relevance of certain traits. Using the example of women with perfect teeth in "'a terribly inbred town in the Appalachian mountains'", Brian emphasizes the importance of the environment as "'the external part of the interface'" which makes "'certain elements plentifully available, and other fairly absent'" (250): that is, the conditions for perfect teeth. Brian then maps this comparison onto being a woman, "'a complicated genetic interface'", living in a body from birth, "'growing up in the world, learning to do what you do ... with and within that body'" (251).

While Brian's explanation seems at first to be an argument for the complex interrelation of environment, phenotype and genotype in the production of experience, there is something more troubling going on here, highlighted by her ultimate belief in the stability of the category of 'woman'. Brian's explanation articulates the explanatory void around which biologized descriptions of identity circle, in an attempt to retain the supremacy of scientific reason. Subjects end up being left out of their decisions. Due to the complex interface she has described, "'you will never be a 'complete' woman,'" says Brian, the word 'complete' carving out a space in existence that Bron cannot reach. Chan notes the 'technical sophistication with which the [transition] operations are done' and – as an aside – that this implies 'some interesting things about the intersection of business, technology, and public opinion' (2001, 194). That is, the reason these individual decisions about identity do not matter is first, because they are tied into a social obsession with individual typology which is itself shown to be a fiction, and second, because the manipulation of surfaces is bound to an economy fuelled by scientific rationalism. While Brian is careful not to reduce traits to genes, *à la* Dawkins, her account of the difference between gender and sex marks a troubling essentialism, where 'the environment' becomes a site of determination and fixing. Her invocation of an isolated, 'inbred' community in a remote and peripheral area shows how Triton's analogies and comparisons derive from modern cartographies of geographical and cultural difference that seem resolutely Earthly and imperialist. Triton's transition technologies are premised on a feedback loop between an individualized biomedical infrastructure, and public consensus around what 'being a woman' constitutes. The peculiar circumlocutions of Brian's explanation, while promising an account of biological plasticity in the making of gender, end up collapsing this promise into modern colonial arbitrations of gender and sex, using the sociobiological chronopolitics of development as an alibi.

This is not by chance. Brian's explanation is intimately connected to military datalogics, a means of weaponizing individual uncertainty into apathy towards mass destruction and genocide. In these moments of obfuscation and indeterminacy, Delany's interrogation of colonial epistemologies of gender, sex, sexuality, race and ability is most apparent. It is not just the categorization and typologizing of life itself that needs dismantling – liberal governmentality – but the proliferation and de-signification of data that this inevitably leads towards. To follow Chan and Pearson, what the heterotopian narrative highlights is not so much an ideal of endless personal choice, but rather the limited efficacy of technologized personalization in producing collective iterations of freedom. The instrumentalization of personalized decision-making becomes a way of holding off transformations of bodily affinities and temporalities, for the sake of upholding techniques and technologies of mass surveillance and control. Read this way, the interplanetary war is not a backdrop, but constitutive of Bron's crisis. At the end of the text, reduced to a sociobiological account of herself, Bron's choices disappear. As Pearson puts it, 'Bron is caught in the tensions between [biological] destiny, destination, and *destinerrance*; this, quite ironically, makes him in many ways the most utopian character in this ambiguously heterotopian world' (469). Her nostalgia for patriarchy – a world in which her preferred type of masculinity can flourish and reproduce – is still 'a blueprint for a better world', which her peers seem to have given up on (469). Instead of realizing this utopia, she is lost in a hinterland of monologues and parentheses, still trying to make sense of the past.

The lure of a typological multiculturalism is an abstruse cover-up for parenthesizing crimes against humanity. Dean Spade and Craig Willse identify something similar in their discussion of multicultural imperialism, and a troubling complicity between the promotion of the United States as the centre of the 'free world' along the lines of progress made towards equal rights for racialized minorities, women and LGBTQ+ people, thereby justifying continued military intervention and imperialist expansion abroad. For Spade and Willse, multicultural imperialism describes the reduction of potentially transformative, wide-scale identity movements to a typology of state-sanctioned identifications, in turn used to bolster an explicitly 'Western' construction of liberty. The rhetoric of liberated subjects deployed around gender and sexual politics is used to produce a divide between modern and anti-modern states – as in Samuel Huntington's 'clash of civilisations' thesis (1996) – and to justify military interventions. In the case of the construction of the Middle East in post-9/11 Euro US, in which women's rights and LGBTQ+ rights are suppressed under a monolithic Islamic, heteronormative patriarchy, the West is promoted as a site of liberated subjectivity. Multicultural imperialism does not function outside the restrictions of sovereign typology, but places a multiculturalism of fixed types in opposition to repressive uniformity.

Sam represents a conflicted alternative to this, a character who gradually moves from the periphery of Bron's lifeworld into the centre after her transition. When Sam is first introduced, Bron 'hates' him. An intermittent resident of the one-gender, nonspecified co-op that Bron lives in, Sam is worldly, brilliant and powerful – 'Sam had about as much power as a person could have, in anything short of an elected position' (26). He is also plural and expansive in his practices of intimacy: 'one of the reasons that Sam was away for so long between visits (Sam explained one evening) was that he was part of a thriving family commune (the other fifth of the population) of five men, eight women, and nine children in Lux' (26, 27). The parentheses here look like anxious annotations as Bron attempts to find a place to put Sam. Sam seems to resist these attempts, which ends making him irresistible to Bron. Sam spends time at Bron's co-op because in his other places of habitation, he cannot get away from politics; the Serpent's House is, for him, peacefully apolitical. Sam does not share Bron's need for cohesion, but is interested, rather, in local forms of synthesis. Nor is he performatively obscure, as is The Spike. Sam's mystery, we realize, is derived from the limits of Bron's own capacities to read the world. Sam is a product of Bron's bad reading, and his refusal to do 'practical social reflection just in finding ways of being queer', instead, 'avoiding such a self-understanding and the social reflection it would imply' to borrow from Michael Warner (1991, 6).

Sam does not live in the same time-zone as Bron. He has cultivated a way of being that 'exceeds the present', in Freeman's words, surviving not through a masculinist logic of heroism and destruction, but 'through the ability to invent or seize pleasurable relations between bodies . . . across time' (2005, 58). Instead of sequestering, silencing and holding back, Sam lives across multiple worlds and is able to move between them. This movement is neither painless nor innocent, but means that he is able to inform and warn – and save – those who have made a life out of sticking to the pantomime theatrics of Triton's death-worlds, trapeze artists and war heroes alike. Sam is constantly surprising Bron, taking him out of his nervous classifications. This is not for the sake of power games, as Bron tries to do with Miriamne; Sam answers questions, but he does not want anything from Bron that Bron can comfortably recognize or give. Meeting Sam by chance in a bar soon after her final conversation with Brian, Bron asks to come and live with Sam: '"Let me come and live with you and your family"' (261). Sam turns her down, and Bron is devastated and confused:

> *Why* had she been approaching Sam?
> Sam was no more a man than she was a. . . . No. She had to stop that thought; it could lead nowhere. Still, again, she had been about to sacrifice all her ideals, her entire plan, just for an . . . emotional whim! Yet, while it had been happening, it had seemed those ideals were just what she had been pursuing. . . .
> Sam?

Here, '. . .' takes the place of parentheses. Bron is fully within the confusion of her thoughts. 'Stopping the thought' becomes literal: she is thinking about stopping thinking, so that that the absent end of the thought that has been stopped is emphasized: 'woman'. She thinks she is not a woman, and being 'not a woman' at this point could lead her to nonbeing. This is a moment where Bron's refusal to learn how to be queer takes up expression in the main. Was her 'plan' to save the species always to become a woman so that she could be with Sam, a trans male queer? The sequence extends and expands to encompass her querulous and fearful question, parentheses of nonbeing temporarily held at bay by a visceral working-through.

The question mark suggestively gestures to a different kind of proximity between private and public experiences of time, and how this proximity might bank onto another set of possibilities for survival. This proximity is not based on a collapse into surfaces, but on what Tyler Bradway – reading Delany's queer experimentalism – calls 'the hermeneutic relation to embodied uncertainty' which 'keeps open the possibility for dialogic history to emerge' (2017, 64). This is in contrast to the 'forgetting perpetuated by narratives predicated on the myth of historical objectivity' (2017, 64). This historical objectivity and its deliberate amnesia are figured in *Triton* across both the social and biological. Delany's heterotopian narrative shows the contradictions involved in the dissolution of a chronopolitics of development, when the main instrument to perform this dissolution is a string of disassembled code. Bron's prolonged inability to relate to others outside a conceptual matrix of gender binaries (being a 'complete' woman), a matrix which continues to determine social relations even as its central subject – the male hero – does not, ultimately, matter in terms of changing the broader historical narrative of the planet, which is its war. As a playful compromise, the text leaves a question mark over forms of kinship that might be forged, instead, through the messier meetings of politics, care, health and transition, without closure.

Lessing and Delany's novels chart the disintegration of liberal developmentalism (sociobiology) into a neoliberal logic of exchange and substitution (the selfish gene), which also shows the collusion between these ideologies of the self and social organization. In *Memoirs*, this disintegration is bound up in eugenic models of social organization, which typologize humans into genetic categories through which relative productivity and usefulness can be measured. At the same time, eugenic practices make possible maintaining the supremacy of heteronormative whiteness at a point of socio-economic crisis. *Trouble on Triton* riffs on the ruse of completion, and of being a whole subject in time, dividing its protagonist across indices and syntax, luring her through narrative possibilities that never materialize. Genetic engineering represents a set of practices of biological self-fashioning, and a formal analogy for subjects that live between full expressions and parentheses, unable to distinguish or decide on what is most relevant for their sense of ontological security. Both show the complicity between biological constructions of the self and governmental control. Metaphors of biological programming in the 1970s offer an alibi for, if not total, then certainly endless war. This emphasis on security and a self that is no longer 'itself', but subject to and participant in the endless exchange and rearrangement of information, is a crucial context for the development of the Human Genome Project, which I turn to in Chapter 3. In the following chapter, I consider a different context for genomics, on the other side of the Iron Curtain.

2

# Cultivating dreamworlds

Genetics in the Soviet Union underwent a different trajectory in the post-war period, split into two areas of research – molecular biology and plant breeding – directed towards two different areas of Soviet development: military defence and agriculture. From the mid-1930s to the early 1950s, the latter faction dominated, leading to 'informational starvation' for geneticists trying to keep up with the rapid advances in the increasingly global and industrialized field of molecular biology (Levina and Sedov 2000). During the 1930s, Trofim Lysenko, the now-infamous amateur botanist, led a campaign against genetics and geneticists. This led to the banning of genetics in 1948 (which he denounced as a 'bourgeois science'), and the exile and expulsion of prominent Russian geneticists out of the Soviet Union or to gulags. While 'Lysenkoism' became a synonym for pseudoscience across the world, the exiling of molecular biology from Soviet science was by no means total. This was largely due to the development of biological warfare programmes in the interwar period, which picked up pace with the advances in biotechnology following the discovery of the double helix. Molecular biology in the Soviet Union continued under the secretive and often remote aegis of national defence. The so-called Fifth Problem – creating protective barriers for biological warfare from other nations – ensured funding for molecular biology in the post-war period.

At the same time, Soviet biology was also marked by the powerful metaphor of cultivation, part of a utopian vision where Soviet workers would nurture resources collectively (industrial and agricultural) and where the biology of workers might be cultivated at a mass scale. The biology of adaptation was applied to the figure of the New Soviet Person, a vision of a Soviet subject emerging out of Soviet environments, transcending differences of culture, language and land across the Soviet Union: a unified and collective subject formed by the Soviet state. Biological and aesthetic forms were placed on a continuum as tools of cultivation. In this imaginary, the Soviet state was akin to a soil in which crops could be cultivated in the right environmental conditions.

By the era of the genome, molecular biology in the Soviet Union was organized principally around the creation of biological weapons in secret laboratories, a history that is still marked by gaps. The Soviet biological weapons programme meant the development of a large workforce of expertise in molecular biology, and by the 1970s, this included methods of engineering bacterial and viral genomes through cloning and replication. Alongside this, the environmentalism of Lysenko still wielded influence over the experimental imaginaries of Soviet biology, exemplified in the genographic studies of the 1970s. At stake in both strands of Soviet biology was contributing to national projects of defence and agricultural production. This is key: while this was going on, the Soviet Union was heading into catastrophe, unable to withstand the pressures of the global financial crisis during the early 1970s, and ultimately losing its position as a viable political and economic alternative to the Euro-US.

This conflict exposes two opposing metaphors of biology in policymaking in the post-war period: engineering and cultivation. While molecular biology offered tools and techniques for isolating parts of the genome, cloning them and joining them to other parts (of the same genome, or of other species), plant breeding was wedded to pre-molecular ideas around environmental conditioning that also predated Soviet governance. Here, I look at two texts of the so-called Soviet 'Thaw' period – Boris and Arkady Strugatsky's *Roadside Picnic* (1972) and Kir Bulychev's 'Another's Memory' (1985). In their different representations of adaptation and molecular biology, these texts offer an alternative to the selfish gene, while also registering the dissonance between cultivating Soviet futures through a synthesis of collective, environment and individual, and engineering them at molecular levels. This was also a tension between biology as a technology of production and as a strategy of defence.

These texts are part of a body of Soviet sf that made its way into Anglo American publishing through various English translations during the 1970s and 1980s. Istvan Csicsery-Ronay describes this period of translation of Russian sf into English as a temporary creative boom between West and East: 'Soviet sf represented an alternative tradition altogether, and ethical-literary environment far different from the fast-forward techno-modernity of most Western and Japanese sf' (2004, 337). He reads this as part of a movement to frame imaginary futures for both West and East, at a point when neoliberal globalism had yet to sediment its ascendancy. Mikhail Suslov and Per-Arne Bodin have argued that during the 'golden years' of Soviet sf – from the 1950s to the 1980s – 'sf gave the intelligentsia an instrument to reflect on the technological optimism and the Communist teleology of Soviet modernisation' (2020, 6), in a trajectory markedly different from those of other post-war industrialization projects.

Crucial here is the importance of literature as a technology of national cultivation. In these texts, narrative is part of an environment that cultivates new subjects, a theme in Soviet dream-making from its inception. Soviet sf of this period reckons with what Susan Buck-Morss has called 'the passing of mass dreamworlds' (2000, 276) – dreamworlds initially imagined in social realism – and looks towards new possibilities offered by new globalized technologies. At the same time, they depict the future of humanity as an ambiguous landscape fraught with contesting visions of its use-value. Are bodies machines for dismantling, cloning and rearranging, or is the collective one holistic organism, moving in all its complexity towards realizing new possibilities for life itself?

Both Bulychev and the Strugatskys consider the failure to the imagination posed by the disintegration of Soviet utopias, and the fallacy of naturalism as a principle of truth under Stalinism. These are lifeworlds where the chronology of world-building is reversed, upended or held suspended. Fragments of shadow worlds slice into the present, from ambiguous origins and with unclear purpose. The West appears in these texts as a monolithic, shadowed entity, modelling biotechnological infrastructure. Uses of this apparatus remain veiled behind obscure state interests. Narrative form and biotechnological infrastructure are placed in uneasy concert, while contesting visions of the human fragment chronology and resuscitate forgotten or repressed pasts. The possibility of cultivating dreamworlds haunts the margins: a spectre of collective consensus that never really was. These texts explore the chaotic sorts of dreams that occur in the imaginative configurations of environment and body, at borders which might destroy, speed up progress, or which hold characters suspended in abandoned and disintegrating terrains where nothing grows.

## Mutual aid

Collective cultivation was a central metaphor in Russian life up to and during the Soviet period, whose economy was heavily dependent on agricultural production. The land and climate of Russia were constituent parts of Russian biology, in ways that diverged considerably from Anglophone interpretations of Darwin, which emphasized the organism's individual strategies of survival – for itself and its closest biological kin. The idea of an immutable line of inheritance passed down from one generation to another contradicted systems of common and collective ownership in both imperial and Soviet Russia, and these models of ownership – if only in theory – formed methods of experimentation in biological research. While Western genetics came out of a Lockean ideology of private property, with the figure of the capitalist-as-patriarch as a central character, Russian biology was organized around agricultural practices that involved larger numbers of people, often necessitating the collective pooling of resources.

The history of biology in imperial and Soviet Russia offers a frame for understanding the prominence of environmentally induced, collective adaptation in Soviet biology. Russian biology had taken up a different Darwin in the mid-nineteenth century, a version much more focused on collective adaptation than an individualistic version of natural selection. Russia had a harsher climate and larger terrain – a four-month growing season and vast areas of land where nothing grew at all (compared to England's eight-month one). After the abolition of serfdom in 1861, rural peasant communes were sites of technological innovation and, eventually, political resistance. There was no central jurisdiction, and often communes were doing the best they could with what little tools and infrastructure they had, closely attuned to the unpredictable conditions thrown up by the environment, year after year.

Post-abolition Russian agricultural production was characterized (though unevenly) by a system of common ownership, collective forms of cultivation and a system of sharing risk, in ways that were incomparable to what was happening in Western Europe. Cultivating the land was both materially and imaginatively crucial in the emergence of widespread resistance to imperial rule; this resistance was built in part through the autonomy offered by the proof that lifeworlds might be adapted and engineered through collective practices, even with limited resources and in harsh environmental conditions. While in the West, evolutionary narratives were centred on the struggle for existence at the level of individual, Russian interpretations of Darwin were more interested in the question of transformation at a collective level. The biologist Dmitri Pisarev criticized the 'rational egoism' of Darwin's Malthusianism, and Nikolai D. Nozhin adopted the French politician Pierre-Joseph Proudhon's notion of *mutualité* in arguing that biological organization is fundamentally cooperative, rather than competitive, when it comes to the distribution of resources. (Malthus had argued that given the scarcity of resources, 'natural checks' to populations – famine, disease – were not only inevitable but to be welcomed, and demanded no state mitigations.) The organization of peasant unions at the end of the nineteenth century demonstrated the influence of collectivist methods over pre-Soviet labour struggles. Scott J. Seregny argues that these countryside coalitions drew peasant concerns into the wider upheaval and unrest of the moment, in 'the first relatively successful attempt to establish a mass political movement in the [Russian] countryside' at the turn of the twentieth century (1991, 377). Mutual aid as a technique of cultivation moved across social and agricultural practices.

Pëtr Kropotkin took up the idea of mutual aid at the turn of the twentieth century in his essay collection, *Mutual Aid: A Factor of Evolution* (1902). While socialist revolutionaries believed that mutual aid was primarily a social phenomenon, Kropotkin was concerned with proving that mutual aid was an inherent feature of biological evolution, in ants as much as humans:

> The ants and termites have renounced the 'Hobbesian war', and they are the better for it. Their wonderful nests, their buildings, superior in relative size to those of man; their paved roads and overground vaulted galleries; their spacious halls and granaries; their corn-fields, harvesting and 'malting' of grain; their rational methods of nursing their eggs and larvae, and of building special nests for rearing the aphides whom Linnaeus so picturesquely described as 'the cows of the ants'; and, finally, their courage, pluck, and, superior intelligence – all these are the natural outcome of the mutual aid which they practise at every stage of their busy and laborious lives. (1902)

Kropotkin's vision of ant-worlds is akin to a far-off utopia on another planet, one built to ideal specifications, spacious and deliberately conceived, and more advanced in design and ritual than human ones. The reference to Thomas Hobbes stands as a rebuke to the latter's bio-mechanical theory of innate violence, his claim that there is no objective value-system outside human worlds, and his political arguments for absolute sovereignty as the only way of preventing perpetual war (2017 [1651]). Instead, Kropotkin joins Darwin in a fascination with cooperative systems among nonhuman species. Like Herbert Spencer, he is interested in the tendency of certain species to help each other, but unlike Spencer, this does not indicate a 'natural' division of labour analogous to that of industrial capitalism. So steep and serious are the obstacles that living groups have to overcome to survive, that – he writes – 'no progressive evolution of the species can be based upon such periods of keen competition'. These are examples of decentralized, nonhuman communities that make decisions through consensus, and shape habits around the constraints of the ecologies they happen to inhabit or move through; for Kropotkin, this is an example for human praxis.

Writing just before the fall of the Berlin Wall, Stephen Jay Gould – in accord with Daniel Todes – situates Kropotkin's arguments in *Mutual Aid* within a long and popular history of anti-Malthusianism in Russia: 'Kropotkin was part of a mainstream flowing in an unfamiliar direction', which represented 'a standard, well-developed critique of Darwin, based on interesting reasons and coherent national traditions' (1988, 16). The question of resources, selection, and adaptation had a very different kind of relevance in 'an immense country [and] also, over most of its area, a harsh land' (1988, 17). On the steppes, under brutal conditions, it is the battle between groups and environment that might determine survival, rather than individual fitness. Malthus's principle of overpopulation was cultivated in the increasingly dense urban environment of 1790s London characterized by segregated deprivation, with seismic and transformational revolutions happening in Haiti and France. It did not map onto a sparsely populated area of vast distances whose landscape necessitated community survival in isolated areas, human and nonhuman alike. And as Kropotkin points out, it was under-population, not overpopulation, which was 'the distinctive feature of that immense part of the globe which we name Northern Asia' (Kropotkin 1902). As Gould argues, Russian critiques of this Malthusian, selective Darwinism were attentive to the difficulty of translating Darwin's construction of organic processes to other geological and meteorological environments. Recognizing Darwin's regional biases did not mean throwing his ideas out entirely, but adapting them into local practices.

## Cultivating humans

Narrative and cultivation were closely aligned in the Soviet project. Soviet ideologues knew that to transform everyday processes of production – and, through this, to mould a new kind of citizen – it was necessary to tell different kinds of stories. The stories of the nation would be responsible for cultivating its subjects, across divisions of biological and social. At the Soviet Writers' Congress in 1934, Maxim Gorky decried the detective story as the paradigmatic genre of bourgeois literature, where a solitary detective ignores 'patent crimes against working people' in favour of 'mysterious crimes of the imagination' (1977). He reminded his audience – which included Karl Radek, Nikolai Bukharin and Andrei Zdhanov – that stories about stealing depend on an idea of private property that upholds a bourgeois fantasy. Literary and biological technologies for what the novelist Yury Olesha called 'engineering the human soul', a phrase taken up with enthusiasm by Stalin, were placed on equal footing. Socialist realism foregrounded labour processes as the primary narrative principle in the struggle for existence, eschewing bourgeois narratives organized around ancient times, single heroes, epics and romance. Likewise,

Soviet biology centred the figure of the collective as an agent of evolutionary change (human and nonhuman), a line of thought that dates back to nineteenth-century anarchist writing on mutual aid as a primary mechanism of evolution (over natural selection).

Soviet biology offered an alternative evolutionary framework for cultivating new social subjects under Stalin; while this was not strictly eugenic in the sense understood by Galton, this framework underpinned Soviet experiments in human biology, whose focus was the cultivation of the New Soviet Person. The banning of genetics in 1948 was partly a response to the instrumentalization of Gregor Mendel's laws of heredity by Nazi scientists to bolster their racist pseudo-science during the 1930s and 1940s; even earlier than that, in 1927, the biologist Clarence Dunn visited the Soviet Union; there, he found that his 1925 textbook *Principles of Genetics* had its chapter advocating eugenic policies removed. According to the translator's preface, this was because 'its outmoded bourgeois capitalist ideas ... have no relevance for our body of citizens' (in deJong Lambert 2013, 19). Instead, Soviet eugenicists 'aimed at establishing a Marxist, Soviet eugenics movement as part of a vision for a scientific organisation of society' (Pers Anders Rudling 2014, 46). Eugenics in the Soviet Union was interested not in racializing populations into a superior/inferior hierarchy, but in studying purported racial differences among the different territories of Soviet dominion for the sake of eventual incorporation into the Soviet project as New Soviet citizens as part of the collective productive force of the new nation.

This form of eugenics was drawn into the larger centralized vision of a Soviet dreamworld under Stalin. Human biology became part of the technological apparatus for achieving this utopia, through the idea of environmental cultivation. Model citizens might be cultivated through conditioning. The land was a key site of transformation in Soviet realism, with human and nature closely entwined. Soviet biology was less about dividing humans into component parts, and more attuned to possibilities for harnessing biological processes in technologies of collective cultivation. Biology was to be a domain for producing (and reproducing) the New Soviet Man and Woman: a new kind of human for the possibly endless prolongation of the Soviet project. The rise of Lysenko was made possible by the belief that humans – like plants – might be cultivated into being more productive and healthy, and bio-psychically sublimated into an ideology of selfless collectivism. Lysenko's theories were banked in a longer history of environmental influence over biological development in Russian biology, and the broader programme of Soviet biosocial engineering. While his agricultural experiments were generally failures, his political influence in Stalin's government during the 1930s and 1940s reflected Stalin's wider ambition to engineer the soul of the Soviet subject.

Lysenko was an anti-Mendelian and a proponent of the theory of the inheritance of acquired characters in his agricultural experiments. He wanted to foreground the Russian biologist Ivan Vladimirovich Michurin's 'Creative Darwinism'. In his 1948 Lenin Academy speech, the same speech in which he banned genetics, Lysenko dismissed what he saw as Darwin's errors – the Malthusian influence, the struggle of the species and its contribution to natural selection and evolution. He argued that the environment is 'the sole force that drives organic change and evolution' (Schneider, 147). Through Michurin, Lysenko resurrected a form of Lamarckism in Russian biology (although he denied this was the case); he believed that organisms evolved through the inheritance of acquired characters in response to environmental stimuli.

The son of a kulak, Lysenko was working at a research station in the Caucasus to find crops suitable for freezing conditions in the early 1930s. His father Denis had sown winter wheat in the spring after keeping seeds in a sack under snow (he had been hiding them from grain collectors during the grain crisis). Upon planting, he saw that these seeds produced exceptionally high yields. Lysenko expanded this into a method of cultivation he called 'vernalisation': 'the transformation of winter-habited plants into spring habit' (deJong Lambert, 22); literally, 'making spring-like'. The idea was to promote the accelerated development of wheat plants by adapting seeds to sprout in colder temperatures, for the sake of fast and large-scale production.

The influence of Lysenko on research in genetics was by no means total; genetics was not eradicated, and when it reappeared as a legitimate field of research, it remained allied to the project of Soviet industrial development. Susanne Bauer argues, 'Despite Lysenko's influence on the Soviet life sciences, the terms genetics and cytogenetics began to reappear in medical research during the 1950s, yet they remained an "underground science"', moving to radiation biology and mutations research (2014, 164). By the mid-1960s, Lysenko was declared a fraud and was condemned by Soviet geneticists for 'causing great damage to Soviet agriculture' (Graham 2016, 1). Despite Lysenko's fall from grace, his influence over Soviet biology – namely, his stance on the importance of the environment in shaping evolutionary change – influenced subsequent research in Soviet biology. The interim period between the banning and reinstatement of genetics as a legitimate area of scientific research produced something new and quite unlike anything that was happening in mainstream Anglo American biology at the time: a fusion of developmental biology and genetics.

By the era of genomics, this vision of the New Soviet subject had faded into the crumbling infrastructure of the global post-war boom. While the Soviet project was another decade from being over, the global financial crisis of the early 1970s ricocheted across the world, affecting both East and West, but the Soviet Union did not have the same capacity to overcome it as the West did. Later, the forcing of post-socialist regimes into IMF debt rescheduling and free markets – and the consequent challenge to workers' rights – led to the diminishment of Soviet dreamworlds. The global influence of emerging genomic technologies placed pressure on these alternative strands of biological thought, as well as the national drive to keep up as competitors in the various international techno-scientific races of the time. Not least of these was the development of biological warfare programmes, as I explore in a reading of the Strugatskys' *Roadside Picnic*.

## The Fifth Problem in *Roadside Picnic*

*Roadside Picnic* depicts a dreamworld collapsing into rubble, where invisible toxicity seeps into the bodies of a peripheral blue-collar community – ostensibly in the United States, a small town in a former industrial state, or 'possibly Canada', speculates Ursula Le Guin. The novel can also be read as a story about the disappearance of Soviet utopias, as mysterious, illegible, immeasurable alien forces contaminate an industrial township. An unknown event – known as the 'Visitation' – has left six zones across the world with collections of enigmatic objects, powers that cause the dead to rise up from their graves as living corpses and mutations in the genetic code of those who go into the zones, expressed in their offspring. The zones are sites of a nameless catastrophe, steeped in Old Testament metaphors of divine retribution for human shortcomings. The living world at large is exposed to its fallout. If the narrative takes place around the date of its publication – the mid-1970s – then the zones appear in the early 1950s. This dates back to the death of Stalin and the subsequent Khrushchev Thaw period, which saw the softening of restrictions around information and infrastructure exchange from West to East, the discovery of the double helix and the development of post-war biological weapons programmes across industrialized nations.

Here, I read *Roadside Picnic* as an analogy for the Soviet biological warfare programme, its shrouding in secrecy and its experiments conducted in remote areas of the empire, a programme which connected Soviet development in material ways to modes of production in competitor industrial nations. The biological warfare programme was one of the only sites of Soviet governmental investment that continued to allow an infrastructure for cytology and genetics within the Soviet Union; officially, genetics remained banned for another decade. Genetic research, still considered a Western import, was to remain in the laboratory. The first Soviet biological warfare programme ran from 1928 to 1972; along with Japan, it was the largest and most technically sophisticated in the world, and there was traffic between the two nations through shared infrastructure and knowledge exchange. As well as Japan, there were joint programmes between the United States, the United Kingdom and Canada, and China had its own. Many of the details around this first phase of the programme are unknown, because there was a moratorium on information and many records were destroyed. It was primarily a collaboration between Soviet military and Soviet industrial science. Biological warfare research was a significant source of funding for molecular biology institutions in this period, leading to what E. S. Levina and A. E. Sedov describe as 'hidden strings of compromise' between Soviet molecular biologists and the Soviet Department of Science of the Central Committee (2000, 425).

What is known is that the purpose of the programme was twofold. The first and most prominent strand of research was the development of strains of model bacterial organisms – foreign DNA – that would cause biological damage among enemy populations (weaponized pathogens). The second was to develop vaccines that would combat them; the code name for these efforts to create protective measures against biological warfare was the 'Fifth Problem'. For this, they needed test sites. In the early years of the programme, before the Second World War, three open-air test sites were established: the first at Tomka (later Staryya Shikhany) in 1925, near Volsk – just over 900 kilometres from Moscow – covering 100 square kilometres, first used for military training and then, from 1933, becoming a testing ground for chemical and biological weapons, home to 1,000 personnel and eventually extending to 600 square kilometres (Leitenberg, Zilinskas and Kuhn 2012, 23). Two further testing sites were established on islands: Gorodomlya, north of Moscow (about 10 kilometres square), and Vozrozhdenhiye Island, in the Aral Sea. The former was to become the go-to site for testing weaponized pathogens, 'so isolated that it afforded a high level of biosafety to open-air test sites, eliminating the need for additional open-air sites' (Leitenberg, Zilinskas and Kuhn, 23). Isolation was not only a matter of biosafety but also a way of keeping these activities relatively secret.

By the 1970s, according to science historians Milton Leitenberg, Raymond Zilinskas and Jens Kuhn, the Soviet biological warfare programme 'probably had a validated biological weapons system based on the *variola* virus' (smallpox), as well as a number of other biological weapons (45). The spectre of the early phase of extractive and settler colonialism through the transmission of smallpox to Indigenous populations is part of the muscle memory of militarized offence strategies, a global mode of territorial acquisition for the duration of colonial–capitalist modernity, a history in which the Soviet Union was also embedded through imported scientific infrastructures, and international knowledge and technological exchange with colonial powers. In *Dreamworld and Catastrophe* (2000), Buck-Morss describes the modelling of Soviet industrial townships in the 1920s and 1930s on those of American industrial cities that became epicentres of Fordist production, places like Gary, Indiana, and Detroit, Michigan. She details the visit of a group of Soviet engineers to Detroit, and their meeting with the architects who designed Henry Ford's River Rouge car assembly plant, and other prominent engineering companies (General Motors, Packard and Chrysler): 'this meant that a US capitalist firm [became the] designer of Soviet socialist industrialisation' (Buck-Morss, 165). This was not just knowledge exchange: in 1929, an entire Fordson tractor factory was constructed in Detroit and shipped to Stalingrad. Other similar imports resulted in what Buck-Morss describes as 'the largest technological transfer in capitalist history' (168). For Soviet ideologues this, too, represented a kind of alien contamination: could capitalist infrastructure be imported without its attending ideology?

*Roadside Picnic* offers an imaginary of biological warfare after something has gone wrong, when its effects are all that are visible, and the causes remain obscure and indecipherable, while set in a town that looks remarkably like one of the imported townships of Soviet industrialization. As Viacheslav Ivanov observes, the Strugatskys are particularly attentive to 'the flavour of contemporary science', particularly around theories of time and energy, and the social control of reproduction (2011, 9). These two themes merge in *Roadside Picnic* in its interest between the interaction of foreign code and environmental influence, the cultivation of biology through infrastructure, and vice-versa. The narrative begins with a promise of scientific hypothesis: an interview with Dr Valentine Pillman, a Nobel Prize-winning physicist, with a correspondent from Harmont Radio. (Harmont is the fictional town somewhere on one side of the Canadian border, possibly near Detroit, where the United States's Zone appears.) He is known for the discovery of 'the Pillman radiant': a theory of the Visitation's provenance and the spacing out of the six Zones across the globe. He describes the radiant acerbically, denying that it is either an important discovery, or really 'his' at all ('the radiant was discovered by a schoolboy, the coordinates were published by a college student, and yet it was named after me' (RP, 1)):

> Imagine taking a large globe, giving it a good spin, then firing rounds at it. The bullet holes on the globe would fall on a certain smooth curve. The crux of my so-called important discovery is the following simple observation: all six Visit Zones are positioned on the surface of the planet like bullet holes made by a gun located somewhere between Earth and Deneb. Deneb is the alpha star of Cygnus, while the Pillman radiant is just our name for the point in space from which, so to speak, the shots were fired. (2)

Two interwoven anxieties stand out here: the arbitrariness of language and warfare as targeted contamination. In this logic, the toxic Zones have appeared seemingly at random, the result of some unknown presence firing shots across the earth, presumably colossal, if the proportions of spinning the world like a globe are kept in mind: an act of unprovoked, extraterrestrial violence on a global scale. In this new state of affairs, national borders are also arbitrary: there is no superior nationalism that can save the world from this attack, the implications of which, thirty years on, remain elusive. It is a crisis of language and any sense of human ownership over knowledge, too: Pillman's ambivalence about the 'discovery' being a 'discovery' (resisting the implicit coloniality on which international recognition of individuals is premised), about this 'discovery' being 'named after me', and his caution against placing too much faith in scientific vocabulary (a radiant is 'just our name' for a place that can only be hypothesized about) reflect a global crisis of epistemological coherence.

This ambivalence is lost on the interviewer – 'Dear listeners: finally, a clear explanation of the Pillman radiant!' – who goes on to remind these listeners that two days' previous was 'the thirteenth anniversary of the Visit' (2). The radio host stands in for a more general effort to make meaning out of the crisis, weaving disparate and incommensurable details into narrative out of which some kind of culture might be forged: anniversaries, prize-winning theories and famous scientists. Making sense out of the crisis is key to keeping some semblance of normality, and it is science that – at least initially – is asked to give these assurances. This is a globalized effort involving ongoing promises of deduction and deciphering. There may be some grander secret to be revealed at a later date, or mystery to be solved: making the Visitation into culture places it in a logic of cultivation.

At a local level, these culture-making efforts make less sense. *Roadside Picnic*'s protagonist is Redrick Schuhart, who enters the text as a laboratory assistant on a scientific investigation for the Harmont branch of the International Institute of Extraterrestrial Cultures (again, mapping the event as culture – as Visitation – to hold off uncertainty). This involves going into Harmont's Zone to collect data. In time, these investigations are outlawed when the biologically deleterious effects of Zone begin showing up in the children born to those who enter it. Schuhart needs money; he has a young family, and his daughter has been born with some kind of mutation that means she is covered in fur and resembles a monkey, gradually losing her powers of human communication. He takes on work as a 'stalker', which became the title of Andrei Tarkovsky and the Strugatskys's loose adaptation of the novel in the 1979 film: a rogue agent who enters the Zone illegally to source some of its mysterious objects to sell to informal markets that have sprung up around the Zone along the edges of the Zone, extraction on the sly. The objects have no obvious meaning or purpose, but this uncertainty keeps value attached to them: they may well become useful at a future time.

If the Zone represents some kind of code inserted or spliced into particular sites across the globe, an illegible 'treasure trove' (110), then these objects are its unidentified sequences: a white metal bracelet that spins endlessly (89), and beads that become known as 'black sparks' that are used for jewellery (137). There is a genomic analogy here fused with the cultivation metaphor of Soviet biology – the Zone-code as cipher, producing forms that are in turn determined by external influences. Pillman conjectures that these sparks 'are actually vast expanses of space – space with different properties from our own, which curled up into this form under the influence of our space' (137). There are two things to note about this conjecture and its double helix lexicon: first, scale. The idea of small objects containing vast expanses of space corresponds to a biogenetic imaginary of the helix as a site of evolutionary time, extending well beyond the lifespan of an individual. Second, influence. The form of these objects, Pillman is suggesting, is in part influenced by the spatial dimension of Earth. Code can be localized, producing forms that are relevant to its environment, but also which are in some way determined by the configurations of this environment.

This fusion of code and cultivation was made possible by the kinds of cross-fertilizations of Soviet biology and Anglo American genetics throughout the course of the twentieth century. What is important in this discussion is the narrative ambivalence towards maintaining a distinction between the Zone and the context in which it has arrived. The border between the Zone and Harmont is more of a cultural articulation, which gradually erodes as the text goes on. This is a narrative about influence, its vagaries and incalculability, its seemingly arbitrary effects and the way it extends across biological and social realms – a theme which VanderMeer uses as an intertext in his Southern Reach trilogy, which I consider in the final chapter. The narrative momentum of *Roadside Picnic* is not generated by an architecture of causality, but by fragmented accounts of its effects. Amy

Ireland notes how this is registered through ecological transformation: 'the environment changes suddenly and inexplicably, and cause-effect relations are indecipherable, if they even apply at all' (2019, 67). This indecipherability gestures to an indeterminate traffic between phenomenology, epistemology and ontology in the text, between what is actually going on, constructions of reality and what this means for being. It seems that for the characters that hypothesize around the Zone, descriptions of its architecture and processes and the projections and expectations that its visitors place on it constitute what happens within it. In very literal ways, narrative structures outside Zone cultivate the parameters of reality within it.

Redrick's daughter – nicknamed The Monkey – only comes into the text twice, directly. But her appearances gesture to anxieties around new forms of warfare that might cultivate new forms of human life, or – in the case of The Monkey – scramble the supposed phenotypic chronology of evolutionary time, taking humanity 'back' to earlier lifeforms. Returning home from the Zone one evening, Redrick passes his daughter's bedroom door where she is sleeping, 'covered in warm golden fur': 'he really wanted to pick her up, but he was worried he'd wake her, and besides, he was dirty as hell, drenched in the Zone and death' (73). At no point do Redrick or his partner Guta describe The Monkey as a throwback or mutant; whatever she is, she is loved by them. Outside the home, she is a statistic of the Zone's effects on generations born after its arrival, but in this domestic space, it is Redrick who is the contaminant – harbouring death – rather than the daughter being an evolutionary aberration. There is an acceptance here that the Zone in some way has transformed her, and that going into it means bringing back some of its influence into the home. More than this: Redrick does not have a choice. The income of his family depends on it. There is no longer any other way of making their life as a family work.

Redrick's dilemma – being exposed to the Zone and reliant on it for income – reflects the longer-term precarity of Harmont, predating the Visitation. People cannot leave Harmont, because there is nowhere else to go. Part of the Zone's toxic lure are the forms of income to be made from remaining close to it. A blue-collar town in the American semi-periphery (or a Soviet synecdoche) learns to make its living from the tourist attraction that sits right next to it. The Zone's use-value as a cultural artefact becomes an economic necessity. Its topography helps retain a sense of mystery, exuding a mystique of extraterrestrial precision, its border marked by a 'black thicket along the road [that] looks almost mowed' (21). It helps the younger, childless Redrick in the novel's earlier parts anthropomorphize whomever or whatever has been responsible for its construction:

> These aliens must have been decent guys. They left a hell of a mess, of course, but at least they put clear bounds on their crap. (21)

Here, the younger Redrick imagines a dilapidated moral economy of mess and boundaries. The Zone is figured here as a private space, where anything is permissible so long as it does not seep past these borders into the public. It rehearses a fantasy of benevolent colonialism, where settling might be morally justified as long as settlers do not impose their standards (codes) on others. The fantasy of this equilibrium collapses, partly out of necessity and partly because Redrick comes to know better, but this early description corresponds to a strikingly liberal understanding of the division between public and private, and the basis for cooperative forms of social liberty.

This moral economy corresponds to the one that Evelyn Fox Keller identifies as 'the mirage of a space between nature and nurture' in her 2010 book on epigenetics. Nature is the space of the private – the 'mess' and 'crap' that needs bounds to be set around it – and nurture forms the boundaries of cultivation that enable this division. In this model, nature is innate and more or less immutable – the aliens cannot help their 'mess' – but nurture comes in to regulate its potentially damaging effects. Keller traces the emergence of this disjunction to Galton, and the point at which 'innate' comes to be synonymous with 'heredity'. In historical terms, it is most unambiguously a concept of imperial Britain, a way of theorizing social differentiation as biological difference. In the Soviet context, something different is going on, but Redrick's invocation of boundary-making as a condition of 'decency' corresponds, in this light, to a quietly eugenic management of heredity and public space, whereby those with messier (less fit) hereditary stock might be encouraged to keep it to themselves by not reproducing. This imaginary reinforces eugenics' global appeal: the assumption of a legible correlation between heredity, phenotype and fitness that might be harnessed for the sake of social progress.

If Soviet eugenics was a matter of cultivation rather than selection – hereditary material and environmental influence coextensive – this put the status of genes on more difficult terrain in the Soviet Union. Of greater significance was the question, to borrow from Keller, of 'causal interactions between DNA, proteins, and trait development' (2010, 50). Redrick's perspective shifts through the course of the narrative from this liberal division between public boundaries and private mess, refracted through the infrastructure of Western scientific infrastructure, to a more complex understanding of the forms of entanglement that the Zone exhibits, makes visible or produces. These illuminate not only a different epistemological field but also the toxic lure of a reductionist framework, how it keeps people fixed on its mysteries while perpetually holding off any finite answer. Reduction needs uncertainty in order to generate profit; what would it be to admit to huge gaps in understanding? How can culture be built around the absence of words to describe what is happening, even if those words are part of a lexicon of absence and lack? And if culture cannot be constructed, what happens to the idea of the human, let alone 'progress'?

No definitive explanation for the transmission of damage between the Zone, Harmont and the world beyond ever arrives. The meanings of its objects continue to vacillate in more or less arbitrary ways, temporary placeholders of function: "'We use them, although almost certainly not in the ways that the aliens intended,'" says Pillman, years on from his interview, but this is the equivalent, for him, of "'using sledgehammers to crack nuts'", the implication being that humans have no idea about the scale or force of the objects (136). In the electronics' salesman Richard Noonan's words, any hope of acquiring "'something fundamental from the Zone . . . that could revolutionise our science, technology, way of life'" diminishes as time goes on (135). While the Zone's energies remain inscrutable, their deathly effects travel beyond the perimeters of Harmont, transmitted like a contagion when its former residents who lived through the Visit move away. Pillman explains to Noonan,

> We don't know what happened to the poor people of Harmont at the very moment of the Visit. But now one of them has decided to emigrate. Some ordinary resident – a barber. The son of a barber and the grandson of a barber. He moves to, say, Detroit. Opens a barbershop, and all hell breaks loose. More than ninety per cent of his clients die in the course of a year; they die in car accidents, fall out of windows, are cut down by gangsters and hooligans, drown in shallow places, and so on and so forth. (139)

All this, and an increase in municipal and natural disasters: gas pump explosions, flu epidemics, tornadoes and typhoons. The mess of the Zone spreads out, a contamination characterized not by DNA sequences, but by a principle of disorder, disrupting human-made infrastructure and destroying ecosystems. The biological changes in those who have been in contact with the Zone register across both phenotype and genotype, and genealogy ('son of a barber, grandson of a barber') offer little in the way of stability or certitude.

These descriptions of death and catastrophe are terrifying not only because of their scale but also because of the apparent arbitrariness of this devastation. The only causal principle is proximity to the Zone and the time of the Visit, as if some invisible force extends over the whole of the Area, binding all of those in its vicinity to its violent energies. And as Pillman notes, it is not the objects or ghostly resurrections that pose the greatest threat to the idea of humanity; these are to an extent imaginable, if not explicable. Rather, the Zone represents 'the violation of the principle of causality' (141): not so much an extension of the principle of influence, but rather a confounding of the logic of cause and effect.

To return to the argument with which this section began: the Zones as open test sites for biological weapons. There is a shift in the narrative from metaphors of exposure to metaphors of proximity. Bodies are not exposed to, or cultivated by, particular environments (political, social, ecological) – or vice-versa. Instead, the narrative becomes a site where the contingency and unknowability of what it is to exist with others becomes visceral; that is, detached from inherited infrastructures for seeing and knowing the world. The great project of cultivation cannot survive this transition. It is one thing to be cultivated within boundaries; quite another to be in proximity with all kinds of unknown entities and forces with different origin points and unknown trajectories.

This is not a misplaced romanticization of human, nonhuman and inanimate cohabitation. If experimentation with biological weaponry has the potential unleash catastrophic and unknowable effects, despite the assumed isolation of test sites, then thinking with proximity – rather than cultivation – becomes a political necessity. When considered not just in terms of their horizontal devastation (across space, in the present), but also their vertical damage (across time, annihilating futures), new tools of biological mass destruction necessitate new metaphors for thinking about the scale of consequence when something goes wrong. The binary of cultivation/heredity does not go far enough: it is not just that organisms are cultivated by their environments; rather, these forms of warfare introduce new temporal and spatial proximities that subvert established frameworks for knowing the world. This proximity is not just biological: it includes the forms of uncanny proximity facilitated by globalized biotechnological and industrial infrastructure, and the forms of competitive nationalism (both financial and territorial) that promote the endless production of defensive and offensive weaponry; it is the constant proximity to states of war, and forms of destruction that cannot be regulated and managed by enemy lines or national borders.

*Roadside Picnic* ends with this transition from cultivation to proximity. In the final section, Redrick is paid to go into the Zone with Arthur Burbridge, the son of the local mob boss, because Arthur wants to find a legendary golden sphere that other visitors to the Zone have talked about. The golden sphere is supposed to grant wishes, a transcendental object capable of communication with those who seek it. When Redrick and Arthur find it, in something like 'an abandoned construction site', there's nothing golden about it; it looks like a piece of junk, 'closer to copper, reddish, completely smooth, and it gleamed dully in the sun ... cozily nestled between the piles of accumulated ore' (188). At first Red notices nothing unusual about it, but soon 'looking at it became enjoyable', and he wants to get closer to it.

> It suddenly occurred to him that it'd probably be nice to sit next to it and, even better, to lean against it, to throw his head back, close his eyes, and think things over, or maybe simply doze, resting. (189)

There is a toxic lure about the sphere, a dance of beckon and threat, to borrow from Mel Chen's theorization of toxic animacies. Chen discusses toxicity as a condition of sociality, rather than simply a property of an individual, group, or substance (2011, 272); a toxin 'is not necessarily alive, yet enlivens morbidity and fear of death' (265). Toxins can be thought of as 'conditions with effects, bringing their own affects and animacies to bear on lives and nonlives' (282). Toxicity involves different kinds of sociality, 'straddl[ing] boundaries of "life" and "nonlife", as well as the literal bounds of bodies, in ways that introduce a certain complexity to the presumption of integrity of either lifely or deathly subjects' (279). Chen gives the example of 'labouring or literally intoxicated subjects' – factory workers, agricultural workers surrounded by pesticides, residents in industrial and heavily polluted areas of the city – who 'tak[e] into their bodies what their better-vested employers can avoid' (276). The toxins inhaled and consumed by these bodies, as they destroy bonds of biological life (nerve endings, organ function, brainpower), produce other kinds of bonds that 'link these groups, bonds that are recognized in the potent affinities of labour and immigrant activism, have been laid there from without, to suture and reinforce multiple transnational systems of racialization, labour hierarchy, and capital – and ultimately of affection or nonaffection' (276). For Redrick, this proximity transforms his desire: from deciphering and extracting objects, to being absorbed by them, and from the certainty of cultivating boundaries to a liminal lingering.

Whatever force they find themselves near is neither to be trusted, nor a place to rest; rather, it re-enforces the violent forms of the system ostensibly outside the Zone. The sphere does not produce something new, nor bring something into being that was previously unavailable. Its animacy is generated through its absorption of systemic dysfunction. Redrick's experience of a transfer of desire from extraction to absorption is followed by a kind of response, the only action in the narrative that comes directly from the Zone. As Arthur leaps towards the sphere, ecstatic, shouting the entrepreneurial promises of the American frontier, 'Happiness for everyone! Free! As much happiness as you want! Plenty for everyone!', he is snatched up and squeezed to death:

> Redrick saw the transparent emptiness lurking in the shadow of the excavator bucket grab him, jerk him up into the air, and slowly, with an effort, twist him, the way a housewife wrings out the laundry. Redrick had the time to notice one of the dusty shoes fly off a twitching foot and soar high above the quarry. He turned around and sat down. There wasn't a single thought in his head, and he somehow stopped being able to sense himself. Silence hung in the air and it was especially silent behind his back, on the road. (190)

This encounter establishes a direct relation, a response from some invisible force to the humans who have come close to it. 'Transparent emptiness' and 'silence' become characters in this description, agents with suggested intentions and depth, rather than abstract placeholders for human perception – an emptiness in human form – a set of hands that can twist, something harbouring an intention to conceal itself, and a surrounding silence composed of corresponding intensities. The environment takes on a different meaning here: not just atmosphere or sonic waves, but something deliberate, attentive and responsive to human presence. This response does not induce a doubling-down on selfhood and individual preservation, but an evacuation of both: Redrick's sense of himself extends into what is close and near – the silence, the road and the sphere.

The movement from metaphors of exposure and cultivation to those of proximity breaks with a certain way of understanding bodies 'in' contexts, whether cultivated by an environment, or by mysterious objects whose functions and effects cannot be deciphered. Looking at Arthur's dead body, Redrick notes the younger man's matted, tangled hair. The moment gestures back to The Monkey's soft fur, and creates an unacknowledged affinity between these children of Zone adventurers, both on their way to becoming detached from human appearance in manner and body, proximate to a biological future that has not been planned for. An evolution resulting from unknown causes, in an environment that cannot cultivate the kinds of bodies it needs to move history forward.

In the next section, I consider Bulychev's short story, 'Another's Memory' through this crisis of cultivation in Soviet biology, alongside the making of so-called genographic maps of communities living under Soviet rule in remote areas of the empire during the 1970s. These maps were explicitly for the sake of charting and cultivating a productive workforce as Soviet growth declined as a result of global economic crisis, for working out the genetic basis for certain 'healthy' or 'unhealthy' populations, and for making policy recommendations in response to these data. At the same time, the dream of Soviet Man was fast disappearing as a horizon of possibility.

## Genogeography and Kir Bulychev's 'Another's Memory'

Bulychev's story charts the dissolution of a eugenic dreamworld: the death of the New Soviet Man. 'Another's Memory' is set in a science institute for biological research, somewhere at Moscow's periphery, sometime in the early 1980s: the final decade of Soviet rule. The barracks village surrounding the laboratory – residences built for its workers in the 1930s – is beginning to crumble and is in the process of being torn down. A new building, promised for five years, has not yet been constructed. A crane 'with a huge cast-iron ball dangling from a cable' swings over the remaining barrack buildings, which have been gutted for glass and iron, and deserted (135). The city has 'engulfed' the institute, once in the countryside, and undeveloped land sits at its edges: 'a creek remained, surrounded by tall banks of new buildings' (136). The institute is a scientific island gradually engulfed by urbanization, disintegrating in the process. Barracks suggest a former military presence now in the process of being erased, a backdrop that foregrounds the collusion of scientific research and national security. The crane forecloses a moment of destruction, but it is as yet unclear what will take its place.

The famous biologist Sergei Andreyvich Rzhevsky observes this as he makes his way into the institute, coming in on the bus, forced to take public transport for the first time in a long time because the institute car did not show up that morning. He is introduced as character complacent to his surroundings and accustomed to the perks of the job: a chauffeur-driven car, access to international research (afforded only to Party members at this point in time), and his own research programme in genetic cloning. On his desk as he walks into the office are 'several official-looking envelopes', 'a new English journal' and 'an abstract, from Leningrad' (136). He is someone to whom official mail gets sent, who is keeping up with international science, overseen by state observation, and a member of the Communist Party. The implication, then, is that Rzhevsky's success has been premised on his role in the Soviet Union's efforts to compete internationally in the production of biological research. The plot follows Rzhevsky's experiments with cloning: first, of a chimpanzee, and then of himself. He is able to produce an adult clone using only his own genetic material, bypassing sexual reproduction and the womb.

This clone, named Ivan, comes to consciousness with all of Sergei's memories fully intact, nothing repressed or forgotten, because he does not have the need to forget anything. This means that all the things that Sergei has had to forget in order to ensure some kind of psychological and professional cohesion come into his life: unwanted reminders of regrets, mistakes and the hurt he caused others. Ivan becomes a detective on a self-initiated investigation into Sergei's past, befriending one of Sergei's long-lost friends: a dusty archaeologist at the natural history museum. Much to Sergei's chagrin, Ivan chooses to train in archaeology rather than to follow in his father's footsteps and become a molecular biologist. The narrative accents Ivan's attention to history, rather than Sergei's experiments in technologized reproduction.

The story takes place at the tail end of post-war development of Big Science in industrial nations – particularly the United States, Japan, Germany, the United Kingdom and the Soviet Union – by which time Big Science had transformed the infrastructure of science research. Big Science carried a wartime legacy: military funding was key to the construction of big machines (the Large Hadron Collider in Geneva) – lots of them – and big laboratories (CERN). Sergei's cloning project is part of a global race to the finish: the Japanese are the Russians' closest competitors, "'close to success'", while an article from the United States is "'claiming some success with dogs'" (144). Sergei needs to justify funding, and there are comparisons made between cloning and atomic research. His board is interested in scaling up: "'Someday we will learn to do it on a mass scale,'" says the secretary of the biology division (144). The reference to mass production harks back to early years of Soviet production, here joined to the vision of reproducing a sublime body through the creation of 'a material environment whose larger-than-life proportions would allow . . . new super bodies to move in and take up residence' (Buck-Morss, 149). Sergei's experiments gain support through their nostalgic reference to an earlier phase of Soviet world-building, even as the infrastructure designed specifically for this purpose disintegrates and is shut down, replaced by the promise of laboratories that can rival those in the West.

At this juncture of degeneration and urban sprawl where socialist projects of industrial science are engulfed by capitalist rhythms of accelerated urbanization, suburbanization and unchecked speculative expansion, Soviet cultivation sits uneasily with Western reductionism: a model Soviet citizen to take the Soviet

Union forward into the next century, now expected to compete in a post-Soviet world economy. By removing the need for the unreliable mediation of the female body (as it appears to Sergei), and – literally – annihilating the space of the domestic, Soviet development can extend across both biological and industrial spheres by replicating the forms of its great men. Cloning would ensure maintaining the cultivated Soviet Man even as the ideological borders of the bigger Soviet project were in the process of disintegrating. Bulychev's story dramatizes the tension between molecular biology's future-oriented present – directed towards a looming global horizon at the fringes of Soviet science – and the ideology of cultivation in Soviet biology by collapsing them together. To clone Sergei is to clone the ideal Soviet Man; he is already perfectly adapted to his environment, or so it seems, a model citizen and the pinnacle of Soviet cultivation.

Cloning – a speculative technique of mass reproduction – suggests a particularly cinematic imaginary: the replication of images indefinitely, and the disappearance of the individual into a hall of mirrors. For Buck-Morss, the development of cinema at the beginning of the twentieth century offered a way of capturing '"the mass" as a coherent visual phenomenon . . . an imagined space where a mass body exists that can exist nowhere else' (147). In both the super-projects of socialism under Stalin, the attempt to create a material environment to house new super-bodies – 'the revolutionary mass along the expansive boulevards of Soviet cities' – meant that the individual becomes lost (Buck-Morss, 149). She notes,

> The Soviet citizen, like the Western man in the crowd, is exposed to a specifically modern anxiety of the meaninglessness of the individual that leads to enthusiastic endorsing of the process of doubling. (149)

As a technology of doubling, genetic cloning would make the socialist project real – the imaginary mass projected onto cinematic super-space – while also erasing any sense of individual outside this form. Sergei's project is couched within the dream of the Stalinist mass body, replicating the 'sublime body of the leader, the gigantically proportioned image of Stalin himself' (Buck-Morss, 145): a workforce of replica Stalins.

The fusion of cultivation and replication had a historical precedent in Soviet science policy, exemplified in the Soviet Union's large-scale population studies during the International Biological Programme (IBP), under the banner of 'human adaptability' studies. The IBP ran between 1964 and 1974, and was initiated by C. H. Waddington, who by this point had already coined the term 'epigenetic landscape' to describe the developmental pathways open to an embryo during foetal development (Waddington 1957). The IBP was a response to the call from leading ecologists to reroute the focus on space and technology and instead to develop 'a synoptic collection of observational data on a global scale', an attempt to put the biological sciences on the same kind of footing as the physical sciences (Aranova, Baker and Oreskes 2010, 183–4).

Genogeographic maps produced during this period were part of a number of public health policies in the Soviet Union geared towards the optimization of the workforce. Bauer notes that while Western approaches to population studies were more focused on heritage, and on 'preserv[ing] the alleged backwardness of the populations they termed "unique", Soviet science policy was geared towards drawing these communities into the wider labour force of the Soviet Union' (Bauer 2014, 168). Soviet biomedical studies in the 1970s targeted different professional groups for the sake of increasing their productivity – most notably, factory workers, railway line workers and construction workers.[1] Soviet biomedical anthropologists worked with computer-aided modelling techniques which 'rendered "populations" as systemic entities and enacted specific cybernetic versions of population, evolution and difference' (Bauer 2015, 146). These studies often focused on communities living in 'extreme conditions', which might undergo forms of accelerated adaptation to changed environments – industrial exposure or extreme climates (Bauer 2014, 167). In 1977, a study was carried out on the adaptive physiology of high altitude populations, measuring their capacity to work, physical performance and adaptive capacity, and whether these high altitude conditions might have therapeutic effects (Bauer 2014, 168).

These maps were produced to track 'humankind's capacities to respond to changing environments and aimed to find physiological principles on adaptation to new conditions, which included contemporary and future workplaces and, possibly, outerspace' (Bauer, 168), part of the broader – and temporary – optimism about new Soviet futures. What is important to note here is that these studies suggested a fusion of health policy and labour reform, geared towards optimizing both working conditions and the adaptive physiology of the workforce. Fast adaptation to changed environments was not only a national concern but a feature of evolution that could be manipulated to

---

[1] One study followed the workers who moved with the construction of the Baikal-Amur Magistrale, a railway line going across Russia, from Tayshet to Bratsk. Construction of the BAM line began in the 1930s, with the Tayshet to Bratsk section of it being built by inmates of the Bamlag gulag. Construction of the railway in the 1970s opened up the BAM service area to thousands of young people, with new settlements and bridges built.

match productivity with health policy, recapitulating earlier Soviet dreamworlds through new biomedical technologies.

Bulychev's story is less interested in Ivan's physiology than the two-part question of whether the idea of the New Soviet Man could survive if this figure no longer had relevance to the next generation, and whether this citizen had ever appeared in reality. Upon what elisions and erasures was the cultivation of this subject premised? In a story organized around memory – what it is and whose it is – something has been forgotten. Rzhevsky's cloning project is criticized by one of his colleagues via a Romantic critique of Enlightenment optimism, which attends to the darker possibilities latent in harnessing biotechnology to competitive nationalism. One of Sergei's colleagues, Sidorov, 'opposed to Rzhevsky's methods', asks, "'Where's the guarantee you're not going to create a monster?'" (144). Mary Shelley's *Frankenstein* (1823) is invoked as an example of such an experiment going dangerously wrong, with catastrophic effects for its protagonist and his creation. The reference positions the laboratory in a history of colonial–capitalist innovation, in which the production of human-adjacent lifeforms that are not counted as human is paramount for the reproduction of labour power.

The laboratory figures as a site of enclosure, a place of private decision-making, while the domestic residences surrounding the laboratory contain fragments of practices of communal negotiation. The laboratory does not have the resources to sustain itself, or to make improvements without the intervention of a manager. Sergei relies instead on the laboratory to stand in for the general Soviet project, a synecdoche for the Soviet whole. This compartmentalization has meant that his life has split into fragments – what is expressed (his intellect, his ambition, his scientific vision) and what has been silenced (his family, his friendships, any sense of communal organization beyond leading a laboratory team). The form of the text mirrors the constant interruption of the code of Sergei's life – his job, his work – by external details: the car that does not arrive, the cage door prised open, the clone who remembers everything. The short, concise, numbered sections are snapshots of his life reconstructed from essential details. When other details and characters attempt to exert influence or interrupt his stream of activity, they are abruptly parenthesized: the critical colleague, concerned friend and various unwanted reminders of past mistakes.

This starts to change with the arrival of Ivan. Ivan not only expresses Sergei's genes, but also has all of Sergei's memories. Unlike Sergei, Ivan has no reason to repress them. Instead, he becomes increasingly preoccupied by the life of his genetic original, and by what he sees as Sergei's grave mistakes and long-buried pain: 'Rzhevsky's fatigue, the exhaustion of his nervous system, was inherited by Ivan' (201); the passive construction emphasizes the psychic weight of living with and in someone else's mistakes, and without having any context in which to situate them. Ivan's waking life is dominated by Sergei's past, which presses at the limits of his brain function.

To mitigate this, Ivan takes on the position of internal spy on behalf of the reader, doing the detective work that the reader is sealed off from. At this point, this science fiction story incorporates another genre: detective fiction. This is the genre that makes it possible for him to reconstruct the past, while the hyper-realism of science fiction seems only to offer the redaction of the past. What has been forgotten? Ivan only has Sergei's side of the story and finds himself emerging in the middle of the narrative that he only half understands, and in another genre. It is a love story and – apparently – a tragic one: Sergei loved a woman called Liza, who had a daughter from another relationship – Katya. The three of them lived together in the barracks, but he could not make it work; he was too insecure in his career and in his capacity to love them. Ivan tells Nina, his own love interest in the story:

> 'Rzhevsky wanted terribly to be alone – without Liza, without Katya, without anyone. He felt like a caveman whose life was over before it had begun. And he would never be a scientist. He was irritable and unfair to Liza.' (188)

The necessity of taking responsibility for women makes Sergei feel like throwback in a time where survival is reduced to primitive technologies without a fully formed linguistic system. For him, having a family means being unable to evolve. Liza left, taking Katya with her. She went to Vologda, a northern city with various industrial plants – a site of production, rather than innovation; a city of political exile, too, and the last metropolis before Siberia. Liza's flight to Vologda corresponds to the years of the gulags, with Vologda positioned at the fringes of the Soviet dream, at the borderland between fast-track industrialization and its human cost. Sergei's loss of memory corresponds to the deliberate forgetting of this longer history.

In Ivan's inherited memory, Liza's departure is bound up with sacrifice, indentured labour and tragedy: forcing out the demands of the domestic in order to fulfil the dreams of the new nation, with women's lives as collateral damage. Speaking to Nina, Ivan tells her that a few years later, Sergei had heard that she had been run over by a train – "'or something like that'" (189). Nina picks up on the intertext immediately, responding excitedly, "'She jumped in front of a train. Like Anna Karenina! He did kill her!'" (189). Sergei's account of Liza's fate – and his responsibility for it – is drawn from another text, where women's bodies line the tracks of national progress. Viktor, also in love with Liza, paints Sergei as a character akin to Alexander Pushkin's Yevgeny Onegin, someone who '"has gone all the way to the tragedy of solitude"', an aristocratic anti-hero shaped by his sense of himself as a character larger and more fearsome than domesticated forms of love (197). The cultivation of a collective workforce gives way to an imaginary of a maniacal egoist, antithetical to the ideals of communal labour. In Sergei's case, this is under the guise of serving the Party while ensuring his own professional ascendance. Read this way, Sergei's creation of Ivan appears as the final desperate act of a megalomaniac, the only way he can try to ensure some kind of lasting legacy for himself.

Disrupting this narrative does not involve attacking the source – that is, on correcting Sergei. Instead, it involves moving the narrative from individual tragedy to communal comedy. It turns out that the other side of the story is not nearly so dramatic as Pushkin and Tolstoy's tragedies. Ivan travels to Vologda to find Katya, Liza's daughter, who tells him that far from being guilty of her mother's death, that Liza '"wasn't mad at him at all. Not in the slightest"' (211). Liza wasn't hit by a train, but by a drunken truck driver while crossing a street; this is not giving up the body to technological progress, but accidentally being taken out of it. Katya tells Ivan that the relationship would not have worked, because '"he loved his work more. And Mama knew that"' (213). Digging up the past, Ivan does not find as much tragedy as Sergei's repression had him believe he would find. Rather, he finds a kind of tacit communal effort, and life carrying on past the model of the patriarchal family. What Liza remembered – what she passed onto Katya – was that Sergei gave Liza a biography of Pushkin as a gift, and that they went to the movies, and that they visited Leningrad. Smaller events, where literature and life move next to each other in easier accord: no longer enclosed within the private sphere, enabling the sharing out of error and grief.

This resolution echoes the uneasy coexistence of forms of communal and enclosed production throughout the history of the Soviet Union, where 'the environment' is not the Russian landscape, but rather techno-capitalist forms directed by Party interests, infrastructure imported and harnessed for Soviet purposes – as if arriving from an alien planet. 'Another's Memory' asks what re-reading the environment would mean at the tail end of the Soviet Union. The answer it gives – if ambivalently – is through archaeology, in the form of Pasha Dubov, the awkward, earnest, ageing archaeologist whom Ivan befriends in the local natural history museum, and one of Sergei's old university friends left behind in his climb up the ranks. Ivan's choice to follow in Dubov's footsteps positions him in the collaborative work of excavation, where the future is put on hold, and policy held off.

As well as offering a site for imagining Soviet techno-modernity, Suslov and Bodin suggest that Soviet sf allows for retrospective gestures at the latter end of Soviet dominion, to 'roll back history to the 1960s and push it in a different direction' (2020, 8). The story ends with a comic tableau. Ivan is recovering from an illness, visited by Nina – who, for reasons that aren't made clear, has lost interest in him in a way that seems more incidental than tragic – who is followed by absent-minded and noisy Dubov arriving with full shopping bags, and a bellowing Sergei comes in last, demanding to know why Ivan wants to give up science. The staging of the scene allows for a temporary truce between these converging and incongruous interests, without their curation into something productive. It is a scene of suspension, where various possibilities of national determination at a point of historical transition are held alongside each other. Sergei retreats from his position at the forefront of Soviet development, and a new generation with its eyes on lessons and objects from a complicated and troubled past are placed at the centre.

Through its strange collusion with military agendas even while officially outlawed as a research area, molecular biology in the Soviet Union by the time of genomics expresses a fusion of environmental and genetic accounts of human cultivation, vying between two constructions of time: the immediacy of DNA and the longer-term temporality of development. *Roadside Picnic* and 'Another's Memory' are two of a number of science fiction texts from the Thaw period that register anxieties around the status of national culture – and the suppression of bad memories – as the Soviet Union's global power started to wane. What good was the cultivation of new Soviet subjects when Communist dreamworlds were passing away? To whom, and for what purpose, would this subject have relevance? And on the other side, how could Western biotechnological infrastructure offer a solution, when this involves the disappearance of subjects – and collective organization – into masses of data? It is to this question of memory, data and subjectivity that I turn in the following chapter, in a discussion of memoirs of the Human Genome Project and the generation of fresh fears about the annihilation of memory (and lives) deemed irrelevant or superfluous to the dreamworlds of futures free from disease, even death, that some of its key protagonists purported to offer.

3

# Memoir and the laboratory

The Human Genome Project took place in the same decade that saw a proliferation of popular memoirs in Anglo American publishing, heaving on airport bestseller shelves and piling up on buffet tables in chain bookshops. The extension of chain bookshops from the high street to warehouse superstores in shopping parks on the outskirts of cities meant a boom for popular non-fiction. Biotechnology was also going through a moment in the sun, with billions invested in laboratories around the world working to sequence the human genome, and the bulk of funding coming from the United States. To justify massive amounts of funding, and to ensure a legacy for the project and its key players, several of the Human Genome Project's main protagonists published science memoirs of the project. These memoirs – particularly James Watson's *DNA: The Secret of Life* (2003) and J. Craig Venter's *A Life Decoded: My Genome, My Life* (2007) – quickly ascended bestseller lists, sandwiched between sports stars and film actors. Venter and Watson draw techniques from the blockbuster memoir: a constant (often explicit) refrain of '*you won't believe what happened next*', cascading vignettes of overcoming obstacles for the sake of a higher goal, shock twists in the tale and a cast of protagonists, antagonists and commodities plucked from the thrillers and romances that competed for shelf space. These included men in dark suits from the US Department of Energy, billionaire investors, mad scientists, yacht races and motorbike accidents, and the spectre of Soviet biology.

Two decades on, it seems inconceivable that the Human Genome Project might not have happened, but its huge technological and ideological victory in the 1980s and 1990s was made possible by a constellation of factors: the end of the Cold War, the acceleration of global neoliberal consumption through a handful of brands targeting every level of salary, and deregulated finance capitalism becoming the basis of the world-system. These factors were not only instrumental in allowing the Human Genome Project the scale and global reach that it achieved, but also became part of narrating why and to whom the project mattered and – at a formal level – what a genomic world looked like, its science-fictional forms and utopian promises.

These narratives were instrumental in transforming the genome from a strange, distant object in laboratories to a technology of post-industrial domesticity, and prepared the ground for direct-to-consumer DNA testing from the early 2000s. The genome changed the terms and possibilities of the bourgeois private sphere even as it eradicated the subjects it targeted, as Kazuo Ishiguro's *Never Let Me Go* (2005) and Andrew Niccol's *Gattaca* (1997) show. This was also connected to an often-haphazard collocation of national and international governance structures, where genomics offered technological shorthand for ethnonational investigations of population and phenotype. These investigations took existing descriptions of national identity as their starting point, privileging eighteenth-century mappings of individual traits onto national character.

Jenny Reardon situates this turn from ungovernable international programmes to national imaginaries in the wider context of creating value and meaning in the afterlives of decolonization and deindustrialization. By the mid-1990s, she argues,

> Genomes, in turn, appeared to promise nations the opportunity to create new natural resources out of the bodily tissues of their citizens when resources in their lands and seas were disappearing. (2017, 94)

This links the shift of genomics from obscure laboratory practices to the domestic sphere via the promise of disease-free futures, facilitated by the instrumentalization of national exceptionalism (as in the case of Iceland's deCODE project) to new forms of accumulation. Giovanni Arrighi figures this transformation through the internalizing of transaction costs by the post-war US regime, and the creation of 'economies of speed' rather than 'economies of size' (1994, 247). These economies of speed have been characterized by – following Alfred Chandler – 'the development of new machinery, better raw materials, and intensified application of energy, followed by the creation of organisational design and procedures to coordinate and control the new high-volume flows through several processes of production', and the development of managerial hierarchies (1977, 244). US-driven globalization promised a multiple modes of national identification programmed within this structure, and genomics was no exception. Collecting DNA and tissue was a way of promoting national sovereignty while making this data available for global biotech (Reardon 2016, 102). This global-national model of exporting raw resources (in the case of national genomics projects, of biodata) levied with population-level ethnonationalism helped foster the recent rise of various fascisms across the world. Through these new extractive techniques allied to logics of national sovereignty, a new form of worker emerged: one whose biomatter could be extracted as flesh-made-data, a donor for the bio-consumption of other people's bodies.

This depended on micro-level assemblies of national character, embedded in longer projects of modern European self-narration and its attendant distinctions between flesh and body (Spillers 1987). In this chapter, I consider the memoir form as central to the imagining of a composite genome as a normative reference against which new revolutionary health care practices could be measured. These practices were increasingly organized around an idea of personalized or individualized medicine, representing what Aravinda Chakravarti identifies as 'a fundamental change in medicine that has long relied on the idea of a typological patient' (2015, 12). A crossing place of aesthetic and political formations of the subject, memoir is tied to economies of property and genealogy. It is a genre for writing the self as a legible participant in public affairs, offering a set of discursive techniques for attaching this self to the development of consciousness in literary form.

The turn in medicine from typological models to individualized ones is two centuries behind literary culture. Jerome Hamilton Buckley charts a turn in late eighteenth-century literature from the type to the individual, the novel-form as a 'gallery of eccentrics, whose conduct may image the peculiar foibles of the presiding novelist', and when biography 'moves from the depiction of general human nature to the portrayal of a distinctive individual' (1994, 14). This allowed new forms of value to be attached to the self, which could be rearranged and reorganized, iterations of subjectivity as means of attaining access to the bourgeois public sphere. These new forms depend on a normalization of certain forms of sociality, with the nuclear family often at the centre of what makes the visibility of self possible: its facilitation and perpetuation. When Jürgen Habermas notes a correspondence between 'the autonomy of property owners in the market' and 'a self-presentation of human beings in the family' (1989, 46), this depends on a certain arrangement of private relations that can be narrated as chronological, reproducible and – crucially – believable. These forms are part of the legislation of a set of social relations that became central to participation in a market economy. They offered an alibi for 'a private autonomy denying its economic origins . . . provided the bourgeois family with its consciousness of itself' (Habermas 1991, 47). This is ultimately tied to the creation of a national body politic, a conglomerate character made up of idiosyncrasies, nuances and recognizable traits. In this oscillation between conglomerate and individual, the narrative integrity of a subject developing through chronological time who is pervious to various kinds of influence as they move through their environment disappears. In place of this, the individual becomes a storehouse of data, unmoored from typology and an object from which information might be extracted, or a subject who might extract information from others.

Part of the Human Genome Project's victory was making whole-genome sequencing seem as if it was a historical inevitability. Miguel García Sancho notes that sequencing was positioned rhetorically as the culmination of the DNA revolution that started in the 1950s, a strategy that kept DNA central as molecular biology's principal object of study (2012, 7–8). In Chapter 1, I considered how Doris Lessing and Samuel Delany explored this transformation first as (in Lessing) a reconstitution of whiteness during a crisis for Anglo American post-war hegemony, and second as (in Delany) the formation of a neoliberal subject who can choose between a myriad of identifications, genomics as a technology of personalization. By the 1990s, the Human Genome Project had brought something different into the centre of focus: the idea of genetic disease.

As well as its domination of biotechnology, the long-term impact of the Human Genome Project was also in transforming the social space afforded to genetics in culture. Feminist scholars of biology writing during the 1990s argued that genomics was formed in part through a masculinist co-option of life processes into the rhetoric of automation, entrepreneurialism and engineering. Hilary Rose observes that the 'political interventionism of the new genetics, the product of an alliance between an aggressively entrepreneurial culture and the life sciences, fused the conservatism of biology as destiny with the modernist philosophy of genetic manipulation' (1994, 173). For Rose, the Human Genome Project was not only embedded in the political economy of the 1980s but also 'unquestionably marked the self-inserted entry of molecular biologists into runaway industrialised science' (1994, 197). Writing in 1992, Evelyn Fox Keller stresses that the expansion of molecular biology from the 1970s onwards 'was not just technical', but that there was 'an ideological expansion of molecular biology into both popular culture and medicine' (1992, 291). For her, the idea of genetic disease is key to this. Expanding across health and behaviour, genetic understandings of disease came to dominate both justifications for funding and popular imaginaries around the power (and relevance) of genetics. While this was organized rhetorically around the individual – adhering to the neoliberal privileging of individual choice – this resulted in something different: the creation of a genomic norm, which derives its value from its elusiveness and intangibility, an elusiveness that nonetheless came to 'implicitly define the concept of abnormality' (Keller, 297).

Under the terms of neoliberal subjectivity – the individual as consumer – this elusiveness drives investment in the idea of the genome as a technology of self-fashioning. Keller also gestures, if obliquely, to a new kind of governmentality for which sequencing became a prototype: what Antoinette Rouvroy has called 'algorithmic governmentality', which replaces the individual (and liberal concepts of commons, public and the idea of project itself) with an amorphous 'data-body' with no fixed average or norm (2012; Rouvroy and Berns 2013). This data-body is premised on the forgetting of non-calculable data, and it in turn puts forward its own précis of reality (which is, in turn, constantly shifting). While mass genomic sequencing gave way to the development of precision medicine organized around an individual human subject, this technology has also precipitated a more fundamental shift in the way this subject is constituted, both technologically and ideologically.

The laboratory was a key space in transmitting this new genomic imaginary, and the memoir a crucial form. Here, I look at both fictional and non-fiction memoirs emerging around the Human Genome Project. I consider how memoir – a form that is explicitly about personal memory – becomes the generic totem for a science that tends towards the annihilation of any kind of memory (cultural, social, biological) that cannot be captured by sequencing. In these texts, the memoir becomes a kind of laboratory for experimenting with narrative forms generated by the syntax and technology of sequencing: what the objects and objectives of genomics were, and what subject these practices imagined on the other side of the first draft. Rather than collapsing the story of the Human Genome Project into a more general narrative of technology having its own logic and rhythm separate from ideological interests, I consider how the laboratory and its literary counterpart – here, the memoir – function as sites of ideological production. The laboratory is not restricted to places where (mostly) men in white coats look into test tubes through microscopes; in *Never Let Me Go*, the laboratory is extended to the boarding school – one of the classic monuments to liberal education given up to the mass production of organ donor clones; and in *Gattaca* to the domestic sphere, with hand-held DNA sequencing kits (a prescient foreshadowing of home DNA testing kits in the 2010s). Memoir becomes crucial in sustaining a sense of developmental time, a form that allows a subject to narrate themselves as a character on a trajectory, moving from point A to B. But these texts, in different ways, expose this effort as futile. Post-war domestic and developmental utopias disappear, infiltrated by outsourced biotechnological production, and with it, the aspirational fiction of a subject able to improve their lot through hard work and buy-in.

These texts stage the disappearance of the subject privileged and foregrounded in post-Enlightenment modernity into Big Data: what Sylvia Wynter calls Man 2, or the biocentric descriptive statement of humanity (2003). In its creation of a composite reference genome the Human Genome Project upheld an idea of the normative subject as bourgeois, male and white, even going so far as to use Leonardo Da Vinci's Vitruvian Man as its logo, but this subject could not survive the more compelling and world-dominating possibilities afforded by sequencing. Rather than upholding the colonial episteme of aspirational whiteness as a global standard, sequencing offers an infrastructure for reality as proliferating and endlessly shifting – all that is needed is more technology to identify 'good'. This 'good' is not fixed to something external, but to feedback loops generated by self-learning algorithms (Rouvroy 2013). Memoirs of genomics are monuments to the ideal subject of the European Renaissance, but also register (knowingly or not) the disappearance of this ideal into what Rouvroy calls 'data behaviourism' – the pre-emption of individual and collective behaviours 'to cope with the complexities of a world of massive flows of persons, objects, and information, and to compensate for the difficulties of governing by the law in a complex, globalised world' (2012, 143). Genomics became the technological prototype for the algorithmic data-body.

The question of legality is key: as Ruha Benjamin notes, data worlds are by no means free from the kinds of ellipses and blindness that constitute racial capitalism, and they actively perpetuate it (2019). Rather, the challenge of the present moment – which both these texts anticipate – is the increasing irrelevance of state legislations of human freedom documented in national and international texts of human rights. Rather, the question has returned to the relation between flows of labour and violence, across borders, wherein legal parameters of citizenship can only go so far, as I explore in Chapter 4. The ideological disintegration of Man 2 has been facilitated in part by a technological system that was designed – paradoxically – to facilitate not only this figure's technological perpetuation, but also its immortality. Genomics is part of a new panoply of technological possibilities that bring about the accelerated destruction of liberal humanism, by introducing a new grammar of existence.

These texts trace how the sequencing imaginary of the 1990s emerges out of the homonyms of the Human Genome Project: code, pairs, clones, overlaps, map and sequence. Loss of memory is implicit: the reformulation of words corresponds to what Hans-Jörg Rheinburger and Staffan Müller-Wille have called the 'partial amnesia' of the genomic revolution, when 'the gene' as a concept starts to dissolve, replaced by 'complex assemblages of diverse activating and inhibiting mechanisms' (2017, 108, 68); alongside this takeover of language, there was a forgetting of older models of systems biology. They cite the work of French biologists Francois Jacob and Jacques Monod on the *lactose* operon during the 1960s, a gene control mechanism in *E. coli* and other bacteria that facilitates the transport and metabolism of lactose. The broader influence of their work has resulted in 'the findings of how many different ways such transacting events can be molecularly mediated', in Stephen Baylin's words (2016, 2060). It is not so much that Jacob and Monod were not taken seriously at the time; rather, these sorts of regulatory mechanisms were less easily determined from a genetic blueprint. In a critique of the gene-centrism of personalized medicine, Charles Joseph Kowalski and Adam Joel Mrdjenovich note 'even if it were possible to know the exact sequence of A, C, G, and Ts comprising the DNA of a "normal" human being, this could tell at most a limited part of the story of that person' (2017, 79). Nonetheless, telling this story of a 'normal' human being through their code was a central component of the Human Genome Project and the promises it heralded for Big Bio (Garay and Gray 2012).

The figure of partial amnesia offers a trenchant point of departure for considering how memoir functions as a technology of forgetting, the neurotic inscription of a liberal subject on the surface of a present in the process of subsuming this subject into data. *Gattaca* and *Never Let Me Go* are both interested in the body as a machine – a syntactical unit whose actions can be pre-empted – as well as the engineered inequity programmed into the system. And because genomic data-bodies do not exist 'in reality', they cannot die. Hence, individual death in these texts is outsourced or made invisible: what matters is that information keeps moving across systems, extracted and displaced from an assumed material source.

## Metaphors of the Human Genome Project

The Human Genome Project began in the early 1980s, and it ended in 2003 with the first draft sequence of the human genome, fifty years after the publication of the double helix. Watson recalls bets being taken on the human gene count:

> At the Cold Spring Harbor Laboratory conference on the genome in May 2000, Ewan Birney, who was spearheading the Sanger Centre's computer analysis of

> the sequence, organised a contest he called Genesweep. It was a lottery based on estimating the correct gene count, which would finally be determined with the completion of the sequences in 2003; the winner would be the one who had been closest to the right answer. . . . I was able to get in on the ground floor, putting $1 down on 72,415. My bet was a calculated attempt to reconcile the textbook figure, 100,000, and the new best guess of around 50,000, based on the chromosome 22 result. Birney announced the result in May 2003: 21,000 genes – many fewer than anyone had guessed. (Watson 2004, 197)

The emphasis on number, on winning and losing, and on the correspondence of human complexity with a higher number of genes gesture to the expectation that the sequencing genome would tell us *what makes us human* in the new language of genomics. Bets are a good analogy: Watson describes a moment of speculation in which all the assumptions of some of the Human Genome Project's leading scientists and proponents became temporarily visible. Namely, that complexity equates to the amount of genes amassed, couched in a stock-market imaginary for envisioning genetic identity.

This bet also registers a shift in economic metaphors around biological life: from property to trading. Whereas genetics had been based on an older model of property relations attached to particular persons and lineages, genomics is attached to an economic model of neoliberal mutability, in which stock can be isolated and traded, moving around the system, to be implanted or subtracted according to investment. If imagining genetics was about the combined sum of individual stock and the discipline of individuals, genomic sequencing became a technological prototype for imagining individuals as conglomerations of shared (and tradable) code. The individual disappears, their property (as inherited genetic code) subsumed into extractable components of use-value (as tradable genetic commodity). The metaphorical power of the genome as a script for life bridged the classical concept of genes as immutable inheritance, and the post-Synthesis concept of genetic mutation as calculable.

The turn of the twenty-first century saw the publication of numerous first-person accounts of the project, from some of its key players: most notably, John Sulston, Venter and Watson. Memoir became a way of controlling the narrative in the Anglophone world about the Human Genome Project and its legacy, and one of its big selling points was the acrimonious cross-Atlantic drama between UK and US laboratories over the question of whether genomic information should be for public good or private profit. This drama went some way in obscuring the relatively underwhelming results of the project. Far from offering a map of human complexity, the first draft sequence of the human genome showed that humans share a similar number of protein-coding genes to *C. elegans*, type of worm. Nonetheless, these memoirs became bestsellers, and Watson's *DNA* and Venter's *A Life Decoded* continue to stand as the definitive popular accounts of the project's history, aims and long-term vision. The focus of these texts is placed squarely on the dawn of a new age in biotechnology and on the unlocking of human potential for new routes in healthcare and reproductive technologies. Social welfare competes with state security, with molecular biology becoming increasingly tied to military budgets from the early 1950s onwards. By the late 1970s, the unmooring of science from its social implications (or the reduction of the social to national security) became part of the broader project of neoliberalism, with scientific expertise increasingly drawn into private capital flows.

Mike Fortun has addressed the importance of paying attention to 'the affective register of scientific developments' (2016, 7). Although in memoir, affect isn't always trustworthy – even when it is positing itself as such – it indicates the affective register the Human Genome Project's main players wanted to associate with the project, and how this register shaped both its technological and epistemological stakes. Building the imaginative infrastructure of whole-genome sequencing through memoir cemented the project's ideological underpinnings: in the United States, private entrepreneurialism organized around a neoliberal subject. While there was some resistance to this in the UK – Sulston considered genomics as a potential instrument of state welfare and therefore public good – the genome came to stand for individual potential, broken down into its component parts. In Sulston, Venter and Watson's books, a string of personal memories threads together the narrative of the Human Genome Project's main events, interwoven with details from the author's lives: Venter's experiences as a young medic in Vietnam; Watson's intransigent Scottish mother; and the motorbike accident that took Sulston away from the Sanger Institute for extended leave at a crucial moment. These details communicate some of the stakes of the project for its main proponents: for Sulston, taking responsibility for a team and sharing out the work, as well as the data, was central to his methods and hopes for a truly public science. Watson positions himself at the centre of the consortium, diplomat and antagonist across the public-private divide: the old guard keeping pace. And from a medical tent in Vietnam, Venter tells the story of the race for the genome as a race against death, building an implacable defence system that might extend human life indefinitely through big business.

It was crucial to tell a story about the genome for a number of reasons: to garner public support for its uses in biomedicine, important in the generation of further funding and legacy work. In Sulston's case, public opinion was vital in his (and others') efforts to keep the data of the reference genome public. But above all, this was a crowning moment for technological modernity: sequencing the genome was a Copernican overturning, repositioning the human in space and time, unravelling the mysteries of human complexity and instrumentaliing these answers for a better future. Thematically, these books set the terms of the Human Genome Project's drama (whether or not to patent genes, and who won the argument) and formally, they recapitulate the value of the individual as the fundamental unit of biological calculation. They present the genome project as a paradigm of academic-industrial cooperation, and centre DNA as the governing interest of molecular biology (Sancho 2012). As Sancho argues, this 'oversimplified' view centring DNA 'marginalises other disciplines, along with other historically relevant molecules, e.g. proteins' (2012, 8). But for reasons that others have noted (Keller 2000; Rajan 2006; Fortun 2008), the story of DNA was the one that sold, rather than more complex accounts of intracellular interactions between proteins and segments of DNA. In the latter decades of the twentieth century, the molecular of molecular biology was the gene, and ways of isolating, cloning and modifying it was where the funding was. In the new era of biological citizenship described by Nikolas Rose, 'vitality is decomposed into a series of distinct and discrete objects – that can be isolated, delimited, stored, accumulated, mobilized, and exchanged, accorded a discrete value, traded across time, space, species, contexts, enterprises', processes which have meant the inextricable intertwining of biopolitics with bioeconomics (Rose 2007, 7). Memoirs of the Human Genome Project situate the project as the first Big Science project of the neoliberal era, promising new frontiers for health. 'We can never turn back,' writes Watson at the end of *DNA*; 'what the public wants is not to be sick' (174). Questions remained around who and by whom this 'public' was constituted.

Rose uses the word 'decomposed', a suggestive adverb steeped in a gothic imaginary, calling up an image of a body decaying around genetic objects which it both houses and which are uncannily alien to it: the irreversible breaking down of an organism into smaller parts of matter. Here is the contradiction of neoliberal subjectivity: value in the system relies on sustaining an image of the individual subject and its augmentation through biotechnological intervention, while simultaneously breaking this subject down into exchangeable material, genes as commodities to be copied and sold on the market. The promise of precision medicine is that the patient-as-consumer can choose from a range of options specifically designed around their genetic make-up, as long as they buy in to donating their data and biomatter. But Rose suggests that there is something deathly about this situation; as the patient is co-opted into this way of reading themselves – as collections of genetic segments that might be rearranged, exchanged and can be ascribed particular values – the living matter of their body decays. In this sense, genomic subjects do not inhabit whole bodies. The environment is side-lined as a constitutive influence over development. Character becomes genetic blueprint, without any potential for development, a collection of parts that might be extracted and exchanged.

## Welfare, profit and ethics: The Vitruvian Man

The symbol chosen to represent the Human Genome Project was Leonardo Da Vinci's Vitruvian Man, an image of a universal human body that symbolized the birth of a new world-system in the sixteenth century, at the dawn of a new age for scientific and artistic creativity. As others have noted, the driving force of the Human Genome Project was based on national competition as much as transnational collaboration, and dominated by interests, ideologies and agendas of Anglo American biology. Beyond this, the project combined the moral economy of eighteenth-century liberalism and twentieth-century neoliberalism into new valuations of living a good life for the twenty-first. The central ethical question of the project was derived from the transition from liberalism to neoliberalism: whether the genome was a public good (data to be released for public use), or private property (broken up into exchangeable commodities). But this obscured the political gesture that made this debate so charged: the assumed reliability and efficacy of the genome as an instrument of universal human progress, even while the longer history of genetics has been embedded in histories of racialized exclusion (Saini 2019; Rutherford 2020). The false binary of welfare/profit came to define memoirs of the Human Genome Project, concealing the deeper ethical and epistemological questions around the genome's status as a universal description of human biological history, privileging genetic heredity over other forms of influence and change, and attaching a new standard of individual moral choice to its legibility.

As a moniker, the Human Genome Project stands in for a consortium of research centres across the world working on sequencing the human genome – the International Human Genome Sequencing Consortium (IHGSC). The project began officially in 1990, but it had been in development since the mid-1980s under shifting terms of negotiation between different scientific bodies and funding sources. The aim of the project was twofold: to determine the sequence of DNA base pairs, and from this to map the whole genome to determine both the place and function of certain genes. The two strands of the double helix are made up of chemical links between them (nucleobases), called base pairs. The four nucleobases are adenine (A), thymine (T), guanine (G) and cytosine (C). Like rhyming couplets, A always goes with T, and G with C. Sequencing these means working out their order in a molecule of DNA. By the end of the project, 3.5 billion base pairs had been sequenced. The final draft sequence was not from one individual, but an aggregated collection of genetic material composed of genomes from anonymous donors, all with European ancestry. This continues to be the reference genome in human genomics.

Due to the complex arrangements and negotiations around attracting and sustaining funding, the technological demands of the project moved at pace. Venter developed a method called 'shotgun sequencing'. Shotgun sequencing involves isolating parts of the genome, cloning them, sequencing the clone and comparing these to other clones to determine their overlaps. This method was not as precise as the slower process of 'walking the genome', but it meant much faster results. Venter's haste was driven by a division among key players in the project over the question of whether cloned segments of DNA could or should be patented. Venter felt that they should, and he set up his own private biotechnology company – Celera Genetics – to continue sequencing. This was in the context of a broader proliferation of private genomics laboratories across the United States, which would become the infrastructure for new techniques of precision genomic healthcare from the early 2000s on. This proliferation was enabled, in part, by a landmark ruling in the US Supreme Court in 1980 over whether a genetically engineered bacterium could be patented in *Diamond vs. Chakrabarty*. A legal team representing the microbiologist Ananda Chakrabarty successfully argued that the bacterium was not a naturally occurring substance, but rather his own product, and should be awarded a patent. This ruling paved the way for an unprecedented new standard for biological innovation: the ability to patent and profit from engineering organic matter. While it was not possible to patent unaltered genetic material, it was – in theory – possible to do so for engineered DNA.

In the early 1990s, Venter was still employed at the United States's National Institute of Health at Bethesda, Maryland. When he proposed to patent gene fragments (expressed sequence tags, or ESTs), there was a big pushback. This was a turning point for the Human Genome Project in terms of speed and stakes, pushing the debate over whether sequenced data should be made publicly available immediately for the sake of the development of the field, or whether it should be classed as the intellectual property of individual laboratories. Venter was unsuccessful: the Pharmaceutical Manufacturers' Association argued, 'a governmental policy of ownership and licensing of gene sequences would inevitably impede the research and development of new medicines,' and that access to ESTs should remain publicly available. For Venter, this threatened to damage America's lead in the race for the genome (publicly available meant internationally available). Wallace Steinberg of venture capital group HealthCare Investment Corporation agreed with him, and awarded Venter $70 million to set up his own institute: the Institute for Genomic Research (suggestively shortened to TIGR) in Maryland. TIGR was linked to a sister company – Human Genome Sciences – whose purpose was to develop products out of TIGR's research. In 1995, Venter's team – including Hamilton Smith and Claire Fraser – published the first whole sequence of a bacterial genome (*Haemophilus influenzae*) in *Science*, an opportunity for Venter to place whole-genome shotgun sequencing at the forefront of genomic technology. The race between public and private genomic sequencing was unambiguously on.

Meanwhile, in the UK, John Sulston's group at the MRC Laboratory of Molecular Biology in Cambridge had been working on another model organism: *C. elegans*, a worm. Sulston's team was interested in working out the genetic programming that caused a worm to develop across its lifecourse, as well as basic tasks like feeding, moving and reproducing (Sulston 2002, 39). How were living things put together, how did they do the things they do and what ensures the relative stability of such processes and functions? These were research questions the bridged the supposed divide between molecular and evolutionary biology, placing the issue of development at the forefront of investigation. On the subject of so-called junk DNA, Sulston writes that it is 'a collection of fossils from our evolutionary history, which makes it interesting in the same way that a midden is interesting to archaeologists' (2002, 40). At the time of writing, it was not yet widely appreciated how much more significant this 'junk' was, but Sulston's description is not meant to be dismissive: he was keenly aware of the importance of attending to the archaeological as well the futuristic when it came to molecular biology's history. Outlooks like his – broader and longer than some of his peers – kept the imaginary of evolutionary history alive. When it turned out that this supposed junk played a much more active role in genetic expression, and particularly for complex organisms like humans, the language of disuse and recycling – or, perhaps a better metaphor, the sedimentation of older genetic material – came into its own. What was key for Sulston was that excavating our evolutionary past was not restricted to protein-coding genes and that non-coding DNA could also tell us important things about human history. The difference between humans and worms, it turned out, is not the number of protein-coding genes, but the relatively large amount of non-coding DNA held in human genomes.

Sulston's memoir documents his concern with the increasing focus on genetic material as an extractable and exchangeable commodity. The issue of patenting was, for Sulston, a moot point: there is 'no invention in finding [genes]', and owning them would be 'rather like owning a piece of the moon' (2002, 87). But he, too, recognized the stakes of the Human Genome Project, and that the outcomes of debates over ownership and profit would set the tone for years to come. Echoing Watson, he wrote, 'You can never go back' (2002, 104). Sulston was instrumental in setting up the Wellcome Trust's Sanger Centre at the outskirts of Cambridge, which was the largest centre involved in the project in terms of the scale of its sequencing output. The Sanger Centre was the only non-US centre involved in the G5, and while laboratories in France, Germany and Japan also played significant roles in the broader consortium, 'there was no doubt at all who was in the driving seat' (Sulston and Ferry 2002, 195). But the involvement of Wellcome in its funding of the UK contingent – a private funding body with a focus on public health – as well as the relatively smaller role of the British government when compared to the National Institute of Health in the United States brought a slightly different vision to the G5. As time went on, the focus of the group became beating Venter to sequencing the genome first.

Speed and competition drove the narrative of the Human Genome Project, despite the reservations of its more cautious and publicly minded leaders, Sulston included. This public-private debate reflected, to some extent, the different agendas of the Human Genome Project's forerunners, and became its key source of tension and disagreement. By 1998, Venter had set up a new venture – Celera Genomics – which he continues to head, and which is now owned by Quest Diagnostics. The last couple of years of the project were fraught with fears over lost time, and high stakes in getting there first. In the end, it was declared a tie, with Bill Clinton effectively calling for a truce between private innovation and public good. In 2005, Celera announced that it would make all of its data public, partly because they realized soon after the first results came in that 'the promised profits were not going to materialise' (Marris 2005, 6).

Where promises of revolutionizing healthcare fell short, genomic imaginaries still held huge commercial potential. Genomics might not have been in a position to cure cancer, but it could tell different kinds of stories about human connection, social organization and family history, and it was clear that during the early 2000s, the cultural power of the gene as a kind of transcendental signified – a keystone for life itself – was not going anywhere. For Watson, the metaphorical power of the genome was even greater than that of the double helix. His account in *DNA* is full of the drama of that decade, with a larger and more glamorous cast of characters than the comparatively small-scale fallouts between small research teams in small laboratories at Cambridge University and King's University London during the early 1950s in his earlier book, *The Double Helix* (1968). *DNA* blurs the script of the Human Genome Project blockbuster with the script for life itself, and cinematic metaphors proliferate: the book is a screenplay for a film, just as the genome is – for him – 'life's screenplay' (2004, 164). No longer just a work of modern art suspended from the ceiling of a lab, the genome enfolded all kinds of genres into its realm of possibility: forensics and the thriller, aptitude and Bildungsroman, reproduction and romance, paternity testing and reality TV, DNA fingerprinting as 'the ultimate in infotainment' (293). While unevenly and not-always-reliably critical of Venter's patenting, Watson shows a keen awareness of the commercial possibilities of the genome, because he realized that it fed into powerful and pre-existing imaginaries around human relationships – personal and ancestral.

The phenomenal imaginative power of the genome stems in part from a merging of scales, and the ambiguous relation between the macro and micro: worlds in grains of sand. The possibility of these worlds is allied to older narratives about transcending bodily matter, intellect taking the body to new heights of potential. The genome holds the largest secrets of life itself in the smallest molecules of the body, the key to existence packed into the tiniest of spaces. What was key was to imagine what these possibilities for human progress might be. After the political vacuum left by the end of the Cold War, the early 1990s was a critical time for imagining other worlds. This moment saw a rejuvenation of science-fictional imaginaries, where outer space marked the limits of the Western frontier, rather than East Kreuzberg: new territories for expansion. The Human Genome Project coincided with the recapitulation and extension of the American frontier as a metaphor for technological progress.

Watson is fascinated by modes of transport – Venter's yacht and Sulston's motorbike – and describes the genome as something akin to the American Mid-West:

> Studded with noncoding segments (introns), genes can sometimes straddle enormous expanses of DNA, the coding parts like so many towns isolated between barren stretches of molecular highway. (199)

This is an image of settlement in vast open spaces, the gene not so much a finite entity but whole region, with remote sections split off from each other. 'Molecular highway' is a particularly suggestive and fantastical image of white noise in uncharted space, closer to postmodern video game visuals than the naturalism of genealogical trees or the elegant modernism of linked helixes. It imagines the genome as vast as a sparsely populated continent, (almost) terra nullius, whose transport infrastructure resembles that of industrial modernity. In this eerie landscape, the intervention of modern science serves to light up these dark spaces, tracing connections and working out their relation.

The power of the genome also pivots on the borders of modern fears – life/death, knowledge/ignorance, connection/isolation. Mediating these fears required creating a language of precision, in which messy matter could be reduced to function or image, using familiar vocabulary: 'code', 'segment', 'pair', 'clone', 'overlap', and 'sequence' were repurposed for genomic descriptions of spatial organization, no longer just descriptions but also performative utterances that bring a novel way of seeing into language. New figures for managing, viewing, reproducing and profiting from life abound: forensics, cloning, trading and disease elimination, each attached to different kinds of biotechnical management. Forensics relies on a database of DNA to identify certain biological traces, particularly in the realm of policing and security, which Carlos Novas and Nikolas Rose link to a growing infrastructure of biological citizenship founded on the collocation of healthcare and security (2005). Sequencing technology developed around copying segments of DNA (cDNA), which then are then analysed as discrete units, swapped and traded with others to account for certain parts of the code. Out of copying comes cloning and exchange.

These words engender a reformulation of subjectivity, which is connected to a broader transition in the ways that the human body is understood as distinct and exceptional in the realm of living matter. Part of the radical suggestion of the Human Genome Project in its creation of a new reference point for comparing humans with each other and other species was that 'the individual' as such no longer really matters. What's key instead is the ability to compare and aggregate shared elements – segment, pair and strand. In this phase of the genomic era, the individual disappears as the primary reference subject; instead, making conglomerations of individuals comparable with each other becomes possible.

The genomic sequencing revolution was organized around new technologies of substitution, embedded in the structural dehumanization of non-European peoples. While the individual disappears into a conglomeration, an imaginary of a model individual remains. This serves to both bolster visions of transhuman futures and to sustain a racialized ordering of human life, to follow Alexander Weheliye, 'disciplining humanity into full humans, not-quite humans, and nonhumans' (2014, 4). Recently, Ruha Benjamin has offered a framework of 'race critical code studies' in her merging of science and technology studies and critical race studies, to 'open the Black box of coded inequity' (2019, 26). For Benjamin, technology does not roll on apace beyond or outside the control of social worlds, but rather, 'social norms, ideologies and practices are a constitutive part of technological design' (2019, 30). Race continues to function as the core organizing technique of biopolitics' right to 'make live and let die', by 'appealing to the principle that the death of others makes one biologically stronger insofar as one is a member of a race or a population, insofar as one is an element in a unitary living plurality' (Foucault 2003, 258). This is also a question of genre, with memoir instrumentalized to reiterate a narrative about aspirational individualism, or to contend this with its presumed alternative: public good. While Venter is for the most part telling a story about himself, Sulston is interested in the question of genomics' potential to be a commonly held resource available to everyone. But what genomics does is actually abolish both the classic liberal, developmental self, as well as the neoliberal entrepreneurial one: it smashes apart liberal humanism, its material referents and the concept of time as teleology on which it depends.

## *Never Let Me Go* and the end of development

Watson's assertions that 'what the public want is to be healthy' and that there is no possibility of going back to a pre-genomic era are repeated almost ad verbatim by the former headteacher of Hailsham, the school for clones in *Never Let Me Go*. Ishiguro's novel is a fictional memoir by Kathy H., relating the story of her childhood and adolescence, growing up with her friends Tommy and Ruth and the gradual revelation of their purpose in the world: to become donors of organ and tissue to prolong the lifespans of the rest of the nation. Explaining to Tommy and Kathy, who have come to request a deferral to the process, why such deferrals never existed, Miss Emily tells them: '"How can you ask a world that has come to regard cancer as curable to put away that cure, to go back to the dark days? There was no going back"' (240).

*Never Let Me Go* is narrated by a character fixated on going back. The plot is carried forward by a series of 'and thens . . .', reminiscences of the past that Kathy tells us often she has gone over again and again. As Tia Byer points out, the fragmentation of Kathy's memory 'suggests that certain aspects have been overemphasised during their retelling' – like the song of the title being played over and over again in her childhood – and that as a consequence, 'we do not know what has been left out' (74). This anxiety of amnesia and erasure derives its power, then, from a fixation on information as an economy between reader and narrator: what can be read, and what remains illegible or uncoded, in a text that is constructed via the gulf between code and context.

This gulf between code and context is mediated by an enforcement of chronological time, which gradually becomes a signifier of unreliable narration as the text unfolds. In memories carrying particular emotional weight, Kathy is brought into the present, where she works as a carer for donors, helping them through their process of donation. Some live through three or four donations (we are not told which organs or matter are being extracted), some through one or two. In Kathy's present, there is no room for chronology, save for the 'then' of another extraction. The past, on the other hand, can be narrated in chronological time: 'my approaching Tommy that afternoon was part of a phase I was going through', she says at the beginning of the second chapter (12). Going through a phase suggests a particular kind of developmental time, a sociology of growing up, a subject undergoing psychological changes. This banks onto a broader post-Enlightenment construction of human subjectivity, attached to the political metaphor of individual freedom: liberal humanism. The 'public' is not a commons, but rather individuals with access to the public sphere, based on ownership of property. The students of Hailsham are not considered human, because this biological property is not 'theirs': they are copied from genetic material of anonymous others. In liberal humanism, public desire is not collective or commonly held, but the desire of propertied humans, if 'property' is extended here to mean ownership over materiality: of shelter, of labour, of biology (Arendt 1958). This public is a liberal elite with access to corporate and state forms of healthcare, whose lives are sustained (economically and biologically) through the production of an underclass.

The novel only gives one name and date: 'England, late 1990s', with a number of references to years passed that permits a reconstruction of the time-span of its events to the late 1970s. The 2010 film gives four dates, charting the transition from the post-war consensus to neoliberalism: 1952, the year of the 'medical science breakthrough' that allowed us to 'cure the incurable' (the year before the double helix); 1978, when the students are at Hailsham (the year before Thatcher came to power); 1984 when they are at the Cottages (the year of the miners' strikes); and 1994, when Ruth and Tommy die (the tail end of almost two decades of Tory rule). The film depicts this move through the sepia-toned public-private welfare utopianism of Hailsham, to the muddy greens of working-class rural communities in the dilapidated Cottages, to the greys of the Brutalist tower block that becomes Kathy's home while she works as a carer, and the blue corridors of the hospitals where Ruth and Tommy die. Kathy's flat number is 52, referencing the film's additional date of the scientific breakthrough that brought her existence into the realm of possibility. The date creates a through-line between scientific discovery and public policy, one of the ways that Kathy's life is determined by past events outside her control or, for most of the text, her knowledge.

The novel situates its critique of liberal humanism as a model for self-determination in post-war meritocracy – its organization first around a creaky consensus of welfare, private benevolence and social mobility, and its corporate reformulation under Thatcher. First, the organs are for public good, but an apostrophized public that excludes those who carry out the labour necessary to sustain it, unevenly written into the social contract via gestures of social responsibility (state-funded education, housing and maintenance benefits). By the 1990s, Hailsham has been closed down, and clones are now bred in 'vast government "homes"' akin to mass animal breeding farms (242). Hailsham was supposed to be a reprieve from the reality of cloning, turning clones into students, even though there was no future for them to prepare for. Miss Emily calls them '"lucky pawns,"' who have been able to build their lives '"on what we gave you"': '"we were able to do that principally sheltering you"' (245). This final conversation reveals to Tommy and Kathy that the provision of welfare was never about proving themselves worthy of a reprieve (a deferral), but a charitable organization's uneven intervention into a system of cultivated inequality.

For much of the novel, meritocracy structures character development, a form of social mobility explicitly organized around heteronormativity. There is a rumour that a couple might be able to 'defer' from donations if they can prove that they are genuinely in love, and same-sex couples are excluded from this possibility. The supposed great betrayal of the text – Ruth keeping apart the novel's 'true' couple, Tommy and Kathy – is premised on an ideal of human community centred on the union between man and woman (Foucault 1978; Sedgwick 1990; Warner 1991). Rachel Carroll argues that in the novel, 'coupledom is understood less as an elective expression of a romantic or sexual affinity than as a necessary assumption of a culturally coded set of practices' (2012, 142). Hailsham is a site of indoctrination into the 'the paradoxes and perversity of heteronormativity', even while its students are incapable of sexual reproduction (144). What is being protected, then, is not survival as such, but rather overdeterminations of normativity that uphold particular taxonomies of human. It is the fiction of heteronormativity – narratively coded as tragedy through Ruth's betrayal – that keeps the clones locked into the mythology of their own necessary destruction. Even as they realize that they are excluded from the script of social mobility, they are still compelled to uphold this in service to a greater purpose, and heteronormativity is central to this compulsion.

Ishiguro also charts the contraction of whiteness in post-imperial Britain, where material and epistemological infrastructures of enslavement – the epistemological field that continues to make enslavement possible – sequester freedom along lines of genetic 'originality', while genetic cloning makes possible the harvesting of body parts for other humans' use. While on the surface meritocracy is an ideology of equal opportunity, Ishiguro shows that this is laced with restrictions that prevent certain subjects from ever attaining it, even as places like Hailsham promote it. Racialization figures in important ways in the text. Ishiguro's world here is not a post-racial nation where 'even' white people now suffer; rather, the text shows how the racializing infrastructure of enslavement coordinates with an updated taxonomy of copy/original and donor/client throughout post-war liberalism and neoliberalism. As Josie Gill points out, readings of the novel as post-racial miss one of the key (and more or less silent) figures of the text, given no space for character development and who, in the film version, is shown only from the neck down, his hands on the back of Miss Emily's wheelchair: George, who Miss Emily describes as 'the big Nigerian man', with no given surname, her live-in care-worker. George never speaks directly; Kathy and Tommy hear 'a gruff male voice . . . so muffled it might have been two floors up' (229). Their meeting with Miss Emily and Madame draws Kathy and Tommy out of the illusion suggested by their being invited in: two couples debating the possibility of freedom in a middle-class sitting room. They are not supposed to be in the more public space of the sitting room, but somewhere upstairs, muffled and offstage. The scene annihilates their hope of attaining some degree of deferred freedom through faith and hard work (their love for each other and their creative outputs); they were never on an upward trajectory of social mobility, but on a continuum of underpaid or enslaved labour, now represented by an unseen migrant worker from a former British colony. Gill argues, 'As bodies that have been created to serve the needs of the "normal" population, the clones' experience appears little different from the contemporary exploitation of the black and minority ethnic workers who are often reduced simply to bodies that carry out various forms of undesirable and poorly paid labour' (2020, 64). They are not subjects with autonomy over their development: they are substitutes who are consigned to a temporality determined by the needs of other people's bodies.

Rather than being set in post-racial lifeworld, the pathos of Kathy's memoir is facilitated by her reliance on individual memoirs of systemic oppression, focused not just on 'documenting the suffering self but also, necessarily, recording the tormenting other' (Mendlesohn 2010). At the same time, these histories are held off and out of sight, the shadows of imperial infrastructure rendered into a perpetual present. Shaping a narrative of development for herself and her fellow students should figure as a mode of resistance, forcibly writing them into history, but Kathy finds herself caught, without the vocabulary to arrive at an end. In her efforts to deal with the past – the constant turning over of what she sees as critical turning points in the complicated dynamics between her, Tommy and Ruth – the wider narrative eludes her:

> As I've said, it wasn't until a long time afterwards – long after I'd left the Cottages – that I realised just how significant our little encounter in the churchyard had been. I was upset at the time, yes. But I didn't believe it to be anything so different from other tiffs we'd had. It never occurred to me that our lives, until then so closely interwoven, could unravel and separate over a thing like that.
>
> But the fact was, I suppose, there were powerful tides tugging us apart by then, and it only needed something like that to finish the task. If we'd understood that back then – who knows? – maybe we'd have kept a tighter hold of one another. (180)

The encounter that Kathy refers to is the penultimate conversation between the three of them before she decides to become a carer. Tommy has shown Ruth and Kathy his animal drawings, his deferred contribution to the artistic endeavours they were encouraged to participate in at Hailsham, which he had refused to do at the time. Ruth encourages Kathy to laugh at Tommy's drawings, and in the churchyard, reports this back to him: "'It's not just me, sweety. Kathy here finds your animals a complete hoot'" (178). At the time, Kathy is unable to say anything, 'like being given a maths problem when your brain's exhausted, and you know there's some far-off solution, but you can't work up the energy even to give it a go' (179). The moment passes her by without telling him that she does not find his drawings worthy of ridicule, and – in the passage above – she attributes this moment to their subsequent separation. Here, as in other moments of going over past hurts, she reads their behaviour as indications of character, and their failure to stay together as something to do with the interpersonal dynamic between the three of them.

Kathy's narrative style is suffused with recursive inscriptions that separate past from present in anxious reverberations – 'as I've said', 'afterwards . . . I realised', 'if we'd understood back then'. These asides enclose the architecture of nostalgia that hold the story together. Memoir becomes a way of documenting regret: missed opportunities, monuments to lost time. The characters live a deferred existence, and when Tommy and Kathy finally come together in the way Ruth feels they should have done to begin with, it is less a narrative culmination than a case of too little, too late. After they start having sex, Kathy notes Tommy's manner 'tinged with sadness, that seemed to say: "Yes, we're doing this now and I'm glad we're doing it now. But what a pity we left it so late"' (218). If only Ruth hadn't felt so jealous; if only Kathy had said something; if only Tommy have forgiven them both sooner. These regrets are given greater poignancy in the present, where Tommy is lined up for a third donation, and Kathy's time as a carer is coming to an end. An alternative set of decisions that might have prevented their unravelling and separation hangs over the text, emphasizing the importance of the individual's autonomy to put things right in the moment, rather than merely waiting for life to take its course. In Miss Emily's words to them when they are children, a '"missed opportunity"' (39). Kathy's efforts of documentation and revision are determined by this fear of missing an opportunity, a fold in the fabric of her life that she might seize and hold onto.

The paragraph break of the passage provided in the previous paragraph breaks up the illusion of personal autonomy, and the (assumed) precedence of this ostensibly private moment between three individuals over the public desire for their biomatter. The metaphor moves from fabric ('closely interwoven') to waves ('powerful tides tugging'), setting up a movement between activities of the private (knitting, weaving) and public spaces (organized – ostensibly – around natural laws, or at least which uphold an idea of natural checks to human freedom). The reality of this private sphere is grammatically ambivalent, disappearing into a horizon of uncertainty. The 'it' in 'it only needed something like that to finish the task', does not have a preceding referent (the waves are plural); 'it' refers to some uncategorised, undeclared relation, too fragile to survive tides. The break between paragraphs is also a break between individual code as a weaving, and the context which determines its possibilities, the tides of a social environment that splits them from their biopower.

On a more prosaic level, public health policy is equated with natural processes; more than this, the material and metaphorical resources of the natural world have been co-opted for human ends. The speculative aside, 'who knows?', undermines Kathy's assertion that they might have acted differently had they realized the bigger picture. But this keeps the three of them stuck in the myth of individual autonomy tied to a meritocratic promise of moving out of their lot, and the idea that simply having access to knowledge equals fair opportunity to make the best of a bad situation: Hailsham's final victory of indoctrination. The final metaphor, 'keeping tighter hold', is a euphemism for acts of apology, forgiveness and honesty, and a gesture to Kathy's own tight hold over their collective memories: it underscores Kathy's narratively suffocating belief that their behaviour can change their circumstances, which ends up preventing her from imagining other possibilities for freedom.

Kathy relies on the fiction of the individual and on memoir to provide a safe structure to demonstrate character development. Her anxious need for her life to move forward in time drives her creation of characters with different motivations, even as these characters tell her that they have no belief in character. For Kathy, survival requires becoming a good user of language and a good reader of people, skills that Hailsham equips her with: she is the archetypal good student, working as hard as she can to follow the shifting paths of the maze into which she has been placed, unable to see the whole picture. In her journeys to the past, she steals back the organs that are being taken from those she loves, seizing them from operating table back to metaphor, using nostalgia like a crowbar to break into wish-fulfilment. For instance, remembering the way that 'Norfolk' became a metonym for the outside world, the chance of a normal life, 'something that was once close to our hearts' (61). Norfolk becomes a possibility of a whole life, a place where they might end up one day, a 'fantasy land' to which one day they will be 'free to travel', but also a place where 'heart' can signify a certain kind of spirit, or – to use Tommy's word – a soul, rather than an organ available for extraction (61). This fantasy is less fearsome that some of the other metaphors that slide across the peripheries of her consciousness, like the helium balloons she sees a clown pulling down a street one day:

> I thought about Hailsham closing, and how it was like someone coming along with a pair of shears and snipping the balloon strings just where they entwined above the man's fist. Once that happened, there'd be no real sense in which those balloons belonged with each other any more. (194)

Character development is a defence tactic to mitigate the logic of substitution and surrogacy that the clones are otherwise forced to participate in. It is a way of forgetting the fragility of their relations with each other, the insubstantiality of their lives and the lurking violence ('shears . . . snipping the balloon strings') which will end them. It is this violence that makes their lives incommensurable with the fantasies that feed them, and Kathy's focus on character means holding this reality at bay for as long as possible.

While, for Kathy, character is a way to speak about desire (and about not having what she wants), Tommy and Ruth have different coping strategies: where Kathy writes, Ruth copies and Tommy resists. This characterization is analogous to moments of genetic programming – transcription, translation and expression; even as Kathy tries to give them full lives, mechanized description infiltrates. Tommy's animal drawings are works of surrealist impressionism, and upon seeing them for the first time, Kathy notes that 'it took a moment to see they were animals at all':

> The first impression was like one you'd get if you took off the back of a radio set: tiny canals, weaving tendons, miniature screws and wheels were all drawn with obsessive precision, and only when you held the page away could you see it was some kind of armadillo, say, or a bird. (171)

Tommy's art plays with the reduction of body to mechanism, placing biological matter (tendons) next to engineering and infrastructural innovation (screws, wheels and canals). The living body is incorporated into the machinery of technological modernity, compressed into an object of mass transmission. This disaggregation of mechanisms is described in a vocabulary that is transferrable between body and technology: the bodies here are reduced to pure mechanism, a collection of separable parts that might be taken apart and reassembled in another object.

Ruth's technique is to copy. For much of the text, the reader shares Kathy's sense of not quite knowing or trusting Ruth, even as Kathy tries to work her out. Ruth is constantly pulling the rug out, keeping Kathy on her toes, rearranging alliances as much as she needs to in order to maintain her position. From Kathy's vantage point – and through her, the reader's – Ruth seems prone to taking away from others (their sense of self, their happiness, their passions). Her efforts to counteract this always seem to fall short; when it's implied that she steals Kathy's beloved tape, she makes up for it by replacing it with a tape that doesn't have the same significance. But this is an instructive error on her part; Kathy recognizes that Ruth does not have the same appreciation for art and music that she does: 'to Ruth, who didn't know the first thing about music, this tape might easily make up for the one I'd lost' (69). For Ruth, one tape can replace another, and that's what Hailsham's market is for: the constant exchange and substitution of things for other things.

For this reason, Ruth's worst fear is different to Kathy and Tommy's. While Kathy fears the insignificance of their desires – nostalgic life-writing as defence, and Tommy fears their reduction to mere mechanism – turning to art, Ruth fears that they are akin to the junk of their small collections amassed at The Sales: easily lost, and easily forgotten. This comes out on their trip to Norfolk, to see someone who their new Cottages friends – Chrissie and Rod – think could be Ruth's 'possible'; here, 'possible' means the person whose DNA might have been used to clone her. This possible works in an office with big glass windows, "'a lovely office'", in Chrissie's words, a white-collar worker in a seaside town (146). Ruth's desire to see the person from whom she may have been copied is linked to a more general desire to have descended from people who are living lives that are cut off to them: people who have used their education to move up the ladder, free to choose where they work. A woman making the best out of the opportunities afforded by a mid-1980s economy premised on aspirational individualism and the ethos of equal opportunity in third-wave feminism.

When it becomes clear that the woman is not Ruth's possible – they follow her into an art gallery – Ruth reacts angrily to Tommy's suggestion that this was "'just a bit of fun'" (151). This is the first moment of the text where Ruth is honest with Kathy and Tommy about what she really thinks about their lives, herself and them. While they have been busy trying to work things out, playing detective (which they continue to do until the final meeting with Miss Emily), Ruth lays out what, for her, is the reality of their existence:

> 'We're not modelled from that sort. . . . We all know it. We're modelled from trash. Junkies, prostitutes, winos, tramps. Convicts, maybe, just so long as they aren't psychos. That's where we all come from. We all know it, so why don't we say it? A woman like that? Come on. Yeah, right, Tommy. A bit of fun. Let's have a bit of fun pretending. That other woman in there, her friend, the old one in the gallery. Art students, that's she thought we were. . . . If you want to look for possibles, if you want to do it properly, then you look in the gutter. You look in rubbish bins. Look down the toilet, that's where you'll find where we all came from'. (152–3)

In the film, this speech is delivered on a beach overlooked by a pier: Clevedon in Somerset, a Victorian pleasure beach which by the 1980s had become part of the UK's forgotten periphery of former holiday towns. This beach is another symbol of a dying post-war consensus, the domestic holiday of the 1950s, 1960s and 1970s in the process of being replaced by cheap travel to Mediterranean beaches further south. They are too late: this trip to the seaside comes as everyone else is moving on into new middle-class dreamworlds. This beach scene emphasizes the recognisability of this place, its allusion to carefree childhood summers

– swimming and jumping into the water – while cutting them off from the possibility of doing the same things, in the same way. The fantasy of the beach gives way as they stand on the sand, as Ruth's speech cuts them out of the scene, its own technology of deletion. Even here, there are not at leisure: their labour is to stay alive and to keep healthy for as long as their body parts are required.

The act of placing oneself in landscapes that are not meant for you is also an intervention in the traffic between sociopolitical formation and aesthetic forms. Being mistaken for art students carries a particular irony, but not the one that Ruth suggests. All three of them are in different ways students of art, adopting distinct styles. Ruth's speech conjures another modernist aesthetic, not Kathy's *Bildungsroman* nostalgia, nor Tommy's surrealist impressionism, but more akin to Brecht and Beckett. The rhythm of her language tends towards annihilation and closing-down – a list of degenerates connected by violent commas – while the imprecision of the ideas and subjects prevents full comprehension: the syllable-heavy 'prostitutes' lining up with the single-syllable 'tramps'; she starts sentences mid-way through, the speech patterns broken into fragments, forcing a reader into tracking the metre of her anger to follow her meaning. Tommy can accept the pretence, having access to an imaginary that in some way allows him to reshape reality according to principles that fall outside realism; Ruth, on the other hand, pushes realism to its limits. In her speech, pretence is not a gesture of resistance, but rather a way of putting blinders on their self-image. Throughout the novel, Ruth fears exposure: her fraudulence, her selfishness, her sexuality, her desire to divide and rule. At the same time, she is the character most exposed to the structural reality of their situation: their bodies will soon be disposed of, flushed away, forgotten; they are marginal, undesired, peripheral nobodies.

The novel is strung together by episodes that come to resemble a long list of anecdotes tied together by Kathy's desire to keep the three of them together – if only in narrative. The plot moves forward at the end of section breaks with repeated allusions to 'what happened next . . .'. This pedestrian plotting, where a truth might be revealed or a set piece staged, draws the reader through the text, going back and forth over anecdotes and their possible meanings. There is the sense of an underlying script that moves event through to consequence, cause and effect, the form of the text akin to a code expressed through repetition and copying; the content changes, but the same basic structure of events is repeated again and again: a mystery, a revelation, a splitting apart and the hope of reconciliation. The episodic form leads the narrative away from Kathy's insistence on finding a greater meaning for their lives, and it is this that makes it difficult for her to see why it would not take that much for their connection to become unravelled and for them to be separated from each other. This form makes the narrative more easily reducible to fragments of memory – snapshots that resemble, across metaphor, the pieces of flesh that will be extracted from the students. It mirrors the disaggregation of parts from the whole.

Repetition as narrative form reveals something about the correlation of memoir with sequencing imaginaries: in terms of structure, there is no real change or development, not so much phases leading to other phases, but different manifestations of the same set of events, responses and outcomes. Remembering the last conversation between the three of them, Kathy notes, 'The way it began, it was a bit like a repeat of earlier' (208). This 'earlier' refers to earlier in the day, but also to the persistence of 'earlier' in the way she keeps time. 'Earlier' recurs throughout her narrative, like segments of code ending and repeating, the beginning a recapitulation of something that has come before.

Gabriele Griffin reads *Never Let Me Go* in the context of debates over cloning in the late 1990s and early 2000s, after the successful cloning of Dolly the sheep. Contending with M. John Harrison's indictment that there is 'no science' in the novel (2005), Griffin argues that Ishiguro's text is not interested so much in the minutiae of scientific process, 'the practicalities of cloning and organ donation', as it is in the effect of 'scienticity as the actualisation of scientific practice' (647). Rather, the text is invested in the effect of these processes on understanding the self as human in the midst of an acceleration of posthuman imaginaries through technologies of genetic modification (2009, 646–7). For Griffin, this comes out in the relation between specialist scientific language and ordinary language in the novel. Following Barbara Duden, this involves both the emigration of scientific terms into ordinary language, as well as making ordinary language strange through its proximity to a scientific and medical (and historical) context which remains mostly offstage (Duden and Samerski 2008). This estrangement of ordinary language is made possible not (only) through scientific literacy, but (also) by socio-economic and political descriptions of human life that have positioned the biological at its core.

Anjali Pandey develops this argument about the relation between scientific and ordinary language further, suggesting that Ishiguro's technique is to reconfigure not only the grammar but also semiotics of life after the genome; that is, the way in which life takes on or sheds meaning, through a technique that she calls 'lexical dissonance' (2011, 394). For Pandey, the power and ambivalence of Ishiguro's linguistic neologisms (donor, clone, carer) are derived from the tension between polysemic intent and polysemic copying: by moving words around the surface of the text, Ishiguro disturbs the meaning imposed by what the clones take as reality. This strategy mimics techniques of copying, insertion and deletion of genetic material in practices of sequencing and modification. For Pandey, this is pastiche: while this model of experience is indomitably grammatical and derived from practices of lexigraphy (rather than biology making grammar), 'Ishiguro's meticulous use of lexical dissonance . . . creates literary cacophony,' wherein what emerges is not similitude or reducibility, but a railing against the attempted destruction of life via euphemism, synonymy, metonymy and sincerity, for the sake of dysphemism, antonymy, synecdoche and irony: 'lexemes in the service of literature' (2011, 395).

Pandey gestures to a form of resistance derived through this strategy of lexical dissonance, and this is registered at the level of semiotics; that is, in the way that the characters are able to hold off, move around, or annihilate meaning. Captured within a lexical form that constantly anticipates their annihilation through repetition and disaggregation, deferral becomes the only mode of resistance left to the students. This, too, has a genetic analogy, but not one restricted to the logic of sequencing. While sequencing technologies of the 1980s and 1990s were organized around what is expressed in the genome – the protein-coding genes – Ishiguro gestures to the deferral of expression, the holding back of meaning, and silences that may or may not be filled. Often, a gap emerges in time between action and response: the time it takes for Tommy to forgive Kathy for laughing at his animals when he shows them to her, after Ruth's completion and in anticipation showing them to Miss Emily: 'I realised immediately that this was Tommy's way of putting behind us everything that had happened at the Cottages, and I felt relief, gratitude, sheer delight' (220). Kathy does not often realize things immediately; many of her realizations up to this point are the result of going over the past, and looking at it from a different vantage point. But the delay between Tommy's first act of showing and this one allows something different to be expressed, despite the formal repetition; instead of bewilderment, 'relief', and instead of guilt or confusion, 'sheer delight'. Tommy's deferral of forgiveness mimics the repetition established in their relationship so far (doomed to miss each other, to misunderstand, to not say the right thing at the right time), but ends up breaking it: some new possibility comes into play between them. It is this moment – as the breaking of habit out of mimesis – that constitutes something new, that allows them to exist, if temporarily, as a pair, in time with one another for the first time in the novel.

This moment is temporary. Deferral strategies cannot work to alter their position. The architecture of memoir – at least in the form it takes here – does not allow space for this. As in *Gattaca*, resistance in these texts is more to do with breaking into the no-time of genomic sequencing, the immanence of their predetermined existence and the capture of ends in beginnings. This restricted field of resistance points to a bigger crisis – that of constructing the self in chronological time. Ruth is the character who understands this crisis most viscerally. The novel ends with an image of rubbish – plastic bags caught on the barbed wire of fences, in an anonymous part of rural England. This image situates the novel, finally, in a history of enclosure that technologies of nostalgia for a lost pastoral cannot fully cover over, and draws the clones into a topography of discarded debris and waste; 'all sorts of rubbish', echoing Ruth (263). This closing image – 'two lines of wire' presided over by trees in which 'I could see, flapping about, torn plastic sheeting and bits of old carrier bags' (263) – looks like a sequence, the lines corresponding to the two lines of the double helix, interspersed with genetic clusters. This material has fallen out of use, no longer required, like bits of redundant information on the nucleotide.

The end of *Never Let Me Go* anticipates the new imaginary for which sequencing offered a prototype, and for which the practice of organ extraction sets a precedent: not the formation of new subjects, not even reducing the body to code, but a new kind of governmentality based on differentiating genomic value via algorithm, rather than subject. Kathy's strategy of trying to make meaning (value) via characterization is futile. This new precedent is a eugenic technology that does not need a single referent or ideal subject, but rather composes and recomposes avatars by aggregating disaggregated and de-individuated data: not the transformation of the (neo)liberal subject, but its disappearance into Big Data, a composite reference, a new normal that is constantly in flux. The liberal fiction of development collapses into what Maurizio Lazzarato calls 'machinic enslavement' (2014), a theme that *Gattaca* takes up through another first-person genre: the Hollywood noir. This time, the detective is displaced into machines, and the subject under investigation has disappeared into data.

## *Gattaca* and algorithmic governmentality

*Gattaca* was released in 1997, six years before the first draft of the human genome was published. Its world is a future version of our own, where it is now normal to sequence the genomes of embryos to determine their propensities towards certain physical and mental diseases, as well as their skin colour and gender. Not only this, but it is possible to select the 'best' of parents' genetic stock to construct genetically superior children. It is still possible to have what are called 'god children' – children conceived without genetic engineering – but these children are usually at a severe disadvantage when it comes to professional mobility and interpersonal relationships. There are personal genetic testing stations where DNA can be sequenced quickly, anonymously and cheaply – in one scene, a woman has the saliva on her lips from kissing her date scraped off and sequenced immediately. It is implied that there is a composite reference genome that makes these practices of probabilization and comparison possible, but exactly what this is made up of and what constitutes 'normal' is never made clear. The cognitive dissonance of this invisibilized reference point goes across the social spectrum and it is the character closest to the current genomic ideal that ends up self-destructing.

The film received a wide release and was aimed at a mass audience already primed for science-fictional forensics by *The X-Files*; this partly accounts for why it does not need to establish the terms of reference for the model of genetic idealism it portrays. But the hype around the Human Genome Project was at this point so fevered, and its promises that diseases would be able to be pre-empted and exorcized at the level of DNA so widespread, that *Gattaca* is also able to skip a great deal of explication. Vincent's narrative emerges in the middle of debate not about the scientific validity of genetic disease, but the ethical quandaries of diagnosis and treatment. The film's enduring popularity as a reference film for future genomic dystopias, where discrimination is reduced to individual code, was made possible in part by its updating of older speculations on cloning, bioengineering and eugenics – notably, Aldous Huxley's *Brave New World* (1932).

The lack of clarity around what constitutes normality in Gattaca extends Keller's argument into the sphere of algorithmic governmentality. Communication between individuals no longer matters. Rather, a genomic lifeworld is 'a scheme designed for communications between machines, where information [is] conceptualized in a manner divorced from content, subject matter, or nature of the channel' (Kay 2000, 97). While liberal and neoliberal forms of governance centre an individual (whether part of a commons or self-fashioned), algorithmic governmentality does away with the need for a subject around which to organize data, and 'carefully avoids any direct confrontation with and impact on flesh and blood persons' (Rouvroy 2012, 157). The (neo)liberal subject located in a body that is considered separate from others, whose freedom is premised on autonomy over action, is replaced by 'a statistical body' composed of aggregated data, 'constantly evolving data-body or network of localisations in actuarial tables' (11). Rather than depending on a fixed norm or average, this points to an 'a-normative objectivity' or 'immanent normativity' which endlessly constructs reality out of data, and which needs to 'obscure social normativities, silencing these as far as possible because they cannot be translated digitally' (Rouvroy and Berns 2013, 163). Insofar as algorithmic governance is 'governance without a subject', it needs to silence and obscure subjective coherence, while abstract normative values emerge in continuing fixations on disability, gender, sexuality and race. Irene asks her boss if she will '"lose her place in line"' by doing tasks below her pay-grade, gesturing to ableist and sexist workplace discrimination without any measures put in place to prevent it.

The disappearance of the subject into algorithms is underscored by *Gattaca*'s first-person narrative, delivered by Vincent – a 'god child' who leaves home to pursue his dream of travelling into space, a future that his genomic identity does not allow for. Vincent's predispositions and the probability of their expression are read out to his parents at birth: neurological condition, 60 per cent probability; manic depression, 43 per cent probability; attention deficit disorder, 89 per cent probability; and heart disorder, 99 per cent. He is given a life expectancy of 30.2 years. When we meet him as an adult, now working at the Gattaca space exploration station under a false identity, he is several thousand heartbeats over this prediction. The film is set in a future Detroit, Vincent telling us that he was conceived on 'the Detroit Riviera', locating it in a history of Fordist production and post-war US urbanization, the institution of suburbia and white-collar professionalism as a new post-war-US normal. This setting emphasizes a future of working-class aspiration that has already fallen into disrepair because of the outsourcing of production to cheaper sites across South and East Asia. In place of manufacturing cars, human beings are now assembled in laboratory factories (whose mechanics remain off-screen), factory managers replaced by biomedical consultants who advise parents on assembling the right constellation of genetic attributes for their future children in rooms that resemble doctors' offices. This is the engineering of a white-collar workforce via a fiction of individual choice, a buy-in model for a disease-free future that is explicitly tied to national development. This workforce will deliver the United States to new frontiers: 'Now we have enough of the right kind of people to warrant a new measuring stick: bodies with minds to match. Essential as we push out further and further,' says Gattaca's CEO.

While this equates to the creation of a genetic elite, it leaves those who for whatever reason cannot fulfil either the social or genetic potential of being human peripheral. It also opens possibilities for an informal genomic market to emerge: 'When the elite fall on hard times, genetic identity becomes a commodity.' With his income as a janitor, Vincent saves up to buy the identity of a man with a '9.3' score on his genome test – Jerome Morrow. The real Jerome was involved in a car accident and has lost the use of both legs, restricted to a wheelchair. A possible plot-hole emerges: why wouldn't authorities have recorded this, and why hasn't Jerome's information been altered on the central database? The post-accident Jerome, who now goes by Eugene (a play on 'good origins', eu-genic), lives alone in a two-storey development, but needs an income to sustain his alcohol addiction, hence selling his biomatter to Vincent. Taking on Jerome's identity involves Vincent undergoing an excruciating regime of daily shedding and erasing, through which evidence of Jerome's identity is placed at strategic locations across his body: blood for the finger-prick identification system at Gattaca's entrance, urine for the regular drug tests, strands of hair placed into the comb he keeps in his office desk. As he takes on the material of Jerome's DNA, Vincent must also vacuum and burn evidence of his own: he scours his skin everyday, burning it in an incinerator (part of his and Eugene's domestic laboratory), sucks up scattered bits of fallen biomatter from his office keyboard with a tiny vacuum, and – after a night with Irene, his office co-worker – carefully plucks a strand of fallen hair from the pillow beside her.

The early reference to Vincent's predisposition towards manic depression is offset by the social pathology this system generates. The idea that the Human Genome Project would lead to new biotechnologies for identifying and treating not only somatic disorders but also mental disorders – schizophrenia and manic depression (the implication being that these were genetic traits) – was put forward by some of its key players, Watson included. But in *Gattaca*, the psychic effort of living in this genomic regime leads to breakdown: despite his near-perfect genes and an absence of genetic predispositions towards depression or alcoholism (predispositions which the film's science endorse), Eugene is not only an alcoholic but also suicidal. His depression is never explicitly named, but it is clear that his genetic perfection has not only prevented but also possibly contributed towards it. When Vincent comes back from Gattaca jubilant at having "'got the job'", Eugene replies – looking away from Vincent, his eyes cast down towards the floor, with Vincent positioned behind him – "'Of course you did.'" He points out later in the film, when Vincent is worried about being recognized, that 'they' don't see 'Vincent' at all – only a pre-accident version of 'him'. Jerome's DNA substitutes for a real body, made to stand for two bodies that are now socially invisible. To follow Rouvroy, Jerome-as-data-body does not represent a hypothesis about what individuals or society should be, but rather is part of a more general system of datamining which serves 'to structure, in an anticipative way, the possible field of action of 'bodies" (2012, 149). This field sets the conditions for reality, and constitutes what she calls system of 'data behaviourism' which causes – following Lazzarato – 'machinic enslavement', rather than 'subjective alienation', when the subject becomes a slave of the machine, in a unidirectional flow of control – not unlike the model of gene action given by Dawkins in *The Selfish Gene* (Lazzarato 2014). In the genomic context, the body is slave to the code; in *Gattaca*, this enslavement equates to the disappearance of the subject into the code.

The film's displacement of racializing infrastructure into the language of genetics does not make race disappear; rather, the reflexes of Jim Crow and the eventual flight from Earth form the film's narrative architecture, while – as in *Never Let Me Go* – remaining offstage. Fears of miscegenation and the one-drop rule are conjured by the availability of instant sequencing technologies, wherein blood and genes are metonyms for the possibility of contamination. During their childhood, we see Vincent's brother Anton refuse to exchange blood with his brother, demonstrating a pre-adolescent understanding of a difference in kind that might be contagious, as well as the spectre of AIDS and anxieties around pre-existing congenital vulnerability to the transmission of particular morbidities. The genetics consultant who attends Vincent's parents is a Black man, who notes with a pause that they have specifically requested a child with 'fair skin' during a consultation. While there is a Black office manager who turns Vincent down for a job, and two Black astronauts who go up at the same time as him, these characters are also peripheral and – aside from the consultant – non-speaking, and in the latter's case, unnamed. Jerome's perfection is still premised on his racialization as someone of European ancestry; Eugene-Jerome is played by Jude Law with a received-pronunciation English accent, suggesting his proximity to upper-class European genomes.

This racializing infrastructure is extended to the architecture of the double helix and the genome, symbols which are everywhere and nowhere. DNA can only be seen and grasped through other materials – the symbol of a circle, a helix-shaped staircase, the string of letters on Jerome's genome sequence. The film's opening credits show what seem to be huge objects dropping to the ground, lit in phosphorescent blue, as if we're in another world. These are nail clippings, flakes of skin and hair of various widths and diameters, strung across the screen like estranged hyperobjects: evidence of a human code, both eclipsing and falling away from the bodies they come from. When Eugene first appears on screen, he is sitting in a wheelchair at the bottom of a staircase shaped like a double helix. Images of mechanical mobility abound: elevators, escalators, tunnels and roads. When Vincent and Irene kiss for the first time, a shadowed lattice appears across their bodies, segmenting them into parts on a grid: a frame that they are not aware of in that moment, but which fixes them into a social field that has been imagined out of the architecture of molecular biology. When Vincent tries to cross a busy road without his glasses, the viewer sees what he sees: the blurred lights of cars coming towards him and passing at great speed. Watson's later vision of a 'molecular highway' is almost literal here – Vincent-as-subject is caught in the blurry and obscure movement of biomatter, alienated from the processes going on in his body which determine his exclusion from the world into which he has been born. The architecture of the genome, as it appears in the film, is always depicted as excluding the protagonists. At a critical moment, Eugene has to haul himself up the double helix staircase with his arms and hands, his legs dragging behind him. The moment underscores the hostility of this architecture of human potential to chance events that might require adaptation and facilitation, and for bodies that are not designed to fit its specifications.

This infrastructural hostility results in forms of social blindness, a motif that repeats throughout the film. Vincent's bad eyesight functions as a metaphor for a more general blurring of people and environment into undetermined data objects, becoming part of a perpetual flow without a central reference point. And in this landscape, acts of not seeing become moments of small resistance: when Vincent's former janitor boss 'does not see' Vincent on Gattaca's back stairs, when Vincent purposefully lets Irene's eyelash blow away in the breeze so that he cannot have her sequenced (and when she, eventually, does the same), and when Gattaca's onsite medic – the person who comes closest to Vincent's fraudulent identity – 'does not see' that all along, Vincent (a left-handed man) has been holding his penis with his right while urinating into a cup. Letting details go under the radar, become obscure, get left out of documentation and evidence, is the single possibility for working the system, and the only way that agency emerges.

This resistance to the genome's status as a truth-object is reflected in how the unpredictable dynamics of social relations also resist the architecture of DNA, refusing the symmetry and linearity of its structure. The story is full of pairs that keep getting interrupted. Invalid Vincent and his brother Anton, then Vincent and Jerome, Vincent-Jerome and Eugene-Jerome, and Vincent-Jerome and Irene. If sequencing base pairs is the primary way of reading genomic code, then in *Gattaca*, this process is constantly frustrated, delayed, or abandoned. The stability of the pair is repeatedly undermined, and splitting things up becomes an act of tacit resistance. Machines that read code can be tricked through the tactical use of waste material: forged fingerprints, fallen strands of hair. Precision can be mediated by disappearance, trickery and – in the film's final moments – empathy. No one believes the fiction, but it constitutes an economy which facilitates national development and competitive science.

While these strategies of not-seeing and interruption give the plot some resistive edge, it is Eugene's death that acknowledges the end of one particular formation of human agency. Eugene does end up committing suicide, locking himself into the incinerator. Before this, he tells Vincent that he has collected enough material evidence of Jerome to 'last you a lifetime'. A Jerome that exists only in genetic data is held in Eugene's home laboratory, while the original self-immolates. This moment outlines the annihilating violence of the laboratory, as well as drawing attention to the domestication of scientific infrastructure, its relocation from laboratories on the outskirts of major research centres (Stanford, Cambridge, MIT), to the homes of consumers. It also construes the disappearance of the neoliberal self-fashioning subject – to whom the domestic laboratory is marketed – into this molecular imaginary. Fulfilling one's potential means eventually getting divided into component parts and getting sucked into an amorphous, anonymous and composite field of data.

Eugene's death represents the death of the neoliberal self-fashioned subject, and its replacement with Jerome – the data-body who exists only as a genomic sequence. This data-body will not develop or change, but will remain in the system as comparative data, part of a deterritorialized assemblage without a fixed point of reference. He could be added to future embryos, or at some point, become redundant as the norm (inevitably) adapts to technological advances. Who knows what will happen in space, and what new kinds of genetic potential might come in useful in the future? What is important is not Jerome's near-perfection in and of itself, but the co-option of 'him' as a data object that remains a perpetual site of extraction. Eugene's final words to Vincent are directed towards a possible future, one in which Vincent comes back from his space mission; similarly, the field of action for algorithmic governmentality is not the present, but the future – to what could become, and in Rouvroy and Berns's words, 'to propensities rather than action taken' (2013, 18). As they note, this eliminates liberal ideals of critique, commons and project, for the sake of a new political regime without historical precedent.

The Human Genome Project destabilized narratives of individual development through its invention of technologies that break this individual up into component parts. This chapter has considered how the Human Genome Project brought both liberal and neoliberal models of humanism into crisis, rendering metaphors of development (as environmental influence), critique (as checks and adaptations) and project (the individual) obsolete. But the data-body left behind already had a historical precedent, in the disaggregation and annihilation of lineage, genealogy, biomatter and history enacted systemically through the transatlantic slave trade. It is to this history and its prominence in postgenomic uses of genomic technologies that I now turn.

4

# Speculative ancestry

The Human Genome Project did not inaugurate ideologies of engineering human biology. While genomics offered new technologies for identifying DNA sequences, practices of breeding humans have been sewn into colonial-capitalist expansion. As a new universal subject stepped out from the shadows of all that was premodern and primitive, humans were being stolen and shipped across the world as enslaved labour. And while European liberalism offered a developmental trajectory for this new vision of humanity as enlightened and in charge of its own destiny, these other humans were disaggregated into useful traits – phenotypic and psychological, body-shape and temperament – and bred by enslavers in ways similar to the breeding of domestic animals. Francis Galton's science of eugenics was as much a product of human breeding projects on plantations and in colonies as it was the application of natural selection – the natural propagation of the best hereditary stock – to social development.

When the Human Genome Project came to an end, it quickly became clear that it would not be able to deliver on the promises upon which much of its rhetoric had been founded, or at least not immediately. Nonetheless, the near-cult like status of the genome in popular imaginaries meant that it was going nowhere in a hurry: narratives of the 1990s had propelled it into global superstardom. There was no turning back. This was a new century, and it was to be the century of postgenomics. In lieu of healthcare applications for genomic science, which were still in their infancy at the turn of the millennium, more immediate uses of personalised genomics came into view. At the same time, the biologists Thomas Wilson and Clarence Grim's genetic account of the inherited effects of trauma and poor diets on rates of hypertension among African Americans situated the descendants of enslaved peoples in a genealogy of horror written into embodied code (1991). While their study was criticized for its (supposed) historical inaccuracies, it articulated an alternative set of concerns that was interested in the relationship between biology and history, rather than the reduction of self to code, and in collective approaches to health based on shared experiences, rather than an individualized model of innate and immutable traits.

Here, I consider how the rise of genetic accounts of historical belonging are registered in fictive and speculative family histories, and how these histories end up challenging an encroaching reliance on genetic origins as a description of kinship. In Saidiya Hartman's *Lose Your Mother: A Journey Along the Atlantic Slave Route* (2006) and Yaa Gyasi's *Homegoing* (2016), DNA testing is not correlated with racial belonging, but is instead part of an apparatus for recomposing the past. The metaphorical power of ancestry testing reorients genomics from improving human futures to reckoning with the histories of brutalization and displacement upon which liberal humanism is founded (Lowe 2015). This reorientation puts pressure on molecular accounts of life and belonging, threatening to undo the premise (and promise) of genomic descriptions of being.

While genetic ancestry testing has promised a vision of genealogical continuity across the Atlantic for Black American roots seekers, it is also a site of inconsistency, imprecision, absence and silences. Inconclusive results point as much to flaws in the technological apparatus as they do to the tendentious incompletions of bio-historical record. This underscores yet another way in which this history – considered from the perspective of lineage – has been deliberately obscured in narratives of capitalist development (Baptist 2014). In the promise to share the burden of healing from history by repairing tears in the fabric of Black time, ancestry testing locates the trauma of enslavement at the level of the molecular, pressing on code as proof of the past.

Ancestry testing and racialization are not reducible to each other; the desire to seek ancestral roots in the genes is not the same as seeking biological evidence of racial identity. But the proximity of these desires begs attention. Finding answers about identity in the genes points to what Paul Gilroy has described as the modern convergence of nature and culture, in which racial difference and racial hierarchy become interchangeable. A protection against 'various postmodern assaults on the coherence and integrity of the self', this convergence enables both minorities and majorities to 'supply vivid natural means to lock an increasingly inhospitable and lonely social world in place and to secure one's own position in turbulent environments' (2004, 6). The popularity of genetic ancestry testing rehearses anxious recourses to deterministic accounts of being as a way of coping with uncertainties and injustices of the present.

Moving within the violence of this convergence, Hartman and Gyasi attend to a different lineage, not one inscribed in the genes in any straightforward sense, but through which 'the strengths passed down . . . the things that helped our ancestors survive in a hostile world' might be found as marks on the body, and in shared practices across diaspora and Continent (Greenidge 2018). While the historical precision of genetic ancestry testing is limited, its cultural power has been made possible in part by the way it draws on the utopianism of Pan-Africanism, dwindling under the pressures of competitive nationalism after global financialization. This gives the politics of reparation a new technological imaginary, even as its value as an empirical form of evidence falls short. While ancestry testing continues to elude empirical and legal constitutions of evidence, its cartographic metaphors bank on reiterations of Black internationalism and African futurism, and the visions these plural movements offered to Black lifeworlds.

Movement is vital. Ancestry testing as Black praxis is not an ontological project, but a cartographic one: remaking annihilated routes. In *Demonic Grounds*, Katherine McKittrick writes that 'concealment, marginalisation, boundaries are important social processes' in the production of space, processes that destabilize the very kinds of predetermined stabilities of 'fixed and settled infrastructures and streets, oceanic containers' (2006, xi): 'We make concealment happen; it is not natural but rather names and organises where racial-sexual differentiation occurs' (xi–xii). There is a rough analogy here between mapping bodies – emancipated subjects able (in theory) to participate place in a liberal commons – and mapping space. The concealment of histories where Black flesh supplements white bodies corresponds to the concealment that shapes Black geographies as absence, for the sake of arbitrating the fault-lines of a monolithic white world. As for McKittrick, the practices of mapping with which Hartman and Gyasi are engaged do not seek to '"find" or "discover" lost geographies' or – in the context of this chapter – lost lineages; rather, their narratives consider how 'space and place give black lives meaning in a world that has, for the most part, incorrectly deemed black populations and their attendant geographies as "ungeographic" and/or philosophically undeveloped' (2006, xii–xiii). Geography and genealogy are intertwined in these texts as sites of uncertainty, attending to the enormity of the project to 'make visible social lives which are often displaced, rendered ungeographic' (McKittrick 2006, x).

These texts imagine kinship as a plural and often speculative making across the inconsistencies and transformations of biological and non-biological ties, not the product of singular lineages reliant on transparent and legible records. This is as much a philosophical intervention as it is an historical one. Writing on human genome diversity research, Kim TallBear notes, 'the faith in origins as molecular origins' is 'at odds with the idea of change over time, of becoming'

(2013, 5; see also Leroux 2019). The bearing of kinship on ontology is carried through tumultuous currents of emplacement and displacement in time and space: what does kinship mean and who can claim it, when rhythms of capture and loss have shaped the contours of endurance? When ancestry testing does not offer the restoration of lost lineages tied to territory, but continues to shroud the past in indeterminacy, some forms of kinship are annulled, some made necessary, and some emerge in new and transformative conditions of possibility. In Hartman and Gyasi's texts, the opposition between origins and relations shifts – to follow Christina Sharpe – 'in the wake' of the ruptures in time and history caused by the transatlantic slave trade (2016).

## Ancestry-making

In *Lose Your Mother* and *Homegoing*, an ongoing crisis of genealogy reverberates across rhythms of leaving and staying, genealogical continuity as lure and feint as much as a promise. If genetic ancestry testing relies on the idea that hereditary material might fix a person to a place in time and history, these texts attach this promise to the ambivalence around biological origins in the wake of the destruction of family ties through enslavement. AbdouMaliq Simone offers a powerful description of what he calls the 'curse and potentials of the abruption of genealogy', rendered through the Koranic figure of triple darkness:

> Slavery was the brutal cut in the connection of a people from their land, culture, and capacity to institutionalise their version of humanity (or a version without it), a people whose 'darkness' threw them into a state of darkness, of separation and condemnation. It compelled their need to reinvent themselves without the certainty of cultural coherence, of the dark remaking a version of humanity in the dark. In doing so, through long periods of suffering, struggle, solidarity, and improvisation, all of the historical narratives that explained how things came about and how the world was made were upended. Those that were slaves consigned these narratives to darkness. (2018, 91)

The effort of enduring the cuts of history makes necessary modes of reinvention and improvisation. Here, genealogy is placed off-centre in an assemblage of practices for contending with a world turned upside-down. It is not that the genetic as such has no purchase. Its architecture is always something to be negotiated and reckoned with, rather than functioning as a central description of being. It is not the repetition of biological heredity that matters, but the resurrection of practices through long periods of time, when no alternative future can be guaranteed or relied upon.

It is in this key that Hartman and Gyasi deliver their reckonings with lineage, with a past that can be traced, and with an aporia between genomic legibility and historical reparation: the genome might be legible, but what can it prove? The texts are connected by the question of what it is to dwell in a collective body that does not know if it is staying or leaving. What does this mean for the idea of the genome corresponding to a particular place and time and history or, conversely, the idea of universal genomic subject? Hartman and Gyasi's narratives dwell in the time of the body – the first-person narrator of *Lose Your Mother* and the third-person collective narrative of *Homegoing* – to consider what it is to 'go home' in the age of ancestry testing, when the possibility of alternative histories have legal and reparative dimensions, but when the technology consistently fails to provide definitive evidence.

Genomics has a strange, even combative, relationship with the past. For the most part, the main players in genomics were not interested in the past, except as proof of natural selection – genetically derived traits whose survival indicates fitness. Heritage is invoked in ethnonational imaginaries, as in Mike Fortun's account of the deCODE project in Iceland (2008). Venter's memoir is interrupted every so often by information boxes about his own genetic inheritance which prove certain autobiographical observations about his tendencies, gifts and – sometimes – his altercations with others. But my claim here – following Alondra Nelson and Dorothy Roberts – is that genetic ancestry testing does a different kind of cultural work in the context of Black American genealogies. Ancestry testing is not being used as proof of the inevitability of human progress along a long-term developmental trajectory – that is, of a racialized human supremacy – but rather as proof of endurance, claiming the need for repair, and invoking the dream of return. It functions as a technology of what might be compared to Hartman's idea of devotional dances to ancestral spirits on the plantations as 'insurgent nostalgia', which 'expressed a longing for home that most could only vaguely recall or that lived only in imagination' (1997, 72), inciting a reckoning, across the waves, between history and memory.

At its most radical, genetic ancestry testing becomes a tool in a broader project of ancestry-*making* – a way of inserting speculative histories into the blank spaces of the past. Hartman and Gyasi's interweaving of fact and speculation imagine the past as a site of multiple crossings – characters that find themselves 'simultaneously in many space-times' (Simone, 55), where people miss each other and fall out of history. They draw on an infrastructure of twentieth-century

Black and African futurist intertextuality – the political demands and aesthetic forms of Pan-Africanism, the Harlem Renaissance, and *Négritude* – to restate the stakes of Blackness into the twenty-first, and to reiterate its contradictions and demands. Genetic technologies of identification are not to do with establishing racial boundaries, but with casting lines across historical waters. While genetic technologies do not – for the most part – offer legal evidence for reparation and return, their promise of calling up the dead produces new kinds of alliances among the living.

Narratives of ancestry-making are constrained by the restrictions of a data-fuelled present, in which (statistically) the data of Black people either disappear and become part of databases for surveillance and criminalization. Ruha Benjamin has called these practices 'the new Jim Code', which use new technologies to sustain and bolster existing modes of racial discrimination (2019, 13). The burden of individuality – the fiction of the self – is a political problem that speculative interventions cannot immediately solve, especially when it comes to racist fictionalizations of Black life into repurposed, racialized narratives of 'natural' inequality.

In this sense, genetic ancestry testing traverses horrors of Black histories and the romance of family origins. Since the turn of the twenty-first century, it has become part of a way of reading Blackness, and its uses indicate the enormity and difficulty of this endeavour. While it offers an 'ethnological and conformist account' of family history, its failure to offer direct lines of descent attests to the silences of history – and memory as rupture, broach and discontinuity (Hartman 2006, 75). And sometimes, the effects of these gaps take their time to catch up in the present. While genomics offers a powerful metaphor for reading the past – 'an autobiography of our species' – it cannot do the cultural work of caring for history. Its emphasis on individual lineage means that it is indelibly linked to an economic mode of existence that has privileged private property. The place of Black folks in this history cannot be rehabilitated through metaphors of liberal humanism.

As a way of negotiating this caesura, and in lieu of a germ-line running in a straight line through time, Hartman and Gyasi deploy recursive modes of storytelling, going back over the same ground, looking for a different opening to the past, and a strategy of enduring the present: to follow Simone, these are improvisations on a theme. These improvisations become a way of reckoning with the difficulty of staying and the pain of leaving, of not being able to exist fully in a body inscribed as the total sum of an illegible and erased ancestral past.

## Genre, genetics and genealogy

Representations of genealogy in these texts fall across genres. These shifts in genre indicate the various and contesting forms of kinship that genealogy needs to encompass in contexts where enslavement is the governing historical narrative. Here, I pay particular attention to the intersection of Black horror and family romance. For Robin Means Coleman, Black horror is a genre born out of exclusion. The fever-pitch excitement around the genome during the 1990s was reflected in a range of popular cultural references, and particularly in representations of the uses of DNA in forensics (detective stories), and bio-engineering (as in *Gattaca*). These representations emphasized the almost-immediate and unquestioned take-up of genomic technologies into the realm of empirical enquiry, with an emphasis on commodification and social control. Black horror is doing something different. For Coleman, Black folks' participation in horror at a more general level registers 'resistance against dominant ideologies' as much as re-inscription into it, and negotiations of representation of Black culture and bodies (2011, 199). A genre that has used Black bodies to represent either a fearsome other or – more recently – gullible fall-people, Black recuperations of horror are doing a different kind of cultural work. In Jordan Peele's *Get Out* (2017) and *US* (2019), this means rearranging cinematic architecture to place whiteness in the position of fearsome other, and to connect this to broader critiques of consumer capitalism, as well as of the erasure of enslavement and genocide as a condition of American settler colonialism.

This is not only a US-centric Black history. The 1980s and 1990s were difficult decades for Black internationalism. Pan-Africanism diminished under the pressures of neoliberal finance capital, and forms of competitive nationalism made compulsory for access to foreign loans from international finance bodies – the World Bank and the International Monetary Foundation. African nations looked inward for cohesion, rather than outwards and across to the diaspora, and political and aesthetic iterations of Pan-Africanist internationalism were replaced by national developmentalism. In the United States, the radical force of Black Studies during the early 1970s was diffused by its co-option into liberal arts agendas (Wynter 2006). In 1999, the Ghanaian government ruled to deny Black American claims to Ghanaian citizenship. This was an extraordinary moment, partly due to Ghana's status as the first decolonized African nation – and long a site for Black imaginaries of Pan-African futures – and partly because it was from Ghana that many enslaved Africans headed to the Americas departed.

In this context, genetic ancestry testing offered to rejuvenate a waning commitment to identification across national borders and the passage of time, hinting at another genre: the family saga, or family romance, the genre of Alex Haley's *Roots* (1976). Matthew Stallard and Jerome de Groot note that assumptions around the 'objective factuality' of DNA in comparison to other historical sources have meant that DNA data 'can be incorporated into genealogical practice as a confirmatory source for "traditional" research' (2020, 278). DNA suggests ways to thread obscured pasts into the present, opening lines of kinship that would trace time back across the Middle Passage. This quickly became commercialized, taking on spectacular forms: through the genre of 'roots revelations' in the nascent era of reality TV in the early 2000s, genealogists 'become performers whose job it is to react to genealogical information that is revealed to them' (Nelson 2016, 96). TV shows on big US networks showed celebrities finding out about their family history via DNA tests, with the promise of finding 'a notable predecessor, a significant historical event, or unexpected affiliations' (96). As Alondra Nelson notes, theatricality is key to this, a way of attesting to both the affective power and return on investment that genetic testing offered.

Roberts notes a resistance in Black history-making to promoting or believing in genetics, given its provenance in white supremacist ideologies:

> Blacks have understandably resisted defining personal identity in biological terms. In America, whites have historically valued genetic linkages and controlled their official meaning. As the powerful class, they are guardians of the privileges according to biology and they have a greater stake in maintaining the importance of genetics. (1997, 261)

Genetics has long been part of a genealogy of Black horror. For Roberts, rather than connoting racial belonging via genetics, group membership among Black communities has been more a question of political and cultural affiliation than any kind of genetically inscribed commonality. This bears on racialized differences in emphasis in uses of genetic technologies; Roberts writes, 'Blacks by and large are more interested in escaping the constraints of racist ideology by defining themselves apart from inherited traits' (261). Roberts was writing before the boom in ancestry testing, but this analysis goes some way to marking a qualitative and historical difference in the significance and cultural power of genetics along the lines of racial identification by the end of the Human Genome Project. Jenny Reardon notes this too, and relates how representatives from a Black community group at Tuskegee were much more concerned by the absence of a hospital and 'basic health care': 'Genetics is not important. And it is not important because there is *so much else wrong*' (2017, 64). There was not only little interest in genetics but also a general suspicion of genetic research, and towards speaking about it in the first place.

The movement between horror and romance mediates the troubled status of a past that cannot be proved – or compensated for – through empirical forms of evidence. Before going into a reading of Hartman and Gyasi, I consider the fusion of family sagas and Black horror, a merging of genre that attends to the continued vulnerability of Black family life, and which undermines the centrality of the nuclear and hereditary family structure as the primary unit of Anglo-European sociobiological lifeworlds.

## Henrietta Lacks and stolen flesh

Black horror registers the scale of theft made possible by enslavement: of bodies, lives, lineages, property, cultures and biopower. This stealing is sustained, rather than repaired, by modern forms of neo-imperial and neoliberal capitalism. It is a genre organized around stolen time, time ripped out of Black bodies to sustain others, and now, in Joy James's words, 'the unrecoverable years stolen or spent surviving warfare and murder' (2016, 254). For Tananarive Due, *horror noire* is borne out of the 'fear that these people are trying to steal our soul' (in Burgin 2019). Biological research agendas that have premised the white body as the recipient of medical care and Black flesh as experimental biomatter are embedded in an infrastructure in which this stolen time is made visible and visceral, while left out of methods and conclusions.

In the era of molecular biology, the extraction of Black flesh for the expansion of colonial-capitalist production took on new dimensions, with biomatter becoming uncoupled from the body entirely. Rebecca Skloot's *The Immortal Life of Henrietta Lacks* (2010), her biography of Henrietta Lacks and the cells that became a global commodity in biomedical research, taken without her permission from a tumour in her cervix, is at once a study in and denial of Black horror. The story of HeLa foregrounds the racialized dimensions of the global molecular biology economy, which – while predating genomics, and with a bigger remit – helps contextualize not only the unevenness of possible health benefits from genomic research, but also grounds molecular biology – and beyond it, genetics – in an affect of suspicion among Black communities. For Alexander Weheliye, the story of Lacks and 'the ongoing narrative of the eternal life' of her cells prove that 'the hieroglyphics of the flesh subsist even in death ... transposed from the outwardly detectable to the microscopic interior of the human' (2014, 80). Weheliye takes the term 'hieroglyphics of the flesh' from Hortense Spillers to describe the transformation of subjects into flesh 'before being granted the illusion of possessing a body', destruction and re-animation, the resuscitation of 'black subjects who have been "liberated" and granted body in the aftermath of de jure enslavement' (2014, 39). Skloot's biography follows this logic, re-animating Henrietta Lacks through the triumph of her cells, shaping a narrative about biotechnological progress through the survival of flesh beyond subject. This difference between body and flesh, for Spillers, marks the difference 'between captive and liberated subject-positions', where the liberation of embodiment is not permitted (1987, 67).

Henrietta Lacks's cells invigorated a branch of science that was in dire need of experimental matter. They were taken without permission by a Johns Hopkins oncologist from a tumour in her womb that killed her soon afterwards. This was a standard procedure in the days before consent was needed for participation in biomedical trials. In the early days of molecular biology, biologists needed to harvest cells outside the human body, but this is a difficult procedure and at the time of Lacks's death, had been largely unsuccessful: most cells extracted from patients died on extraction and could not be reproduced. Lacks's cells behaved differently, reproducing in a petri dish at an unprecedented rate, over a matter of hours.

As her cells divided in the laboratory, Henrietta's tumour spread across her body. She died on 4 October 1951, at thirty-one. Her family had no idea that the cells taken from her body were becoming part of what Skloot calls the 'HeLa factory', otherwise known as the HeLa Distribution Centre at the Tuskegee Institute, 'a massive operation that would grow to produce trillions of HeLa cells each week' (2010, 108). In the midst of a global polio epidemic, Jonas Salk was developing a vaccine, but to do this required a vast amount of cultured cells. HeLa cells were shipped around the country to polio-testing centres, with the centre's employees producing twenty thousand tubes of HeLa every week. Lacks's cells made possible the fast-track development of global exchange in molecular biology, becoming a biomedical object sent to laboratories across the world.

Skloot's book has three key messages: HeLa as a triumph of modern science; HeLa as the contributions of African Americans (however unwitting) to molecular biology ('No dead woman has ever done more for the living,' says Hilary Mantel (2010)); and HeLa and the murky territory of consent. This last message is as far as the political intervention goes. Nonetheless, Skloot layers Black horror into the narrative, even as she tries to diminish or underplay its significance, as if lured by an alternative and undocumented strand of history that keeps raising its head. This emerges through the perspectives of Deborah and Zakariya Lacks, two of Lacks's children, who read the coerced extraction of Lacks's biological matter as part of a longer history of using Black bodies for research, production and profit. It is they who point, repeatedly, to the disconnect between the massive profits generated from Lacks's cells, while Black Americans are prevented from access to basic health care.

Skloot's omissions show the deployment of Black horror as a peripheral narrative, made subordinate to the bigger story of creating value in global science in the form of cures. The dead Black woman at the centre of the story made a certain kind of medical praxis possible, not through her own skills or knowledge, but through the non-consensual extraction of her biomatter. HeLa's later identification as a 'Black' cell line mattered only when identifying it as the source of a global contamination of experimental cell lines; as shipments were sent across the world, HeLa was transmitted into other cells lines held in laboratories by accident, carried through air particles into petri dishes, changing their genetic composition. The story of Henrietta Lacks that positions the horror of white experimentation on Black bodies as marginal is limited to portraying its protagonist as a diseased, over-productive, suffering Black woman's body, whose tumour cells threaten to contaminate the world with their powerful and inexplicable alchemy.

Lacks's children resist this marginalization of Black horror, insisting on its centrality to the story of their mother's cells. For them, the survival of the HeLa cells offers the possibility of resurrection, wherein Henrietta might be brought back from the dead via test tubes – a prospect both fearsome and enthralling to her family. Deborah watches a TV science fiction film, *The Clone*, where a woman's embryos are taken, without her knowledge, to make copies of her dead son: "'That poor woman didn't even know all about the clones until she saw one walk out of a store. I don't know what I'd do if I saw one of my mother's clones walkin around somewhere'" (Skloot 2010, 271). Skloot's interpretation of this is that for Deborah, 'the line between sci-fi and reality had blurred years earlier' (271); this interpretation suggests that Deborah's reading is paranoid or even pathological, a neurotic symptom. Yet, science fiction is able to communicate something about the significance of the HeLa cells in the context of Black American history, and the transatlantic slave trade stripping Africans of their rights over biological and political determination and resuscitating them as dead labour.

Deborah Lacks is neither misreading the situation nor exaggerating it; the cells represent the history of enslavement as recursive, rather than relegated to America's shadowed past. Black women's reproductive labour was central to the development of colonial-capitalism. Roberts writes, 'Black procreation not only benefited each slave's particular owner; it also more globally sustained the entire system of slavery' (1997, 24). Black women's bodies were vehicles of manual production and biological reproduction; the clone imaginary captures the reduction of Black children into economic units, under conditions of rape. It describes a systemic experience of Black American history that is not just fantasy or exaggeration. The stealing of Henrietta's biomaterial from the part of her body identified with reproduction repeats the stealing of Black women's wombs for the reproduction of capital (James 2016).

Skloot's book is a biography of Black horror which tries, time and again, to resolve itself as family romance: a reconciliation between the world of scientific progress and the realities of life for a single Black family. Skloot cannot recognize the genre her book is situated in, and because of this, Deborah and Zakariya's voices are made peripheral. Zakariya tells Skloot, "'You don't lie and clone people behind their backs. That's wrong. It's like me walking in your bathroom while you in there with your pants down. It's the highest degree of disrespect'" (2010, 281). What's at stake, for Zakariya, is a failure to recognize Black lives as worthy of ethical consideration. This is not a 'blurring' of fiction and fact: clones describe a coerced condition of being. The mass production of HeLa cells at a global level is part of the *longue durée* of producing value via Black death. When Zakariya and Deborah talk about clones and ghosts, and tell Skloot about the rumours about that scientists from Johns Hopkins snatched Black children for experiments off the streets of Black neighbourhoods in Baltimore – "'night doctors" who kidnapped people for research' "'They'd snatch em off the street'" "'Snatchin' people!'" "'Experimentin on them!'" (189–90) – this is neither fantasy nor an exaggeration of history. They are telling a story about the way Black life is attached to a necropolitics of experimental practices for the sake of white prosperity, situated in a long history of 'atomizing of the captive body' in which the 'ethics [and] relatedness between human personality and its anatomical features' is lost (Spillers 1987, 68).

## Reparation, romance and kinlessness

The abrasion between personality and anatomy – the severing of the intimate from fleshly elements – bears on the forms of kinship it is possible to declare in public. If to be known is to take a place in a sphere of intimate relations and to offer up that being known to a public sphere as condition of entry, then to be reduced to flesh is to be denied access to both spheres. This, in turn, is a problem of form and genre: in what ways and in which modes should and could narrative stage and subvert this abrasion? The blurring of horror and family history unsettles the assumed primacy of genetic accounts of heredity and kinship, tracing a continuum between contested, obscure or denied kinship networks across the history of enslavement and into modern biopolitical articulations at the border of race, family and community. In Hartman and Gyasi's texts, the family romance cannot hold this abrasion of personality and anatomy. Instead, they explore a condition of kinlessness, whereby all 'future increase' for the enslaved was severed in advance from the lineage of the parent, as Nancy Bentley writes on Hartman (2009, 270).

Bentley identifies two understandings of genealogy that derive from this racialized infrastructure of relatedness, organized around distinct figures: first, the genealogy of genetics, property and lineage (represented by the individual), and second, that of tribe, custom and ancestry (represented by the population). After abolition, this second version equated to 'genealogical debaseness... miring whole populations in a state of genealogical unfreedom and exclusion from the intimate sphere of biological kinship' (2009, 273). For Bentley, following Spillers, this debaseness was not signified by a lack of kinfolk, but rather by the imposed consensus that 'one's ties to kin have "no decisive legal or social efficacy"' (270). Kinlessness is not a historical 'fact' of enslavement, but a condition imposed from above

> to isolate and extract the sheer materiality of a human population – their bodies, labour, and reproductive capacities – from the sphere of the familial, a sphere undergoing its own restructuring as the bourgeois *Intimsphäre* [private sphere] began to emerge in transatlantic liberalism as the touchstone of the human. (271)

The *Intimsphäre* is the site of genetic kinship which determines agency via the property metaphor; outside this are 'diasporic kin worlds ... created and shaped' by this exteriority and 'their forced exclusion from legal, social, and discursive formations of proper familism' (Bentley, 278). Following Gilroy, the attempt to represent kinship in Black vernacular culture is fraught with problems of exclusion from the 'architecture of middle-class kinship' (Bentley 2009, 277), particularly in 'the form of the novel and the different types of memory and remembrance it solicits from its readers' (Gilroy 1993, 218). While the novel form has historically privileged the genealogy of individual property, African American novels representing Black history – for Gilroy – 'all exhibit an intense and ambivalent negotiation of the novel form that is associated with their various critiques of modernity and enlightenment' (218). Carrying this argument into readings of Hartman and Gyasi, I suggest here that their critiques of family romance – its generic impossibility accentuated by the disappearances of characters and ellipses in family history – are organized around kinlessness both as indictment of this history and as the transformation of the terms of bourgeois kinship that produce these distinct genealogical forms.

These critiques are connected to another invention of narrative form in the early 2000s. In its potential to reveal severed kinship ties, ancestry testing heralded a remaking of social life through biotechnologies, as Nelson argues in *The Social Life of DNA* (2016). Genetic ancestry testing was already its own multibillion dollar industry by the time Skloot published her book on Lacks, a way of imagining kinship across the Atlantic, from the Americas to West Africa, offering – in theory, at least – a new evidentiary toolkit for proving the need and validity of claims for reparation. Mario Chandler calls this 'biotechnography', and suggests that this is an example of how 'the dissemination of black narrative has always relied on the use of contemporary innovation and technology' (2018, 32). Genetic ancestry testing offered a tool for social justice when national law failed to account for a *longue durée* of expropriation and enslavement, and – later on – a way of exposing unjust legal processes of criminalizing Black communities via initiatives like The Innocence Project, which uses genetic forensics to overturn wrongful convictions. Nelson argues that matrilineal and patrilineal DNA tests presented 'new language in the long-waged battle over the repayment of a debt now four centuries overdue' (107). If ancestries of enslavement could be traced, new possibilities emerged for holding the descendants of those who profited from the system to account.

This formed the basis for legal cases in the early 2000s. Nelson recounts the example of the insurance provider Aetna Inc. being taken to court by lawyer Deadria Farmer-Paellmann – head of the Restitution Study Group – on the grounds that it had profited from its policies by insuring the lives of enslaved peoples as property of their enslavers. The argument for the prosecution was that a genealogical link to enslaved Africans could be proved by genetic ancestry tests; the case was dismissed because this link was considered not direct enough with regard to family trees. The judge ruled,

> The only suitable means to establish 'a decisive link to a homeland' was DNA evidence that could show an uninterrupted, definitive line of ancestry from

a former slave to an aggrieved present-day descendant or descendants, and simultaneously a direct line of capital gained from an accused corporation to expropriated labourers and their offspring. (Nelson, 135)

This ruling delineates contesting descriptions of genealogy and inheritance, and the imposition of the legal requirement for a direct correlation between biological evidence and historical argument over other forms of evidence. It is a dazzling sleight of hand: the biologization of race as a justification for enslavement disappears into the (assumed) lacunae in genetic evidence of enslavement. This gets to Simone's formulation of a triple darkness, where the loss of genealogical archive is compounded and sustained by the insistence on 'definitive' proof, which here codes as legible genetic code. The fact that the legibility of this code is itself unstable and not necessarily trustworthy is not the point: the underlying message here is not that if it could be proved, reparation would happen, but rather that there is no socio-historical obligation for reparation in the first place.

It is this second message against which politicized – if speculative – discourses of genetic testing set themselves. The case for the prosecution understands the relation between genealogy, ancestry, relatedness and reparation in a much broader sense. What is key here is how genetics, Nelson contends, cannot prove origins but rather highlights the 'social death' that the chattel slavery system functioned on, through the ongoing severing of family ties (Patterson 1982; Gutman 1977; Baptist 2014; Stack 1974). 'Expropriation' in this sense means the severing of enslaved Africans from their genealogical history. Rather than restating the centrality of the genetic as proof of origins, practices of ancestry testing instead challenge the fiction of reducing genealogy and kinship to the genetic. Alternative structures of kinship and iterations of belonging open up where the lure of genealogy falls short. This is critical, also, for the resurrection of Pan-Africanist politics at the beginning of the twenty-first century, a movement hindered by the imposition of finance institutions, rather than shared histories, as the basis for internationalism from the 1970s onwards. Ancestry testing promises a reconciliation between diasporic and continental peoples of African descent, or at least a tool through which affinity can be speculated upon.

Against the rarefication of genetic lineage, histories of adoptive, non-patrilineal and non-biological kinship ties come into play. These also move between genres of horror and family romance, but in ways that do not rest on what Roberts calls the 'cultural artefact' of genetic relatedness (1997, 267). This has complicated legal implications – relationships that cannot be proved or verified at borders or across the movements of history, and the falling away of genealogy. But genetic ancestry testing functions as a route to the ancestral precisely through its resistance to biological descriptions of belonging. In its failures to offer either legal evidence or historical transparency, the metaphor of testing the past is extended out to non-biological kinship. As metaphor, testing becomes an articulation of impossible proofs rather than a technique of reification, part of a longer history of searching for roots via 'cultural, rather than genetic preservation' (Roberts, 261). This conjures a precolonial West African history, too, where children were the responsibility of the whole community, rather than sole property of their parents, and where the primary unit was not the immediate family, but composed of extended kinship relations (Scannapieco and Jackson 1996, 191). These interventions in the historiography and cultural memory of enslavement necessarily involve encountering the anachronisms of decoloniality and the difficulties of sustaining Pan-Africanism amid the pressures of neoliberal globalization.

In these texts, testing for ancestors links poetics to political praxis – horror and romance, folklore and myth – taking chances with the absences of historical documentation. Imaginary lifeworlds push back at historical repetition with the force of resurrection, and going back and back again to find a different way into an inaccessible past is a political strategy: not for the sake of individual development, but for collective articulations of Black worlds outside sociobiological determinisms. Moving between genres is crucial for the kinds of time-travel that genetic ancestry testing cannot fulfil, and for holding open the *longue durée* of enslavement.

On the plantations, there was always the risk that an enslaved person might not recognize their closest kin. Edward E. Baptist notes that establishing new ties of 'pseudo-blood' – through adoption, and the making and remaking of free households – had a speculative dimension to it: those who did so 'chose to shelter under their wings far-off futures that might only arrive long after their own deaths.... For this future to arrive, however, someone had to survive' (2014, 284). Survival here is not genetic, but cultural. That is, it does not equate to ensuring a genealogical legacy in the form of biological property (of name, of finances, of territory); it involves an extended and often unverifiable concept of transgenerational influence that goes beyond the routes of genealogy, outside what it is possible to establish in historiography, because of an absence of record required by the logics of capital under which slavery was sustained. Absences of record are countered by the influence of nameless ancestors on the present. This reparation in advance, a theme that I consider in my readings of Hartman and Gyasi, is a form of speculative ancestry-making that builds futures in the uncertain alliances of the present.

## Leaving: Saidiya Hartman's *Lose Your Mother*

One of the key claims of this book is that the idea of the genome not only offered a description of the self, but also a technology for remaking that self according to new standards of human potential: genomics as fabrication. With this came a whole imaginative apparatus for constructing the self into a coherent narrative, via the lexicon and syntax of the molecular. This takes on a different kind of relevance in uses of ancestry testing, where this personal narrative is attached to the idea of a genetic past – journeys that may or may not be documented, origins that may or may not come as a surprise. The convergence in the affordability of genome sequencing and charter flights during the early 2000s points to a synchronized appeal from private genome companies and tourist boards to middle-class consumers who might be persuaded to take bigger steps across space and time in their annual vacations. Trips abroad need no longer just be about taking time off work; they could be explorations into the shadowed passages of lost time, where personhood might be fabricated during an all-inclusive package tour.

The fabrication of personhood propels the Saidiya of Saidiya Hartman's *Lose Your Mother* across the Atlantic to Ghana in search of lost ancestors. Stepping off the bus in Elmina – the site of a castle with a dungeon where captured humans were held for days on end before ships took them across the sea – she finds herself cast as 'a wandering seed bereft of the possibility of taking root' (4). An African American or a Black American? A long-lost sibling, or *obruni* [stranger] (4)? She is looking for roots, but in this place, she is 'the stranger in the village', a source of shame, a reminder of a past from which the Ghanaians of the present seem to have moved on.

The text is structured like an hourglass. The early chapters on seeking home that form the first half of the book move inexorably towards a narrow channel of impossibility in the centre of the text. In the middle of the book, Hartman expresses the paradox of needing roots while being unable to stay anywhere for long:

> 'Don't go.' 'Stay put.' These are the words of the master. The slave must stay put or stay in her place. . . . But staying is at odds with the very definition of a slave;

the bought-and-sold person comes and goes by way of the transactions of the market. The slave is always the stranger who resides in one place and belongs to another. The slave is always the one missing from home. (87)

Dwelling is not just difficult in this situation; it is antithetical to the dynamics of Black life, historically, in the United States. Genetic forms promise the possibility of belonging to a code, to a family history, and to the idea of being embedded in a place, and tied genetically to a lineage. On the other side of this promise is the severing of the body from genealogy, and – in Spillers's words – the inscription of 'ethnicity as a scene of negation', and the confirmation of 'the human body as a metonymic figure for an entire repertoire of human and social arrangements' (1987, 66). The enslaved body is split between place of residence and site of belonging, chopped into traits by market fluctuations – what might be needed at a particular moment, or what might fall out of use. The body is at once reduced to the biological while split from its processes, which are harnessed for the benefit of the enslaver. In this situation, Hartman says, 'love' is not a remedy; it 'encourages forgetting' and 'extends the cover of belonging and shrouds the slave's origins, which lie in acts of violence and exchange, but it doesn't remedy the isolation of being severed from your kin and denied ancestors' (87).

Isn't seeking the romance of origins inevitable for those 'stranded in a hostile country' (98), she wonders? When you lose your mother somewhere along the passage from village, to dungeon, to ship, to auction block, and to and from plantations, 'the old ways become precious, imperilled, and what your great-great-grandchildren will one day wistfully describe as African' (98). This is a mode of ancestry-making as a speculative gesture towards a lost origin – a fantasy of African belonging sustained through generations. Lineage and descent were not privileges afforded to the enslaved: 'slavery made the past a mystery, unknown and unspeakable' (14). This unspeakability is what initially draws her to the people she meets in Ghana. As she asks questions that her hosts try to divert her from, it becomes gradually clearer that all of Hartman's characters – including herself – are circling round an abyss of unrecorded experience, the silences of people who fell off the map, 'people who left behind no traces' (15).

This is in contrast to the way the present offers up its documentations as evidence – names, passports, archives, photographs, genomes. She reads an article on genetic ancestry testing in the *New York Times*. This is *Lose Your Mother*'s only mention of the practice which, by this point, was taking off in unprecedented ways among Black Americans in the early 2000s, as discussed earlier. While she has come to Ghana to fill in the blank spaces of her history, others are attempting to do this with DNA tests:

> History had failed to solve the mystery of an unknown past, so they had put their faith in science, despite the ambiguous and inconclusive results of the test. One man's words stayed with me. Having discovered that his ancestors were from Cameroon, he remarked that he felt more lost than before. Now he was estranged from an ancestral tribe as well as the country of his birth. 'It's like being lost and found at the same time,' he said. Being in Elmina Castle was like that too. (90)

What's striking here is the sense of commonality Hartman feels with this man, whom she knows only through the mediation of a story that promotes the cultural power of genetic testing, even as it registers its omissions. The idea of the man's words 'staying with me' has a particular force in this context, where words – not genetic evidence – are often all descendants of enslaved peoples have to go on in tracing a route back to the homes from which they were stolen. This is a declaration of kinship between two strangers, both – in different ways – finding themselves further estranged from their ancestral histories, even as they deploy the tools of knowing the self (DNA tests, transatlantic flights).

Key, too, is the movement from science as a site of horror to one of possibility, however 'ambiguous and inconclusive'. The effect of an article like the one in the *New York Times* is at once to validate the science, and to promote public investment in it (whether imaginative, corporate, commercial), while also to keep the spectre of not knowing – the great risk that the mystery will remain unsolved – hovering over the narrative. It positions consumers as detectives into their own past, embedding them more deeply into the logic of a technologized present, while the past is estranged still further. 'Cameroon' is a place on a map not drawn by the communities from which their descendants were stolen. The man and Hartman find themselves lost in maps (genetic, geographic) where other ways of reading land and marking territory do not appear. The man is 'from' Cameroon, in the sense that his genetic origins can be located in a vast area of land that does not offer any kind of route home, or at least in the sense implicitly (and on his side, unknowingly) shared between him and Hartman, across the pages of a global broadsheet.

While this is the only explicit reference to genetic ancestry testing in the book, it is held in the same affect of failure that Hartman experiences while in Ghana – of arriving at a place that you have thought might be some kind of home, and finding oneself in a strange land that does not recognize you. The body and the territory cannot offer ways into the past, or at least not in the places that both Hartman and this nameless man in the *New York Times* article identify: the genome and Elmina Castle. Both sites fail to give an account of belonging; while the man can point to Cameroon on a map and say his genes tell him that he is 'from there', this is not accompanied by any sense of being part of a wider and longer history located in that place. These intersecting failures of territory (molecular and national) correspond to the diminishment of Pan-African utopianism at the turn of the twenty-first century, after two decades of global neoliberalism. The technologies that Hartman and the man have been offered as tools of self-discovery – affordable flights and affordable DNA tests – cannot traverse this. All that is left is a series of disembodied indications towards a possible past, which will never fully be known.

Hartman situates the Saidiya of this text in a generation trying to reclaim history for the present, a generation looking back, looking for 'Afrotopia', using genetics not for the sake of establishing racial lineage, but historical ties. But instead of offering a sense of stability and rootedness, she finds that these ties are fractious and unreliable – just as the man cannot find his ancestral tribe, Saidiya cannot find her kin. Towards the end of the memoir, just before its final act, Hartman notes her feeling of isolation among her Ghanaian hosts and new friends:

> What had I expected of our little African union? I suppose I had wanted to build a bridge across our differences. But nearly two months of working daily together had only made it more difficult for us to find a common vocabulary about slavery, or anything else for that matter. No matter how expansive the category 'sister', I always fell outside its embrace. Whatever remained of Pan-Africanism, which had espoused solidarity among all African people, promoted the idea of continental fraternity and sorority, and encouraged each and every one of us in the diaspora to dream of the continent as our home, no longer included the likes of me. (217–18)

This moment is taken over by another possibility for solidarity, which grows out of the phrase 'working daily together' and the kinds of contingent and unsteady relations that this kind of ensemble work involves. But nonetheless, this admission – late in the text – arrives at a crisis point in the memoir. Saidiya is alone; she has not found what she came for. Her genealogy, whether fictive or real, remains obscure. There is no common way of speaking together – the members of this small group, a 'little African union', have not been able to find the words to express their connection to each other.

This inability to find a common vocabulary of kinship through the wreckage of the past extends between continent and diaspora, and upholds the political borders between nations on the continent, the division of territories into discrete units of GDP, GNP, mortality and natality rates, literacy levels, and other measures of human development: the cumulative barometer of national progress. 'The likes of me' is a colloquialism that transforms a generic 'wrong side of the tracks' identification to 'the wrong side of history', a body that is excluded from a dream of unity. The phrase points to the typologizing weight of Saidiya experiencing herself as *obruni*, an alienation from her fabricated self ('my self-proclaimed African identity . . . my Swahili name' (218)) as much as an externally imposed exclusion, in the place where she has come to seek some sense of shared history, however indeterminate and untouchable. The separation of 'expansive' from 'embrace' is central to this: a shared history should be a way of holding those who experience it in a sense of collectivity, a mode of protection and care; whatever forms of care exist here, they do not include her.

Saidiya wants to touch the dead. If new technologies of identification and transport reduce their consumers to dead matter – to segments of DNA vaguely connected to vast expanses of land, or 'slave babies' (4) – then speculative and recursive ruminations on blank spaces in history give form to acts of resurrection. The slave trade was based on an ongoing economy of ending one kind of life and resuscitating it into another – '[it] annulled lives, transforming men and women into dead matter, then resuscitated them for servitude' (68). Hartman's intervention in this is to replace both action and form: endings are transferred into a mode of recursivity, and resuscitation becomes resurrection. In a place where the disappearance of mass numbers of people had 'no witnesses' (232), she goes back over the same ground again and again. Physically, she describes going back to Elmina Castle, moving around it in different ways, trying to find some key to the past. And formally, the text keeps restating itself, calling on figures of *Négritude*, Pan-Africanism, and anti-colonial struggle in the process: W. E. B. Du Bois, Aimé Césaire, Frantz Fanon. 'I shall return to my own land. . . . I shall return to my native land. . . . Return is what you hold onto. . . . I shall return to my native land' becomes a refrain, breaking into the past and reiterating the claim passed down and across the diaspora, a code that transports the descendants of those taken to other lands back to where their ancestors came from (91, 96, 99). This is not just a promise of resurrection. The intertextuality of Black thought propels her into the past, without the help of flight or test.

She also knows that this return signifies a loss, and that this loss 'inaugurates one's existence . . . it is to lose your mother, always' (99). This lost mother, nameless, sits alongside 'ghostly patriarchs that can be named', who correspond to a line of descent (78). This mother is signified not by a name but by a stamp on the skin tattooed by enslavers:

> The mark of property provides the emblem of kinship in the wake of defacement. It acquires the character of a personal trait, as though it were a birthmark. . . . The mother's mark, not the father's name, determined your fate. No amount of talk about fathers could suture the wound of kinship or skirt the brute facts. The patronymic was an empty category, a 'blank parody', a fiction that masters could be fathers and wayward lovers more than the 'begetters of children'; it was the placeholder of the banished black fathers. (80)

The language of property is explicitly tied to that of heredity, a mark of property becoming a kind of 'trait' to be passed down to subsequent generations. The system of using people as capital becomes embedded in a biological metaphor, an inheritance of anonymity and defacement (spoiling the surface, scratching out the face, reducing the body to a brand). The founding privilege of liberal humanism – the father's lineage, and with this, the claim to personhood – is denied from the outset. The language of placeholder and category runs up against 'the wound of kinship', a new origin formed by the repetition of wrenching away: kinship as the mark of a wound left open down the generations. The idea of the father is voided out of existence, and the enslaved become 'ghosts in the machine of kinship', stopped from knowing and attesting to their own inheritance (194).

The failed witness is an important character in Hartman's text. Halfway through, she describes herself as one: 'Reckoning with my inheritance had driven me to the dungeon, but now it all seemed elusive' (129). The failed witness is reduced to giving endless evidence on injustices of the present, treading the same ground, 'fumbling' with history and 'struggling to connect the dots between then and now' (129). The continuation of racial capitalism voids the power of her arguments about 'the devastating effects of having been property' (129): the dungeon is not a site of memory, but place of origin for enduring inequities. While genetic ancestry testing offers to mend this wound, and to speak into the wake of stolen genealogy, it inevitably fails to do so – to resuscitate the stolen time of the Black Matrix (James 2016). DNA tests are not an impediment to belonging, but a false promise – the biotechnological equivalent of repeated trips to the dungeon, hoping to touch the dead. It becomes just one of multiple streams of return narratives, the arrangement of chromosomes on the surface of the genome failing to match up with the small dots of villages visible from the air, as a plane from the West comes from across the sea: a technology that enables seeing the geographical routes of the past, but which can only ever allude to its true history. The genome is also a failed witness, reducing bodies in the present to the accumulated 'dead money' through the sale and capture of anonymised humans (210).

Instead of what is expressed and visible – the ghostly patriarchs and living Ghanaians – Hartman's narrative begins to attend to silence, and to what remains unexpressed. She begins filling in blank spaces in history, where a historical account ends or falls quiet, or where none exists at all. This, too, has a genetic analogy: the failure of the human genome to provide answers on human complexity. Writing just after the publication of the first draft in 2001, Stephen Jay Gould noted that what was compelling about the relatively underwhelming results of the HGP – that humans express between 25,000 and 30,000 protein-coding genes, rather than the predicted 100,000 – is that human complexity cannot be explained by molecular biology alone, and by the idea that there is one-directional flow of information from DNA to RNA to protein. So-called junk DNA means more than geneticists had long assumed, and biotechnology's assumption that 'each aspect of our being, either physical or behavioural, may be ascribed to the action of a particular gene "for" the trait in question' had been shown to be both 'simplistic and harmful [and] false' (Gould 2001). Complexity is about combinations and interactions, not numbers, and these to a large extent are determined by what Gould calls 'the unique contingencies of history' (2001).

Hartman's turn to speculation in the latter parts of *Lose Your Mother* shares ground with these statements, if indirectly. Rather than dwelling on and in the loss of genetic proof, she moves towards another kind of evidence: the practices of endurance and survival that might have taken place, which are not recorded or written down, but which nonetheless have left traces in the architecture of history. In this sense, the failure of genomics to give a full account of both social and biological worlds does important cultural work: it draws science into the realm of the unverified and speculative, and to the centrality of narrative in world-building. This undermines genomic descriptions of life itself, and makes space for historical silence.

Towards the end of *Lose Your Mother*, the title of the text takes on a different significance: not just a description of loss, but an injunction towards other kinds of kinship that do not rely on property as a claim to belonging. Rather than trying to reconstruct a genealogy, Hartman turns instead to formations of community outside the logic of genetic ties. She imagines what the archives leave out – the junk and forgotten stories that never made it in, or what has been coercively forgotten, or never written down – for the sake of 'the promise of affiliation better than brothers and sisters' (172). Pan-African hopes might be resurrected, but not within the terms dictated by liberal humanism. Central to this is a mode of survival premised on collective ties that extend beyond genetic lineage. In Gwolu, further north, she finds routes that people used to flee slave hunters. There are different stories here, not tied to a 'memory of loss or of captivity, but of survival and good fortune' – those who had 'been able to reconstruct shattered communities' (232). This reconstruction happens, necessarily, beyond the biological family and beyond the borders of individual tribe.

A long passage details an imaginary collective flight, a journey away from captivity, and the fugitive dream with which Hartman ends the memoir:

> Newcomers were welcome. It didn't matter that they weren't kin and that they spoke in a different language, because genealogy didn't matter (most of them couldn't go back three or four generations, anyway), building a community did. If the willingness to receive new arrivals and foreigners was what it took to make a world different from the one they had left, then so be it. So they put down their roots in foreign soil and adopted strangers and intermarried with other migrants and runaways, and shared their gods and totems, and blended their histories. 'We' was the collectivity they had built from the ground up, not one they had inherited, not one that others had imposed. (225)

Here, inheritance does not equate to freedom but to imposition – to something being pressed from the outside, or from above. Genealogy does not matter in more than one sense – either in terms of social organization, or in terms of material inheritance. This is a reading that is making an intervention in the present: we do not really know whether this supplanting of genealogy with community-building was a significant and deliberate choice. Hartman speculates on a way of being in the present by imagining this past, an alternative ancestral history to which she has no biological claim. Kinship, here, is speculative, formed through the difficult social work of living with that which cannot be immediately known, that which is not yet intimate, that which needs translation. This world cannot be found in any straightforward sense, but it reconstructs a history out of escape. It becomes 'the legacy I chose to claim . . . articulated in the ongoing struggle to escape, stand down, and defeat slavery in all its myriad forms' (233). This does not involve claiming territory, but reinstating a dream of flight.

At a moment when genetic ancestry testing promised a route across the Atlantic to precolonial pasts, *Lose Your Mother* appears alongside the failures of genomics to give full or accurate accounts of the past. This makes space for a form of survival that is not restricted to individuals, but which takes the 'messy complexity of social life' as its point of departure and the kinds of tactics necessary to endure it, across multiple generations, involving vast and speculative bounds across lacunae of record and map. In the following section, I consider how *Homegoing*'s narrative energy is derived from the ways that enslavement creates fictions of genealogy, and from the effort of staying – in place, in time.

## Staying: Yaa Gyasi's *Homegoing*

There are no dates in *Homegoing*. It is up to the reader to piece together time from the details of each section. Dates sometimes pierce the surface of the text through bigger world events – decolonization, Civil Rights, the Great Northern Migration – but often characters sit in ambiguous time-scales that correspond to generations, rather than particular years or months or days. This generational time evokes the temporality of a family saga, following characters of the same genealogical tree over a long period of history: here, over four hundred years of capture, forced displacement and migration. The difference here is that family history is often hidden. The family tree on the book's opening pages reconstructs a lineage of which those who form its branches are unaware. The narrative comes either from the realm of spirits – who watch over the movement of the characters on this tree – or from speculation, the possible forkings and splittings of lives that would have remained together if not for the slave trade.

The tree becomes a map for the reader to refer back to throughout the book, an archive of names and the relations between them that roots the stories about individual characters in a context. *Homegoing* is also formed by absences – the brevity of chapters, glimpses of a character's life who we might meet once or twice throughout the book; the way that some members of a generation fall off the tree, while the lineage of others forms new branches. The splitting of biological origins and the displacement of family history are reiterated in the disconnections, interruptions and fragmentations of Gyasi's narrative. The tree structure is repeatedly hacked into by ruptured kinship, both a document of family history, and a monument to lost branches of family history.

This enduring pivot between what is expressed and what remains undocumented roots the narrative in a key of insurgent nostalgia, as opposed to the pay-off of family romance. Neither horror nor reunion, but the pressing insistence of lost history. The past is formed by an absence that structures forms of the present, and this absence is instrumentalized as a tool of narrative rebellion. A form of speculative kinship is modelled from the necessity of adopting other people's children – non-genealogical love as remedy for broken and stolen familial ties – and extends to encompass the kinds of bonds that will permit recursivity, as opposed to repetition. When staying in place is not possible, going back in time becomes essential. The analogy of junk, repressed or forgotten DNA becomes an issue of historical time, not genomic space.

In historiographies of Black American life, fictive kinship is a site of endurance: the adoption of children who are not one's own, to the adoption of a constellation of influences across time. The book is divided into fourteen chapters and two parts, each chapter given the name of someone on the genealogical tree. It follows the descendants of two sisters, Effia and Esi, who never learn of each other's existence, but whose descendants meet at the end of the narrative. Both parts of the novel end by calling up ancestors, through the mediation of a black stone necklace passed through generations – the object that signifies the gene-line. Leaving her home in a Ghanaian village sometime in the eighteenth century, Abena is given the necklace by James – her father, and the son of an enslaver and his Asante wife – who tells her that the necklace once belonged to her great-grandmother Effia:

> It was the first time she had heard the name of one of her ancestors, and she savoured the taste of the name on her tongue. She wanted to say it again and again. Effia. Effia. (152)

At the end of the novel, set in the present, Marjorie and Marcus swim in the sea by Elmina Castle, and Marjorie gives Marcus the necklace, before heading back 'towards the shore' (300). Marcus is scared of water, and Marjorie is scared of fire: they carry the fears of their forebears inside them. Marjorie's grandmother could hear ghosts, 'the people who were stuck on the ocean floor talking to her. Our ancestors' (H, 294). This transgenerational transmission of a ghost story gives Marjorie a sense of being in time. Ghosts in the water break into history's silence.

There is ambivalence among the characters towards chronology and forms of time marked by colonial-capitalism. Ness, Esi's daughter, picking cotton on an Alabama plantation sometime in the early 1800s, cannot remember how old she is: 'Her best guess was twenty-five, but each year since the one when she was plucked from her mother's arms had felt like ten years' (H, 70). Time is measured, for her, in the distance between her and her mother, swelling into decades where she ages at a rate that unwrites the developmental time of human life. The time of enslavement is not included in the temporality of the free world. The stories she has inherited begin in this time, not the memories of a distant homeland. The bedtime stories her mother told her were about 'the Big Boat': she 'would fall asleep to the images of men being thrown into the Atlantic Ocean like anchors attached to nothing: no land, no people, no worth' (H, 70). The time of enslavement becomes the horizon and the origin story.

Understanding the self in chronological time cannot function as repair. Knowing where you are from becomes supplanted, gradually, with forms of what Simone describes as '"rogue care" and strange alliances, inexplicable and provisionary' (2018, 90). When the force of history that keeps time moving forward forces characters to lose each other, forms of care that are on the run, outside the law, become ways of enduring the present. Ness's husband was lynched and her son taken into freedom while the family was trying to escape. Pinky, a little girl whose mother died who '"ain't spoke a word since"', becomes Ness's adopted child (H, 76). Ness remains in the fields of the new plantation, mourning and caring for another child, while her son grows up without parents in the North. Her son's story is held back for another chapter, and Ness's story ends in the cotton field, one eye on Pinky, with a prayer for the safety of her son: '"And protect my son, wherever he may be."' These truncated vignettes of stolen lives engender a form of history marked by continual cuts and abrasions, forced to punctuate itself with prayer, rather than documentation. These simultaneous adoptions – Pinky's and Kojo's – are left out of the record, cut out of burgeoning family tapestries.

The easy interchange between freedom and belonging promised by liberal humanism cannot be counted upon in this text. Freedom is never guaranteed; what becomes more pressing is the passing on of influences – a bric-a-brac of possible ways out – rather than a singular inheritance that might at some point be cashed in. Ness's son Kojo is brought to the North and cared for by Ma Aku – the woman who took him to freedom – in the Chesapeake Bay, working in the shipyards. Ma Aku teaches him to be scared of slave catchers, as well as acting as an interim guide for rituals of the old country, the Gold Coast – taking an offering to a woman's father if you want to court her. She takes on the role of parent and ancestral voice, stealing back time from what has been stolen from them. This 'rogue care' is not attached to genealogy, but uses the ancestral as a borrowed resource in a present that is understood to be fleeting and transitory. What becomes paramount is passing on the lessons that may save a life under the cover of darkness. Creating a passage between old rituals and new enemies is what forms the basis of kinship, a constellation of influences that may or may not come in useful. Any notion of inherited traits – in a biological sense – is superseded by these other codes of enduring.

*Homegoing* laces a suspicion around genealogy into its bursts of direct violence. Genealogical knowledge becomes a weapon of colonial violence for those who are able to keep records, and who uphold and impose a correlation between knowledge of family history and self-determination. Mixing up the two can mean playing into the hands of the enemy. In Akua's section, a white missionary tries over many years to convert her to his Christian God, and refuses to let her leave the orphanage where she has grown up to get married to the Akan man of her choice:

> 'I'll tell you about your mother,' the Missionary finally said. He dropped the switch to the floor and walked toward Akua until he was standing so close she could smell the faint stench of fish on his breath. For ten years, he had come no closer to her than the length of that switch. For ten years he had refused to answer questions about her family. 'I'll tell you about your mother. Anything you want to know.' (189)

Here, discovering her past is only possible on the condition that Akua remain in the infrastructure of colonial violence. Akua is attempting to leave the colonial site in search of her own future, and in response, the Missionary replaces one oppressive tool – the switch – with another. Family history is used as an instrument of restriction, a way of holding off freedom, a method of discipline and control. Akua's wish to know about her mother is subsumed into the Missionary's arsenal of control tactics; 'I'll tell you' is a declaration of absolute certainty, as if he knows all there is to know. His proximity to her at this point is a strategy of intimidation, rather than an offer of repair.

This scene disturbs the idea of family history as a site of refuge, and learning about personal history as a force of liberation. Akua learns the truth about her mother in a set-up that resembles rape – the sadomasochistic overtones of the switch being laid down, a length that holds her at a distance, while extended towards her, across many years, keeping her in place. The Missionary tells her that when he tried to baptize her mother, he had to hold her down in the water to stop her thrashing: 'She thrashed and thrashed and thrashed, and then she was still' (189). This is the legacy passed on from him, the adoptive father, to her: a mother reduced to a body undergoing an extended moment of terror before death, at the hands of a substitute parent. Knowing the truth about one's family history brings with it the danger of resurrecting the violence of the past, within the infrastructure that continues to enact it.

In the America chapters, genealogy is similarly dangerous terrain. The growth in popularity of eugenic science across Western Europe and the United States in the late nineteenth and early twentieth centuries corresponds to accelerating demands for freedom in anti-colonial movements across colonized territories, as well as the groundswell of Black Americans moving from a Jim Crow South to northern cities. These movements were met by a ramping up of racial profiling, under the guise of tracking 'phenotypic diversity'. In Gyasi's text, the assumed confluence between race and heredity is the basis of the narrative's social environment, while never being fully declared. When it comes to Black communities, genetic accounts of race are extensions of blood science, where race is calculated via equations of genealogical proximity.

Willie and Robert's story rehearses the family tragedy of the 'one-drop rule': nineteenth-century race science that categorized a person as Black if they had one drop of 'Negro blood'. Willie marries a 'mixed-race' man – poor, like her – who is 'the whitest black boy she had ever seen' (H, 201). 'Mixed-race' here signifies proximity to whiteness, reifying genetic identity and centring (an assumed) biological heredity as a defining characteristic of both appearance and behaviour. When they move to New York City from Birmingham, Alabama, as part of the Great Northern Migration, 'mixed-race' means that Robert can pass as white, while Willie cannot; and white signifies intellectual aptitude, moral rectitude and with these, the right to access certain spaces. Falling either side of the colour line ends up breaking the family apart. Robert's interest in becoming a mensch of the jazz clubs and white-only shops of the city takes him towards the promise of a family tree with stable roots and visible branches; for Willie, 'her own skin had started to look to her more and more like the thing her father brought home from the mines, under his fingernails and dusting his clothes' (201), another legacy passed on from parents to children: dirt, not blood. In Harlem, the supposed site of freedom for Black southerners, Willie 'cannot move' (209). Robert marries a white woman, and his shared history with Willie and their son is erased, pushed aside for the sake of a new timeline. Willie becomes a cleaner in the clubs Robert frequents with his white work colleagues. Phenotype becomes an alibi for legislating the disappearance of Black women from calculations of social capital, while incorporating them as essential labour to keep new urban dreamworlds moving for those positioned as their protagonists and beneficiaries.

All this places pressure on the nuclear family structure, which derives part of its stability from knowledge of one's own genealogical tree. *Homegoing* underscores the fragility of this as a basis for social organization, because those cut off from knowledge of their biological pasts cannot participate in public affairs. This is a moral economy of lineage. The fragility of the nuclear family is not to do with the way that it excludes those who do not know their history; rather, its exclusions indicate the compression of the public sphere into a very narrow set of social obligations to others, limited in a normative sense to biological offspring. And this compression is what history becomes. Part of the strategy of this text – as in *Lose Your Mother* – is to find a way of pluralizing Black history within incomplete archives and in the absence of names, and to confront the obliteration of these histories in biological descriptions of human destiny.

In these texts, the ambivalence of ancestry creates a politics and poetics of space and time across the cartography of the modern world and mappings of human genealogy. Hartman and Gyasi consider the ongoing crisis of genealogy by subverting its supremacy as a description of human belonging, and a keystone of what it means to stay in place. The idea of the genome as a ledger of the past and its failure to offer new forms of evidence for reparation offer new routes to Pan-African futures. This happens not by proving genetic relatedness, but through exposing the inadequacy of genealogical claims to belonging in a particular place and temporality. In these texts, ancestry is not something to be discovered in code, but is made through practices of making and remaking pasts for the sake of speculative futures. These are strategic uses of genetics as a way of getting to the fiction of national belonging. In the final chapter, I consider other border fictions – empire, organism and species – placing epigenetic imaginaries next to anxieties around the long-term effects of climate change and industrial toxicity.

5

# Toxic infrastructure

By the end of the Human Genome Project, determining the boundaries and mechanisms of heredity and gene expression had taken on new dimensions of complexity. Sequencing the coded regions of the genome did not offer a definitive account of why humans are what they are, and the results did not live up to the hype. Among other revelations, it seemed that accounting for biological complexity would mean understanding the genome as permeable and responsive to external shocks in ways that molecular biology had for a long time considered a peripheral branch of study. Sequencing coding DNA could only give a partial description of phenotype; to what extent are species differences determined by mechanisms of methylation (the silencing of parts of the genome), and the transgenerational inheritance of these genetic states? New questions around the influence of the environment – and the integrity of borders between organism and environment – have emerged (Richardson and Stevens 2016; Müller et al. 2017; Meloni 2019). The postgenomic condition has been characterized not only by the development and increasing availability of sequencing technologies, and the transport of these technologies from laboratories to homes, but also by an epistemic shift in the life sciences, where a panoply of environmental influences on the lifecourse are now scattered around mechanisms of genetic expression.

The large-scale investment in epigenetics and epigenomics over the last twenty years corresponds to an acceleration of anxiety at the level of international governance on the long-term effects of climate change and industrial toxicity. These effects have become global concerns, having been fractiously mitigated at peripheries. Various philosophical considerations of epigenetics have coalesced around ideas of proximity, plasticity and multiplicity. These are metaphors of indeterminacy and plurality, registering the uncertain scales of effect and ambiguities of cause when it comes to biological damage. They are also modes of narrating commonalities across borders of system, species and element in the postgenomic era, and of imagining how these commonalities are communicated across borders. Contrary to a focus on the individual organism as a site for theorizing the unity of life, a shift towards thinking through the interactions and dependencies at the level of ecology has energized much recent critical and philosophical work on questions of relation and influence (Margulis 1991; Wheeler 2006, 2016; Hoffmeyer 2008; Stengers 2010; Thacker 2013; Malabou 2016; Haraway 2016). Opening up the programme metaphor to its investments in ideology, aesthetics and praxis has taken on new relevance in a growing consciousness of ecological emergencies, unevenly differentiated across the world-system.

Laying out the 'deep genealogies' of representational tussles within environmental epigenetics, Jörg Niewöhner and Margaret Lock note with caution the turn/return to 'the social' in molecular biology 'after a phase of largely technologically driven pragmatic reductionism' (2018, 683). To this, they offer the concept of 'situated biologies' – situating the material body in space, 'within different spatial scales' – and in patterns of practice, 'how human practices share the material human body in lasting ways', often at moments of existential crisis (688, 691). In thinking this through, what is important is not typologizing the various and multiple influences that alter and affect embodiment. Instead, they suggest 'the environment' be defined '*in relation* to a second entity to which that environment *can be* environment' (691; emphasis mine). The idea of external environments acting upon the interiority of the organism (reduced to genome), to which the organism must adapt and respond, has shifted to a semiotic account of this process, whereby environments are constituted by relational effects. This is a transitional imaginary, whereby 'environment' is only ever a temporary placeholder for a certain kind of relation, rather than a fixed context determined by the calculation of cause and effect, which also 'challenges the biomedical assumption of a universal body' (682). This marks a very different point of departure from the Human Genome Project. Niewöhner and Lock's approach is useful here because as well as decentring an idea of a universal biomedical subject, they are also invested in decentring the molecular and (as) the biological from accounts of living processes.

At the level of narrative, the texts discussed in this chapter map a tension between an increasingly datafied account of reality, the obfuscation or reduction of accounts of what is called relationality, and the way that moments of sudden change or shock affect and form bodies through space and time. For Wendy Wheeler, 'science, which only deals with material particulars, cannot... offer us an account of relations at all. Neither can it offer us an account of immaterial causes, such as semiotic causes, of which relations are the prime example' (In Beever,

Tønnessen and Hendlin 2015, 178). Drawing on biosemiotics theorists such as Thomas Sebeok and Jesper Hoffmeyer, Wheeler considers the current moment to necessitate a 'new conceptual schemata, and a different grasp of ontology of all living organisms as interpretive makers of their worlds, not as machines but as a kind of living poetry' (178). This turn involves engaging with aesthetic forms as epistemological interventions, 'living poetry' not just as metaphor but as an alternative description of how being takes form. The postgenomic represents both a biotechnological and epistemological shift, and it also brings questions of aesthetic form and cultural praxis to the foreground.

Narratives of emergency tend to organise around plots of relational transformation: the emergence of different ways of being with others, human and nonhuman, often fragile and temporary. A postgenomic imaginary emerged at global scale just over a decade before the end of the Human Genome Project, in the early hours of an April morning in 1986, in the Soviet periphery, when a nuclear reactor exploded in the Chernobyl Nuclear Power Station in Ukraine. I read Svetlana Alexievich's *Chernobyl Prayer* (1997) and Jeff VanderMeer's Southern Reach trilogy (2014) as interventions in forms of writing and narrating community, self and ecosystem after environmental disaster, the hyper-militarization of governmental responses to ecological crises, and the convergence of postgenomic imaginaries with theorizations of care, endurance, responsibility and relationality. These texts are about toxic infrastructure at the peripheries, where the body's architecture cannot be relied upon as a vessel for individual survival, while the genomic information it houses becomes increasingly irrelevant as illegible and unrecognizable forms emerge. Toxicity extends across form – fragmentation, redaction, ellipses, expansions, contaminations – through techniques that play out the slow submerging of narrative coherence. It makes necessary novel forms of characterization that move away from (liberal) developmental paradigms and (neoliberal/algorithmic) disaggregation to render characterization as a transitional process, without a fixed horizon or endgame in sight.

If the age of reductionism is indicated not only in the ways scientific knowledge has been put to social use since the Enlightenment, but also has conditioned the parameters for experimentation and the identification of experimental subjects, then the age of emergence opens the possibility of radically altering the framework within which life itself is understood and managed at the level of community, society and government. Wheeler suggests that this would oppose, first, the neoliberal formulation of the individual and the family and, second, the idea that 'reality is constructed in language' (Wheeler 2006, 26–7). For Wheeler, this shift 'provides us with a new way of thinking, not only about how complex systems work, but about how, in their biological manifestations and beyond, they are inter-related' (27). As questions over responsibility and human survival have become a matter of sociological urgency, biology in the postgenomic era has begun to give alternative accounts of adaptation than those that uphold the selectionist paradigm. These questions shape this final chapter.

## Chernobyl and the postgenomic condition

The fallout of Chernobyl spliced together two branches of post-war industrial science – nuclear physics and molecular biology – while the genomes of those in close proximity to the site and those thousands of miles away were exposed to large doses of radiation. The damage was not only irreparable but also unthinkable. There was no precedent for it, and redressal involved a seismic shift in understanding the long-term influence of nuclear fallout. Chernobyl exposed the brittleness of Big Science's claims to be a facilitator of social development, causing devastation at a planetary scale that has expanded across ecosystems and time in ways that have still not been fully calculated. It was an assault to a coherent sense of form in national, sovereign governance, and the body politic over and outside Soviet borders.

The sovereignty ascribed to both gene and atom over the course of the twentieth century is symptomatic of an accelerated logic of reductionism, blinding some of their chief arbiters to the wider implications and consequences of their science. Chernobyl shook the certainties of both: atomic power as a peaceful energy source, and the genome as immutable code impermeable to external influences. While the genetic effects of radiation had been studied since the United States's bombing of Hiroshima and Nagasaki, radiation exposure at Chernobyl went well beyond these levels. The extent of the damage was, and remains, incalculable, hidden or buried. After Chernobyl, a belief in the transcendence and unilateral good of atomized understandings of the world began to diminish.

While Chernobyl shook the idea of a fixed code more or less impermeable to external influences, it also altered social conditions for narrative, eluding genre. Information and data were either secret or illegible. Books disappeared from libraries, and tools for measuring radiation could not read post-explosion numbers. A cataclysm that brought the latter days of the Soviet Union to an end, Chernobyl fractured an already besieged sense of communal coherence, and represented as much an onslaught to social forms of nation, region, locality and community as it did to biological life. The shock of Chernobyl encompassed health (biology), analogy (culture) and system (politics). The monumental task of repair has involved not only infrastructural mitigation – cordoning, compensation, burial and enclosure – but also grappling with a transformation of the imaginative possibilities of being in the world, more or less overnight. It has been identified as the moment when the fate of the Soviet Union was sealed, exposing the violence of state mismanagement as millions of lifeforms (human and nonhuman) were exposed to nuclear fallout.

Chernobyl was also a global crisis. A culture of secrecy prevailed: what levels of radiation were classed as dangerous, how far had radioactive fallout spread, and how could it be contained – if at all? In the case of Caesium 137, the health risk to humans increases over time once ingested, rather than decreasing. Radioactive rainclouds swept westwards with no regard for national borders or Iron Curtains, reaching as far as the west coast of Ireland. There, Iodine 131, and Caesium 134 and 137 found purchase in soils deficient in potassium and clay, ingested by cows through grass, contaminating Irish milk supplies. The Irish Dairy Board exported a number of dairy consignments to lower-income countries (Mexico, India, Thailand, Egypt, Ghana, Sri Lanka, Brazil, the Philippines and Ethiopia – the latter via famine aid), and some consignments were found to have high levels of radioactive contamination. Northern Sweden had the highest levels of Caesium 134 and 137 recorded outside the immediate disaster zone. Sámi peoples of Lapland were forced to kill and bury the carcasses of thousands of reindeer, harming an Indigenous culture based around reindeer. This posed a threat to their survival as a community with a relative degree of autonomy (Linton 1988, 18), and to 'their political strength and to a Sámi cultural identity bound by material and symbolic connections between humans and reindeer', in Sharon Stephens's words (1987). The crisis redrew maps of environmental influence and biological proximity across the globe, marking a continuation of colonial infrastructures of material, biological and cultural annihilation. What exploded in the periphery of the Soviet Union spread quickly into the peripheries and semi-peripheries of the world-system, highlighting the 'impossibility of predicting the complex global consequences of nuclear accidents as they transform the substance of people's bodies and environments and the meaningful orders of their lives' (Stephens 1987).

After Chernobyl, 'we shifted to another place in history': the history of disasters (Alexievich, 27). The fallout necessitated new forms of political action and citizenship, highlighting the unevenly violent terms of living in the Capitalocene, and the unsustainable demands on all kinds of lifeforms of maintaining toxic infrastructure. Narratives on and after Chernobyl register the uncertainty of the disaster's scale and reach. Who was responsible, and for what? Was the architecture of modern science itself to be brought to account? Responses to Chernobyl move between shadows of secrecy and gaps of illegibility – the cover-ups to mitigate panic and defection, and the lack of precedent and absence of data for understanding the long-term fallout. 'The three dimensional world fell apart,' writes Alexievich in her introduction to *Chernobyl Prayer*; nobody knew what had 'really happened' (26). This was a crisis not only of narrating the disaster (of what to say), but also of genre (of how to say it). Nick Rush-Cooper argues that in the case of Chernobyl, material encounters with radiation in the Zone 'do not take place through modalities of narrative, discourse, or gaze, but through exposure – an embodied vulnerability to that which we cannot sense' (2019, 218). Daniel Bürkner notes a persistent mischaracterization of the accident as 'a superhuman natural catastrophe' facilitated by what he calls Chernobyl's 'aesthetics of invisibility' (2014, 22). In the proliferation of photographic strategies of mythologization and photochemical displays of radioactivity, he argues, human systems fade into the background, the horizon taken up instead by mysterious and unthinkable shapes and substances that confound understanding and generate an affect of morbid wonder.

This embodied vulnerability and invisibility become constitutive of narrative forms marked by what Tamara Hundarova calls the 'Chernobyl Syndrome' (2001), which also deal with the problem of evidence in the post-Chernobyl world: its absence, obfuscation or illegibility. Was Chernobyl a war story, a horror story or a ghost story about vengeful forest spirits? Could it be redeemed through examples of collective heroism and national bravery, or through the effort of documentation as an end in and of itself? What to do now with the environment, with relations between human and nature now mediated by reciprocal contamination? Serhii Plokhy notes that while comparisons to wartime proliferated among locals, 'back then they knew who the enemy was, and the forest provided them with cover. Now danger was everywhere, and the forest, which had helped them survive during the Great Ukrainian Famine of 1932–3 and sheltered them against German reprisals, was the most dangerous place to be' (2019, 202). Central to all this was the evidence of disaster: what it looked like, how it might be measured, and how it could form the basis of legal interventions against the Soviet state, or welfare claims in post-Soviet Ukraine.

In a toxic present, where the periphery is a site of dumping and extraction, attending to the ways that narratives produced within it disturb and resist these processes returns us once more to the question of time. In what forms of temporality can these sites find purchase outside the perpetual present that is imposed by these practices? What futures are possible, and how can pasts be mobilized towards transforming the present, rather than only repeating it? For Hundarova, Ukrainian literatures of the 1990s encounter an 'eschatological sense of an approaching end' in which 'all temporal things seem to be finished and fulfilled, and the present is only a reminder of them, a mere repetition or recombination of the past' (2001, 265). Countering the idea that new forms of time are no longer possible – and that time in some way has already come to an end – Alexievich and VanderMeer posit weird and toxic animacies between humans, nonhumans and the substances that move through them and transform them. As interventions against the philosophical construction of liberal humanism and the consequent order of taxonomies of life and nonlife around this model of humanity, these texts embark on a new epistemological project of humankind.

Imagining worlds where the category of humankind no longer holds the same dominion has become one of the principal philosophical problems of the twenty-first century, as recent work in new feminist materialisms and posthumanisms by Donna Haraway (2016), Karen Barad (2007), and Jane Bennett (2009) has explored. This problem is also thornily connected to the long-term eviscerating dynamics of enclosure, extraction and annihilation of colonial-capitalist accumulation that have brought the current ecological emergency into being, as in Jason Moore's theorization of capitalist modernity working *through* nature, not acting upon it (2013). Sylvia Wynter's call for a new poetics of being human offers a thrilling theoretical injunction for tackling the problem of the human after biocentrism. She imagines a human released from its current biocentric formation, and a 'new and ecumenical human view that places the event of 1492 with a new frame of meaning not only of *natural* history, but also of a newly conceived *cultural* history specific and unique to our species' (1994, 7). She urges as a point of departure 'both the ecosystemic and global sociosystemic "interrelatedness" of our contemporary situation' to 'put forward a new world view of 1492 from the perspective of the species, and with reference to the interests of *its* well-being' (1994, 8). For Wynter, metaphors of interrelation not only facilitate crossings and traffic between humans and nonhumans to trouble the category and supremacy of human. The interrelation of ecological and economic challenges the explanation of human behaviour in an individualized mode of bio-ontogeny, and pushes instead towards understanding it '*in the process* of socialisation that institutes the individual as a human, and therefore, *always* sociogenetic subject' (Wynter 1994, 47; see also Fanon 1952). It is my argument here that the postgenomic does not offer a new ontology of human being, but rather moves towards the recursive opening-out of being towards others as a description of adaptation.

At stake in this displacement, as I have argued throughout this book, is an intervention in 'the history of how we represent the life we live to ourselves' (Wynter 1994, 48). The mapping of peripheral toxic environments *as* peripheries brings the tug of war over adaptation and selection into sharp focus. It is becoming impossible to outsource climate change and industrial toxicity to the edges of the world-system, both practically and imaginatively. Hence, practices that have made survival possible in racialized peripheries now become sites of learning for the so-called Global North. What would it mean to be 'best fit' to survive in a radioactive wilderness, when borders between healthy and poisonous ecosystems cannot be reliably traced? Can an ethos of selection save the species, or does this moment call for a conceptual reworking of 'adaptation' and a reckoning with its modern discontents? These are some of the questions of Alexievich and VanderMeer's texts. Neither gives up on the idea of the human. They work through the long-term consequences of misinformation, exclusion and annihilating dynamics of the forms of governance that both induce and fail to repair the crises of the texts.

## Adaptation, improvisation and epigenetics

While epigenetic research has become increasingly prominent in Anglo American biology since the 1990s, theory now described as epigenetic has developed alongside genetics as a counter explanation for inheritance for much of the twentieth century. Chromosomal rearrangements were first identified by the geneticist H. J. Muller in the 1930s in his experiments on fruit flies in T. H. Morgan's *Drosophila* laboratory, and described as transposable elements by plant biologist Barbara McClintock from the 1940s. Transposable elements are sequences of DNA that move (jump) from one genomic site to another, which McClintock suggested play a regulatory role in determining which genes are expressed, and when (McClintock 1993).

Likewise, the frictive encounter between loss and adaptation has long been a site of literary experimentation: change is often painful, and requires letting things go so that new or different things can take their place. Adaptation has also been caught up in a Panglossian ideology of 'the best of all possible worlds', which Stephen Jay Gould and Richard Lewontin identify as endemic to twentieth-century Anglo American biology:

> An adaptationist programme has dominated evolutionary thought in England and the United States during the past forty years. It is based on faith in the power of natural selection as an optimizing agent. It proceeds by breaking an organism into unitary 'traits' and proposing an adaptive story for each considered separately. (1979, 581)

This programme of reduction is fundamental to the logic of sequencing, isolating parts of the genome and determining their purpose and relative worth (or abnormality). This returns to sociobiology and the selfish gene: trait-thinking as a strategy of a society of control. In place of this, Gould and Lewontin advocate a pluralistic approach which, they argue, is closer to Darwin than the wholesale fetishization of natural selection as the principal mechanism of evolution. Some forms cannot be explained through a logic of purpose or use-value; they occur for reasons that are not always obvious or clearly beneficial, as 'secondary epiphenomena representing a fruitful use of available parts, not a cause of the entire system' (584). Rather than each aspect of a structure having a particular function, best fitted to the environment – natural selection as a mechanism for endless balance between organism and environment – nature has its own by-products: things that look like anomalies or as if they do not fit their context. The analogy Gould and Lewontin use is the spandrels formed by intersecting arches in cathedrals. In San Marco in Rome, these are filled in with incidental artwork, spaces produced by infrastructural constraints but not necessarily (or not obviously) productive.

At the level of literary analysis, this attention to parts that do not seem to serve a purpose is akin to making space for junk: the details that seem to lead nowhere, the red herrings of plot, the characters who disappear without trace. These incidental details play roles that are not always evident, seeming to fall out of significance when a plot takes a different turn – or perhaps even brush the thresholds of narrative rabbit holes that, were a reader to go down, might lead to a textual abyss. In these texts, it is in this sphere of the incidental and miscellaneous where meaning is in the process of being reworked. This is a different kind of adaptation to the one based on selection of those with traits better fitted to the surroundings. It involves an ongoing working out of possible routes: filling in where other functions have left off, not because one mechanism is better or worse than another, but because a situation demands it.

This was a subject Gould would expound on at much greater length ten years later, in his book on the fossils of the Burgess Shale, *Wonderful Life* (1989). The book is as much a philosophical reflection on the role of contingency in the unfolding of life as it is a description of an extraordinary ecological anomaly. The Burgess Shale is a site in the Canadian Rockies which houses the fossils of evolutionary anomalies from the Precambrian era – the era before the Cambrian explosion that brought about the profusion of multicellular (eukaryotic) life through meiotic (sexual) reproduction. These are species that fell out of ecology, creatures with five eyes and phenotypic features with unfathomable functions, 'grubby little creatures of a sea floor 530 million years old' (1989, 52). 'We greet them with awe', Gould writes, 'because they are the Old Ones, and they are trying to tell us something' (52). What is the message they carry? That the unfolding of life is not so much a developmental trajectory as a series of stops and starts – 'a record punctuated by brief, sometimes geologically instantaneous, episodes of mass extinction and subsequent diversification' – an ongoing cornucopia formed by speculative going-towards and moving-aways (54). His most radical deduction from the creatures of the Burgess Shale is that the evolution of *Homo sapiens* was not inevitable, but a phenomenon that emerged out of contingent and improbable circumstances. A parallel world – and perhaps many of them – exists in which the form of life that is called *Homo sapiens* does not.

One of the unresolved tensions between evolutionary and molecular biology is the question of the rate of mutation. If evolution happens via natural selection, and if selection works at the level of genes, the evolution can only really occur slowly, mutation by mutation, over a number of generations. A code fixed at the point of conception does not offer much in the way of flexibility. However, in epigenetic accounts of phenotypic flexibility, genes are activated or silenced by environmental influences. The inheritance of gene *states* as opposed to gene *products* has been theorised as a form of evolution that accounts for much speedier forms of adaptation, and more experimental forms of life (Jablonka and Lamb 2005). This is one way of accounting for the speed at which certain kinds of differential variation occur among members of the same species; or indeed, phenomena of comparable adaptations happening among species sharing the same ecosystem.

Two diverging pathways for genomics emerged in the immediate aftermath of the HGP. The different concerns and preoccupations of these pathways can be understood by distinguishing postgenomics first as a set of practices, methods and technologies within molecular biology, within the infrastructure set up by the proliferation of molecular biology laboratories from the 1950s, and massive investment in genomics from the 1980s; and second, postgenomics as the moment in the history and philosophy of biology that came after sequencing the human genome, particularly in the turn what had been known as 'junk' or non-coding DNA. The tensions between these pathways has led to one of the life sciences' more debated topics – the meaning, relevance and scale of changes in the genome that do not involve mutations in the sequence itself, and that might be induced by influences outside the genome: epigenetics. Taking junk into account means living with the vast contingency of genomic functions – and often, their unknowability and illegibility – and thinking the genome as responsive and plastic, rather than more or less fixed. To use Evelyn Fox Keller's formulation, the study of junk DNA allows a move from discussion of 'gene action', to thinking of the genome as a responsive organ involved in all kinds of interactions in and outside the body (Keller 2016). The focus of this chapter is the profound implications the postgenomic era has had on the kinds of relations that become perceptible, or that take on new kinds of significance; here, through the lens of environmental toxicity, ecological transformation and interpersonal responsibility.

Since the 1990s, epigenetics has referred to the study of heritable alterations to genetic expression that do not involve changes in the nucleotide (DNA) sequence. Classical genetics and molecular biology rely on an understanding of DNA as a coding blueprint for the organism, fixed from the point of conception, based on a one-way flow of information from DNA to RNA to protein; research in epigenetics, on the other hand, has shown that gene expression can be influenced well past the point of conception by environmental factors, leading to heritable changes in future generations. In their thesis of four evolutionary dimensions, Eve Jablonka and Marion Lamb describe this heritable responsivity as a different kind of inheritance system involved in evolution. They argue, 'not everything inherited is genetic'; rather, behavioural, epigenetic and symbolic can have both 'direct and indirect influences on evolutionary change' (2005, 107). This line of thinking would take post-Synthesis evolutionary theory away from a 'gene-centred approach, because it is no longer necessary to attribute the adaptive evolution of every biological structure and activity, including human behaviour, to the selection of chance genetic variations that are blind to function' (Jablonka and Lamb, 2), as in Richard Dawkins's *The Blind Watchmaker* (1986).

Epigenetic descriptions of inheritance are part of a broader epistemological shift that Robert Laughlin has characterized as a shift from the age of reduction to emergence. Laughlin argues,

> What we are seeing is a transformation of worldview in which the objective of understanding nature by breaking it down into smaller parts is supplanted by the objective of understanding how nature organises itself. (2005, 76)

This is a view of life as an emergent process unfolding across various levels of experience – genetic, epigenetic, symbolic and behavioural. While a reductionist standpoint requires that 'physical law is the motivating impulse of the universe' as an ever-present force without origin or explanation, emergent perspectives understand physical law as 'a rule of collective behaviour' (Laughlin, 80). Epigenetics is still heavily couched in the language (and ideologies) of molecular biology, but some of its more radical propositions highlight the insufficiency of the merely molecular to give a full account of life itself. Life cannot be reduced to code; it is thicker, messier and less easy to extract, exchange and manipulate than the rhetoric of industrialized genomics suggests. If the sovereignty of the atom has been challenged by its power of destruction, then the ideological sovereignty of the genome has been ruptured by its permeability to environmental, or non-genetic, influences, and the question of programme by that of organization.

Life is fragile, and change is possible. This is the delicate hope with which Gould ends *Wonderful Life*. Evolution is a lottery, and humans are not its inevitable conclusion or crowning glory: 'May our poor and improbable species find joy in its new-found fragility and good fortune!' (263). This invitation turns the question of humanity from mechanisms of survival to what AbdouMaliq Simone describes as rhythms of endurance among low-income urban communities in the Global South. Rather than building worlds in the name of permanence and improvement, social life among these communities is organized around 'enduring through the absence of a world': a process of ongoing reinvention without a sense of a coherent narrative, or a solid sense of place, nor stable category of home or claim to belonging (2018, 97). While survival – in a straightforwardly selectionist sense – involves a logic of enclosure (through resource capture, habitation, reproduction), endurance is about finding ways to be in time, and with no guarantees that this will ensure lasting security.

Both Gould and Simone attend to the political urgency of thinking with the periphery, whether this periphery speaks from millions of years ago, or from the informal and daily-wage sectors that sustain flows of exchange in megacities in the present. This is not to reify the periphery as a site of theoretical extraction. To attend to how places and temporalities that have been made invisible or unknowable, or seemingly unliveable by the dynamics of history is to come to a sense of the world that is not bound in ontological terms to the selectionist agendas that would perpetuate the ongoing creation of peripheries everywhere, for the benefit of an increasingly limited number of people.

*Chernobyl Prayer* and the Southern Reach trilogy construct peripheral imaginaries in landscapes that have moved beyond the bounds of human control. In these landscapes, modern assertions about species borders, genomic immutability, and the prevailing power of natural selection as the primary mechanism of evolution are all put to the test. Their ultimate inadequacy as trustworthy descriptions of these lifeworlds – or in offering psychical, structural, biological or economic repair for those enduring within them – leads to the unravelling of a particular order of knowledge. Thinking with some of the key voices surrounding this book – and in particular, with Hartman, Wynter and Lowe – as well as to reiterate one of my central arguments: this order of knowledge has privileged a particular conception of the human that is in the process of being reconfigured. In Alexievich and VanderMeer's texts, this destruction involves attending to both the trenchant violence and enduring fragility of human lifeworlds as they disappear into ecosystems. What's key here is to consider peripheral imaginaries – and attending narratives of interruption, contingency and indefinite cohabitation – as a political frame where established categories of knowing the self, body, and world are forcibly suspended, and repositioning other ways of knowing.

Biomorphism is a key concept for the texts discussed here, an artistic and design practice that models infrastructure on biological forms, in the shapes and processes of living organisms. While the double helix has dominated representations of hereditary structure since the early 1950s, this has been accompanied by more unwieldy interpretations of living matter, its contours and connections. As the era of the genome gives way to messier accounts of where heredity is housed, the borders that seal it from external influences, the mechanisms that regulate it, and the influences that interrupt it, the aesthetic sovereignty of the double helix is increasingly being challenged by passages of influence in and out of – and within – cells that carry genetic information. The Chernobyl syndrome is not so much concerned with a logic of exposure (that is, an ideal molecular sphere exposed to the elements) as it is with aesthetics of interdependency – inscription, influence and indeterminate relations that cannot be captured through technologies that privilege enclosure, rather than extension. In both these texts, the periphery – as a site defined by its provision of raw materials (of labour, biomatter, and energetic resource) – becomes a technique of estranging the idea of a core programme or a sovereign code. This is not for the sake of an imaginary defined by networks and flows – that is, the kind of disaggregated model of Big Data where living forms are made to disappear into algorithms. Rather, peripheral biomorphism unravels the epistemological conditions of a world reduced to traits and atoms, making space for complexity as both a political proposition and aesthetic intervention.

## Mutation and fragmentation in *Chernobyl Prayer*

Three themes dance dangerously in Alexievich's *Chernobyl Prayer*: sovereignty, the periphery and endurance. Chernobyl seems like an event from science fiction, and sections of *Chernobyl Prayer* read as if they have been lifted out of *Roadside Picnic*. The explosion site is called 'the Zone', evacuated of humans, filled with the carcasses of dead animals and cement graves, a toxic wasteland waiting to infiltrate the bodies of those who venture to traverse its borders: a sleeping monster. The book is organized into three sections, broken into monologues. These monologues were originally interviews between Alexievich and her subjects, and are presented stripped of her questions, fragments of accounts from a chorus of different voices, summarized by the author in the short titles she gives to each of them: 'monologue of a village on how they call the souls from heaven to weep and eat with them'; 'monologue on something more remote than Kolyma, Auschwitz, and the Holocaust'; 'monologue on a freak who is going to be loved anyway'. Each section ends with a choir – the soldiers' choir, the folk choir and the children's choir – where names become grouped together and the accounts are separated by line breaks.

Igor' Sukhikh calls this form 'collective testimony' (1989), which evades more empirical modes of data capture. Alexievich uses techniques of redaction and postponement to prevent the text standing as legal or medical evidence: delaying naming the interviewees, removing dates of interviews, removing names, recording silences or failures to speak, letting these absences exist in uncertain time. The sparseness of information reaches a crescendo at the end of each section in the choir sections, where the breaks between individual accounts are dissolved, and we are given only a list of names: a literary monument to the dead and dying. The only direct question that appears, from interviewer to subject, is in the first interview, 'The author interviews herself on missing history and why Chernobyl calls our view of the world into question' (24). The text's central question *is* this question – the questioning of human understanding, of the relation between human and world, and of human survival after disaster.

Irina Marchesini reads this as a new genre composed out of the necessity 'to communicate such collective trauma' (2017, 319). For Marchesini, *Chernobyl Prayer* is a 'novel-choir' where 'the voices of the witness sing in tune but, at the same time, are isolated' and also 'mediated by authorial control . . . deeply immersed in them' (319). This arresting description conveys the troubled aporia of agency generated – and exposed – by Chernobyl. Collective forms of memory offset by individual evidence: a strategy of a state in crisis, trying to mitigate disaster by dealing with it on a case-by-case basis. 'After Chernobyl, we began learning to say "I",' says Natalia Roslova, chairwoman of a women's committee of children (CP, 268). Authorial control is powerful, but also in pain, inextricable from the destruction. Sovereignty is in crisis, and this crisis extends across political, cultural, and biological realms: the deep corruption of the Soviet state, the fragmentation of cohesion between different cultures contained within it, and the short- and long-term damage to people's bodies and those of their future children. The effects of radiation sickness spread across the body; those exposed 'rarely had just one disease but instead a complex of illness swarming their bodies like a murder of crows' (Brown 2019, 163). Complexes of illnesses and collectivities of trauma offered new imaginative alliances after Chernobyl, along with metaphors of swarming and contamination – metaphors that resonate with what S. Eben Kirksey and Stefan Helmreich have called 'multispecies ethnographies' (2010): the study of 'the host of organisms whose lives and deaths are linked to human social worlds' (2010, 545), bodies that cohabit with a multiplicity of other creatures, bacteria and chemicals that often cannot be read or identified. This is a conceptual bridge between anthropocentric ethnography and the dissolution of species borders into extrinsic life. In political terms, this would also rupture any kind of typological hierarchy of being fostered through the language of scientific racism. How could form keep up?

The illegibility of Chernobyl meant that there was no fixed genre through which to narrate it. Many of the voices of *Chernobyl Prayer* move their experiences of it across accident, war, horror, and mystery: 'They call it an accident, but it was a war' (CP, 177); 'Horror is our natural habitat'; 'I remember it as a war' (CP, 200). Part of the difficulty of finding forms to imagine the disaster was the reality that there was nothing that could be done to repair it, to dial it back, to save its subjects from the ruins:

> Chernobyl. There is not going to be a different world for us. At first, when they took the feet from us, we gave open expression to our pain; but now we live with the realisation that there is no other world for us, and we have nowhere else to go. The sense that we are now forever fated to live on the soil of Chernobyl is something new. A lost generation returns from war . . . do you remember Remarque? But it is a perplexed generation that lives with Chernobyl. We are dismayed. The only thing that has not changed here is human suffering. That is our only currency – non-convertible, of course! (CP, 179)

Chernobyl is an end in itself: there is no dreamworld in sight, no ideological utopia, no possibility of a different future. World-building is no longer an option. The ground ('soil') renders this obsolete. When wars end, people return – fewer in numbers, accompanied by trauma. But there is no precedent for dealing with a war between the ground and human life. The exclusion from universal currency works as both an economic comment about a lack of access to international finance flows, as well as the non-convertibility of Chernobyl into universal descriptions of human experience.

Here, perplexity rather than loss contours the situation – what to do with the world, in the world, when the future has been cancelled, and when the conditions of the present are fraught with uncertainty and disinformation? This is not just about a lack of information, or secrecy, but the forms in which information arrived – 'in doses', as Anne Speckhard writes, 'often with considerable delay following the accident, and in most cases in contradictory and fragmented ways' (2005). This is a post-truth regime engendered by uneven and unguaranteed modes of transmission and receipt, where everyone is an expert and no one can be trusted. It leaves those who live between informational doses from unverified sources in limbo, waiting for an account of reality that will enable them to reconstruct what has been blown up – descriptions that, when they come, invariably leave them with no place to go.

Having 'no place to go' is one of the recurring motifs in Simone's study, where the value of action and labour is perpetually out of sight and difficult to determine. Instead of this, a sense of being missing in action prevails, amidst 'longings for extinction and desperate boosts of immune systems' (2018, 7). Collectives are temporary and fragile, and any sense of the political is bound up with the radical precarity and uncertainty of dwelling and living. Political declarations and manifestoes only go so far in delineating the scale and spaces and time-zones of political action, tools to be taken up and put down when necessary, as a given situation demands: 'it is necessary', Simone writes, 'to consider the shape-shifting "bodies" of collective enactment, all of the ways in which people and things can and might operate in concert' (127), and in ways that do not necessarily appear as established forms of intervention. Bodies that shift towards, and merge with, and fall away from each other; bodies that are fraught with all sorts of internal contradictory dynamics. Collectives that emerge out of shared articulations of the conditions for enduring the present, rather than in the name of futures that cannot be imagined, much less guaranteed. This is the peripheral imaginary invoked by disasters whose scale and temporality cannot be known or enclosed.

As with genetic ancestry testing, the uncertainty of evidence can be generative of political claims in itself. On the peripheries, evidence has a troubled status: 'what does it mean to collect evidence of harmful situations?' (Simone, 122). In

*Life Exposed*, Adriana Petryna identifies the emergence of 'biological citizenship' in post-Soviet Ukraine in the aftermath of Chernobyl (2002). Knowledge about the impact of radiation on biological processes and health became a political resource, and a way for citizens to 'stake their claims for social equity in a harsh market transition' (Petryna, 4). Access to state welfare was often contingent on proximity to the exclusion zone. Officially, the number of deaths directly caused by Chernobyl remains one hundred; in practice, a multitude of legal, medical and welfare frameworks were put in place for managing its long-term effects.

Petryna's argument is that access to these frameworks – in the midst of all sorts of precarity induced by Ukraine's new dependence on international finance organizations – began to organize a model of citizenship and to legitimize emerging democratic institutions in post-socialist contexts (7). Technologies of diagnosis, knowledge of symptoms and legal literacy formed a toolkit for enduring – unevenly – the new realities of a radioactive present, and for gaining access to welfare (Petryna, 15). Alongside this, the state used images of children born without limbs – humans estranged from recognizable forms – to assert its own claim to legitimacy: these radioactive mutations were the inheritance of Soviet corruption inscribed on the bodies of the young. Biological malformation became a way of asserting the sovereignty of a newly independent Ukraine: 'Such images reminded viewers of the cause of physical suffering. Out of the mire and mess of Soviet mismanagement of Chernobyl had come a dreadful accumulation of diverse malformations' (Petryna, 9). These examples show how Chernobyl was instrumentalized as both national origin story, and strategy for keeping going in a present without guarantees.

This latter point – living without guarantees – gets at the broader ontological crisis posed by the Chernobyl explosion, in the emergence of a reality that did not permit imaginative space for world-building, remaking or repair, much less improvement – in either social or biological senses. People carried on living there because of a lack of options (one of Alexievich's subjects calls the exclusion zone 'the great Atlantis of the peasantry'), and because of the caesuras it placed in cultural narratives of living a good life. The idea that life can be narrated as a series of hurdles to be overcome, or that things will work themselves out in due course, is a hope that recurs throughout the book's fragments, the most proximate sense of a world beyond Chernobyl:

> Our neighbours laid a new floor that year from the local forest, they tested it: the background radiation level was a hundred times over the safety limit. Nobody tore up those floorboards, they just carried on living there. Everything will sort itself out, they reckon. (CP, 131)

This description lends new meaning to ecological cohabitation. Following Moore (2013), the waste products of industrial capitalism work in and through nature, the radioactive trees constituting toxic infrastructure of human dwelling. This periphery's reliance on raw materials sourced locally embeds it more deeply into the violent and annihilating outcomes of core industrial science programmes. The inhabitants of this toxic site cannot hide from radiation, as if from bombs or shrapnel: 'it's everywhere. In the bread, the salt . . . we breathe radiation, we eat radiation. . . . Everything has been contaminated. Now we're faced with working out how on earth we should live here' (CP, 133). 'Here' does not just mean the geographical site, but 'in' the world as such – in bodies that are living with unknown effects, 'here' as in a particular moment in time when the order of things seems to have been suspended and its full weight hangs over the present.

The unknowability of Chernobyl's long-term effects on health had a market logic. In 1992, John Gofman called out the dazzling scale of 'biomedical un-knowledge' around nuclear pollution, which he defines as 'an abbreviation for all the findings which are the opposite of what is true about health and disease' (1992). Biomedical un-knowledge has become a tool for capitalizing on disasters – nuclear-related and others – while the uncertainty around possible health effects enables political apathy around scientific programmes (Yaroshinskaya 1995). It is not in the interests of governments with large nuclear energy programmes for their citizens to know too much about the health risks of their investments. M. Susan Lindee notes that the US government kept information about Chernobyl secret because of its Cold War defence programme (1994, 243). The focus on mismanagement at Chernobyl was not just a way of apportioning blame to a few individuals (or, in the West, the entire Soviet state), but a strategy for not talking about the larger question of how and if nuclear power should be used at all, given its annihilating potential (Yaroshinskaya 1995). The narrative of accident and disaster was a way of isolating and catastrophizing the situation as singular case, rather than a systemic time bomb.

The market logic went further: the Chernobyl explosion 'created a natural experiment with human populations', in Lindee's words (243). Humans (and nonhumans) living in its fallout became sources of data for the effects of large doses of radiation. An unnamed person in 'The Folk Choir' relates finding out from a family member in Russia that scientists are '"using you as 'black boxes'"', making them into experimental test subjects for learning more about the effects of radiation. The person responds: 'We think we are living life like everyone else. We walk around, go to work, fall in love. . . . But no! Actually, we are recording data for the future' (CP, 188). This is the sense of the future articulated for those who lived past the explosion – one whose biomedical, energetic and military infrastructure (its industrial programmes) will be shaped in part by the data of destruction extracted in the nuclear periphery. The more recent emphasis on biodiversity around Chernobyl corroborates this: it becomes an enclosed space for speculating on all kinds of nonhuman flourishing made possible by nuclear modernity, a way of closing down the more difficult questions around the long-term effects on human heredity. There are many data available on nonhuman lifeforms and communities around Chernobyl; the data on humans are less easy to identify.

And yet, people also knew. In Plokhy's *Chenobyl: History of a Tragedy*, the former head of agricultural administration in Kyiv, Vasyl Synko, recalls the speed and force of evacuations: "'Everyone knew that every day and hour spent in the zone would have a deadly effect on the organism of every individual'" (2019, 202). The effect of high doses of ionizing radiation on humans can mean changes to genetic structure, which might be passed down to subsequent generations; that is, the genomes of people exposed to radiation in the fallout of the explosion may alter the genomes of their future offspring, and it is unclear whether these alterations are permanent. Much of this was known before the explosion; indeed, the biological effects of radiation were well known by the late 1940s (Lindee 1994; Shevchenko 1999). Studies on the effects of radiation on genetic structure had been ongoing since the 1930s, in T. H. Morgan and Hermann Muller's fruit fly laboratory at Columbia University. More than this, radiation was developed as a way of treating cancer, 'a technology for the manipulation of the hereditary material' (Lindee, 59). But most pertinently, the genetic effects of radiation on humans had been a large area of study, particularly in the United States, since the bombings of Hiroshima and Nagasaki in 1945. The Atomic Bomb Casualty Commission (ABCC) was set up in 1946 under Truman, with a focus on scientific research rather than biomedical intervention, and genetics was one of its central areas of study. But as Lindee points out, studies on genetic mutation before the development of molecular technologies were hampered by difficulties of evidencing changes, which was done through selective breeding through which genetic structure was inferred.

What does 'mutation' mean in these contexts? In the sense understood by a genealogy of studies on the effects of radiation, it did not mean any hereditary change in genetic material, but a deleterious or 'specifically threatening change' – in Lindee's words, 'a dangerous morphological trait with implications for the future of the species' (170). Survivors of Hiroshima and Nagasaki and their descendants were being scrutinized through a partial lens, which came with all sorts of assumptions about normative morphology, but with a limited purview of what a significant mutation would look like (i.e. not sterility, reduced fertility, 'minor' malformations and so on). The ABCC study was focused specifically on mutations that would add to the 'load of the human gene pool' (Lindee, 191), rather than on events that might have genetic implications, but would not lead to evolutionary changes long-term.

What the ABCC was looking for were not general or already-known issues that might be exacerbated or made heritable through radiation, but for – in Lindee's words – 'genetic monsters' (60). The commission was imbued with a particular imaginary around what genetic mutation meant, more attuned to Godzilla and other science-fictional horrors than to the (supposedly) more low-grade effects already in evidence. The study was criticized for this narrow focus: pouring research resources into work that would not benefit the communities and ecosystems directly affected by the effects of radiation, but which was rather focused on more grotesque manifestations. This highlighted, too, a fixation on the creation of new forms of life through US techno-science.

The Chernobyl Syndrome is a punctuation mark in historical time: the end of a hegemonic order of knowledge that has governed global articulations of subjectivity, selfhood and political participation since the European Renaissance, sustained through colonial-capitalism. This punctuation mark was formed not by the shock itself, but through new intimacies between body and environment, where it became vital to traverse the epistemological rupture between infrastructural enclosure and bodily inscription (the mind-body analogy imposed onto Man's relationship with Nature). These intimacies and their devastating implications about the fragility and unevenness of human sociality expose the infrastructure of the present as unsustainable. Chernobyl was not the exception, but brought the implicit violence of this infrastructure to global awareness. Hence the need to double down on keeping its full implications – and its data – secret.

This punctuation mark appears in a shift in representing biological forms – human and nonhuman. Hundarova defines biomorphism as 'using the morphology of the human body for the topographic inscription of memory traces' (2001, 267). Memory – the domain of the mind – is lured down from its nesting place in the world of thoughts and imagination to form the processes and dynamics that form the body's geometries and, beyond this, the conditions for its interdependencies with and within others. This strange and dangerously illegible memory-scape unravels the idea of far-off signals that encode raw material, bringing the processes that determine our biosocial lives into the warp and woof of the everyday. Memory and morphology are coextensive.

Bodies need to take on new meanings after Chernobyl because the meaning of their bodies after the disaster is required to lose relevance. Bodies become sites of political and economic contestation about the extent of Chernobyl's damage and with it, state responsibility. In 'Monologue on the old prophecies', a mother describes her daughter born 'like a little living sack, stitched up on all sides, without a single slit, only the eyes were open' (CP, 95) – no genitals and only one kidney. Doctors have classed her as 'disabled from childhood':

> What do they mean, 'disabled from childhood'? She's disabled from Chernobyl. I've studied my family tree: there hasn't been a case like this, they've all lived to eighty or ninety, my grandfather lived to ninety-four.... They've called me crazy, laughed at me. They said children like that were born even in ancient Greece, ancient China. One official shouted, 'You're after Chernobyl benefits! Chernobyl money!' I'm amazed I didn't faint in his office, die of a heart attack. But I mustn't allow that. (CP, 96)

This passage lays out four articulations of time: the developmental time of childhood, the genealogical time of family history, time that draws continuity between ancient and modern lifeworlds, and the time of Chernobyl. Chernobyl figures here as an abruption in chronological time, on the other side of which lies a new set of behaviours ('laughed at me') and responsibilities ('benefits! . . . money!'). Chernobyl has been allocated a space in time, but accessing this time is conditional on obscure evidentiary and legal mechanisms of proving causality. The woman's daughter, nameless doctors and officials have implied, is some kind of evolutionary throwback, rather than a new form of human generated out of exposure to radiation through the contamination of her mother's body.

This goes back to Lindee's point about the fixation on (and here, denial of) the creation of novel phenotypes as a result of radiation. An improbable and quasi-mythical evolutionary lineage – the 'old prophecies' of ancient times about children born without organs or limbs – is invoked as a way of minimizing state responsibility. The representatives of conflicting explanations circle around each other in syntax, not touching: the abusive words of the official are cordoned into quote marks, setting down a border between the mother and her claim, 'two states divided by barbed wire: one, the Zone itself; the other, everywhere else' (CP, 268). The psychic cost of living with the perpetuation of state gags around an open secret manifests in faintness, shock and anger, the 'mess of emotions' the mother experiences when she sees other pregnant women, and 'a neighbour's pregnant dog': 'surprise and horror, envy and joy, there's even some vindictiveness' (CP, 97). There is nowhere to put the truth, nor any coherent narrative with which to register trauma. The time of Chernobyl is a restricted zone, and this denial of access engenders testimony with a sense of no place to go, and no time to head towards.

What is interesting here is the articulation of multiple configurations of time – developmental, ancient, genealogical and the time of the disaster – in the attempts by the doctors, and officials, and the mother to try to place the daughter's body in time. There is no finite explanation for her form, and no resolution given in the narrative. In the text, she exists between these time-zones. The biopolitical placement of her body in developmental and genealogical time conflicts with the mythic temporality of prophecies from the past coming true in the present, and atomic time, which is (here) unknown and unquantifiable in terms of long-term effects on biological life. There is an epigenetic analogy: codes that are permeable by influences external to their programme, biological processes that express or silence parts of the genome, that draw old forms into the present long buried deep in the genome's 'junk' DNA, and the speed at which environmental influences (broadly speaking) can lead to alterations in genetic structure. This analogy is made possible by the simultaneity of time-zones in the mother's testimony. The Chernobyl syndrome extends across morphological and metaphorical realms: fast-moving adaptations in the genetic structure, across generations and a synchronicity of conflicting measurements of time that those affected by it are compelled to endure.

The postgenomic condition is not only centred on vast tracts of genomic data amassed through sequencing technologies, new testing devices and precision medicine. It also concerns forms of synchronicity in narrating human experience. In the passage above, the rupture between the biochronology of biopolitics – formed by developmental and genealogical time – the mythic time of ancient history, and the shock-time of disaster are suspended together. This suspension is a site of deep anxiety, and even psychic disintegration. This, as Simone argues, is characteristic of lifeworlds of the periphery: uninhabitable, which 'endure through the absence of a world ... stubbornly holding onto its constant demise' (2019, 94). The postgenomic condition goes beyond new descriptions of ontology: it traverses the edges of biopolitical certainties of management and control, rewriting or writing over scientific justifications for political economies based on survival and selection.

I'll move to VanderMeer's Southern Reach trilogy through an intertextual segue, a moment in Alexievich's text when a biologist describes her thesis on the behaviour of wasps as an analogy for the difficulty of 'breaking away from what you are used to' (CP, 206):

> I spent two months on an uninhabited island. I had my own personal wasps' nest there. They accepted me as a member of their family after a week of sizing me up. They didn't allow anyone closer than three metres, but within a week I was allowed to within ten centimetres. I fed them jam from a matchstick. 'Do not destroy an anthill: it is a splendid alien life form,' was a favourite saying of our lecturer. A wasps' nest is linked with everything in the forest, and I too gradually become part of the environment. A baby mouse would run up and sit on the edge of my trainers. He was wild, a forest animal, but he already saw me as part of the landscape. I had been sitting here yesterday, I was sitting here today and I would be sitting here again tomorrow. (CP, 206)

This passage crosses between two spheres of reality: the language of habitation and property – 'uninhabited', 'my own personal', and 'their family' – and of bordering – 'sizing me up' – transforms into the vocabulary of interdependency – 'linked with everything', 'becoming part' and 'part of'. The 'I' of the passage becomes increasingly detached from a grammar of action. At first, this is a simple reversal between her and the wasps: the nest goes from being 'my own personal wasps' nest', with its stark and colonial overtones, to the habitation of a particular family, with its own logic and regulations around what and whom should be admitted. This sphere of property and habitation fixed to a particular site is marked by affects of suspicion and permission. This is a gentle lure that might make a reader forget the more violent implications of a biologist observing wasps, bracketing her endeavours in a benign form of scientific investigation. There is even a pay-off for the wasps: jam from a matchstick, an image playing on the absurdity of scale as a way of generating sympathy for the encounter between species.

The passage takes a turn in the middle of the paragraph, through a memory of a moment of teaching by an authority figure that, it is implied, is trusted by the biologist. The lecturer's words are delivered like a proverb, an analogical placeholder for a broader moral message. This message is that we do not know the creatures with whom we cohabit ('alien lifeform'), and that they are things of wonder rather than sites of fear ('splendid'), so we should not try to destroy them. 'Anthill' here is less of an architectural description than a synecdoche for a miniature ecosystem and nonhuman community. Like Kropotkin's description of an alien planet based on mutual aid, this quasi-proverb transports the reader – via the biologist – into an alternative social system. Here, the passage moves to metaphors of linkage, rather than property, and of the impossibility of severing the wasps from the broader system they inhabit.

In another context, this might read as romanticizing, reifying or anthropomorphizing, but this example is shared in the context of people getting used to a radical and traumatic change in their relationship with their surroundings. The biologist is asking the listener to bear with her in this scene as she, too, becomes part of the memory. This happens, grammatically, in the gerund, somewhere between doing and being done to: 'I had been sitting . . . I was sitting . . . I would be sitting here again' – a past that continues as long as the baby mouse that has become used to her presence enough not to fear it, to take it as 'part of the landscape', continues to visit the edge of her trainers, and as long as she can continue to narrate this memory. This is a scene of endurance, full of uncertainties and unknowns, upon which the biologist can draw in the present: a memory of a body sitting in the same place at the same time each day, extending across past perfect, past continuous and the future anterior. The emphasis here is as much on the way that time, rather than the space of the forest, becomes a site for articulating modes of cohabitation, or sharing space, between lifeforms organized around different social systems.

## Transitional characterization in the Southern Reach trilogy

The Southern Reach trilogy is also organized around a mysterious event, and the subsequent contamination of an American coastal periphery. The trilogy unfolds on a site of land a few kilometres long – 'part of a wilderness that lay adjacent to a military base' (VanderMeer 2014a, 94) – which the government has cordoned off and designated as 'Area X'. *Annihilation*, the first book, follows a team of four experts, a biologist, a psychologist, a surveyor and an anthropologist – all women – as they head into Area X, and is focalized through the perspective of the biologist, whose name is given much later in the narrative. The first book ends with all the experts dead save the biologist, and the production of her genetic clone in Area X. Original and clone go their separate ways: the biologist stays, and the clone 'returns' to the other side of the border. The team of experts have been sent in by a clandestine government body known as the Southern Reach, 'so secret that it has almost been forgotten', and *Authority*'s narrative is focalized through its new head, Control, whose efforts to control the spread of Area X past the borders manufactured by his organization are failing. The third book, *Acceptance*, follows Control and the biologist's clone into Area X as they search for the original biologist. When they find her – or what remains of her – 'she' has transformed into a massive eco-monster, benign and on the move, a materialization of the larger story the books tell about the forms and practices of slippage between lifeforms laid bare by an unspecified systemic disaster. Like a quasi-proverb arriving unexpectedly in a memory, becoming part of metaphorical infrastructure for living in the present, these forms and practices cannot rely fully on the evidentiary economy of its authority figures (nation, agency or scientific expert).

My reading here will focus on what I call transitional characterization in the Southern Reach series, whereby the stability and reliability of character as a narrative object is placed under various sorts of pressure. This is part of the series' attention to what Jon Hegglund calls 'the contingency of 'human' as a narratological category' (in James and Morel 2020, 42). There are all sorts of transitions, displacements and disappearances in the narrative. For Hegglund, 'the narrative works to erode our confidence in the category of the human through the narrative description of the storyworld, and indeed, through the narrator's retrospective description of her own embodied experientiality within the storyworld' (38). This is a helpful point of departure for understanding what these figures of transition, disappearance and displacement are up to. The word 'erode' is key: across the series, there is a gradual process of cognitive estrangement from the kinds of certainties offered by knowing that a character is human, and all the implications about the sovereignty of information that this category brings with it.

VanderMeer does not give up on the category of human. Rather, the texts are interested in how narrative-making becomes a site for negotiating its borders. VanderMeer's technique of transitional characterization shifts the political stakes of character building to questions of toxic influence and ecological violence, and allows for affect to take up similar demarcations of narrative space as characters do. In these extended possibilities for characterization, discontinuities between character and person open up in ways that are similar to the abruptions to genealogy and property in Chapter 4. As Hegglund argues, in these texts there is 'an openness to the ways in which narrative actively and dynamically constructs distinctions between subjects and objects, figure and background, characters and storyworld' (30). The effect of this openness is not to flatten out relations to a field of radical indeterminacy and to leave it there; rather, VanderMeer is interested in what Beer calls 'the inextricable web of affinities' which 'exists not only as interconnection in space but as succession in time', and consequently, in 'a sense of multiple latent relations which are permitted to remain latent' (2010, 156–7,

161). Relations which are permitted to remain latent offer an extraordinary feint to the demands of making code visible and legible; keeping mystery embedded in narrative, without the grounding of characters taking up and making use of the miscellaneous resources they find themselves amidst, often because they are unable to make sense of them. 'The maze is what matters' (Beer, 167), a gesture that attends to Aran Ward Sell's observation of a distinction in the novels between foregrounding 'malign human influence' in an often correspondingly malign ecosystem, rather than 'human mastery' over a generically 'good' Nature (2018, 98). The texts decentre and regionalize 'human' control, while keeping in sight the muscle memory of destruction that continues to mould experience.

The biologist is an expert in transitional environments: environments that border land and sea. Area X, which the biologist calls a 'rich biosphere', has 'transitioned several times, meaning that it was home to a complexity of ecosystems' (VanderMeer 2014a, 11–12, 30) – there are forests, swamps, salt marshes and beaches in close proximity, low tides that run up to deer and otters, and creatures that have adapted to the post-disaster habitat. The humans have long since left, evacuated by the Southern Reach, and the only ones who go in are those on expeditions. The biologist and her team are the twelfth Southern Reach expedition to Area X, and all the others have disappeared. While in Area X, they are prohibited from attempting any kind of communication to the outside world 'for fear of some irrevocable contamination' (VanderMeer 2014a, 7). How contamination happens, what it is, and what the long-term effects will be are unclear, and this lack of understanding and prevailing sense of uncertainty about what is going on in Area X facilitate an acceleration of emergency powers, and a logic of sacrifice is applied to those going in. If the biologist's team survives, it will be because they are the 'best fit' to survive the environment and to adapt to its conditions. If they do not, the idea is that precautions will prevent them from spreading the contamination further, and the Southern Reach will – at some point – be able to extract the data they collect, just as the biologist's team does for those on previous expeditions.

Placing a biologist at the centre of the narrative – someone who (it seems) could not know more about the environment they are investigating than anyone else, one of the most qualified people for this particular job – heightens the anticipation when inexplicable things start happening. Early on, an enormous wild boar charges down a trail towards them:

> I had the startling impression of some presence in the way its gaze seemed turned inward and its head wilfully pulled to the left as if there were an invisible

bridle. A kind of electricity sparked in its eyes that I could not credit as real. (VanderMeer 2014a, 17)

This description is the first of many in the series when techno-scientific vocabulary cannot lasso the strange forms of Area X. The boar seems to the biologist to be guided by a force that is just about perceptible – 'some presence' – but which remains outside the realm of her comprehension. The idea of an invisible bridle reads as a dark joke on Darwin's co-option of Adam Smith's invisible hand, the mysterious force that guides markets, societies and (for Darwin) evolution towards good outcomes via individual actions (an individualized account of emergence as an equalizing force for income distribution) (Smith 1759). The boar seems possessed: not by a spiritual force, but a manmade one – electricity, or at least a force that resembles it. This moment temporarily expands the compressed mysteries of Area X, mysteries not confined to the site. What unknown futures have been cancelled or sacrificed for the sake of a society that has based its biopolitics on economic metaphors, and its industrial development on the extractive processes necessary to generate electric power? Is it the electricity in the boar's eyes that is not credible, or the eyes themselves; that is, does the biologist's doubt reflect her own uncertainty, or the reality of Area X itself?

The boar becomes a conduit for a swarm of displaced metaphors that fail to carry the biologist over to empirical deduction, figures of speech vying for space as the creature heads off into the underbrush. She tries to find explanations from 'entirely rational biological theories' and past experiences, but finds herself instead 'staring into the future again' (VanderMeer 2014a, 17). This segue – from the natural laws of post-Enlightenment science to new biophysical possibilities in an unknown future – is the epistemological pivot on which the entire series turns. Like *Chernobyl Prayer*, it is the pivot between illegibility and secrecy: what cannot be read, and what cannot be told. Area X frustrates practices of decoding and established parameters of measurement, while being managed (ostensibly) by an organization whose practices are wrapped in secrecy.

What distinguishes Area X from the Chernobyl exclusion zone, or at least that draws out new emphases, is that illegibility and secrecy are not as easily distinguished, as the reader is never entirely sure what is keeping secrets, and what kinds of reading might be possible. This comes out in one of the text's first red herrings: the words on the wall of 'the tower', the ruined building that the team come across early on in *Annihilation* that tunnels into the ground, taken over by massive structures of flora and fauna. Descending a dark stairway covered with 'sparkling green vines' ('sparkling' again conveying a form of otherworldly, or electric, power), the biologist and the anthropologist realize that the vines are words 'in cursive, the letters raised about six inches off the wall':

> As I came close, did it surprise me that I could understand the language the words were written in? Yes. Did it fill me with a kind of elation and dread intertwined? Yes. I tried to suppress the thousand new questions rising up inside of me. In as calm a voice as I could manage, aware of the importance of that moment, I read from the beginning, aloud:
> 'Where lies the strangling fruit that came from the hand of the sinner I shall bring forth the seeds of the dead to share with the worms that . . .'
> Then the darkness took it.

Alongside the biologist's elation and dread, illegibility and secrecy are intertwined at this moment. The words invite decipherment, but they are data without context. This is a meta-genomic image: a script encoded by another script (the vine's DNA), its cursive form shadowing the curves of intertwined helices. In *Acceptance*, the origin of this script is revealed, and it represents the conditions of possibility for the forms that grow out from it in Area X. Part of their lure is that the full picture is not available. Directly afterwards, the biologist inhales some of the matter that comes of out the vines, and this is the moment when she becomes part of Area X – when the possibility of her leaving is cancelled. In many ways, this is the merging of script and growth, a play on the idea of environmental influence insofar as separation of life and genome is figured as impossible. This comes to stand for the moment of the biologist's annihilation, which figures more specifically as the gradual annihilation of her sense of a separate self, as she moves through the landscape and closer to giving up her only motivation for coming into Area X: finding her husband.

Somewhere towards the centre of the narrative lie three love stories: between the biologist and her husband, between Control/John and Ghost Bird – the biologist's clone, and between the lighthouse keeper Saul and his lover Charlie. For the biologist, love is like working out a secret, a process of decoding, turning over data, traversing the distance in her marriage before Area X, in the hope that it might bring her closer to finding her husband inside. Identities and memories pass between these couples – Ghost Bird is born with all the biologist's memories and skills intact; like Ivan in 'Another's Memory', they 'come to her second hand' (VanderMeer 2014c, 30). Her name comes from the nickname the biologist's husband used for her, a reference to her absence in their marriage. Devoid of context, these memories are only useful information to Ghost Bird, which

Control/John attempts to extract from her, first in a series of interrogations, and subsequently on their joint expedition into Area X. She is able to select relevant data without their accompanying emotions: 'The biologist had been married but Ghost Bird wasn't, released from responsibility from any of that' (VanderMeer 2014c, 36). Like Ivan, she doesn't always agree with her original's decisions: 'Why had her other self been so careless with the words on the wall?' (VanderMeer 2014c, 36). Why, a reader is invited to ask, would the biologist be capable of such carelessness at such a pivotal moment of the plot? This sounds like grousing between siblings, the muttered grumbles of one sister to another, not despite their proximity but because of it. But it is also a recursive moment, taking us back to the moment in the first book when the biologist encounters the words on the wall, telling us to go back and reread it, to find something different to what appeared in the first encounter between the wall's words. Why did the biologist lean closer, allowing 'a tiny spray of golden spores' to spew out of a nodule in the "W"? This was the moment of contamination, where the biologist is seduced by the possibility of deciphering a code, while establishing the possibility of Ghost Bird's existence.

In *Annihilation*, relationships are full of silences, made up of the things characters do not tell each other, or the things they do not know that they need to know about themselves. These silences extend to the relationship between reader and narrator. The secrets that the biologist kept in her marriage create a dynamic that encompasses the connection between her and her implied reader: 'At one point', she remembers, 'my husband began to call me the ghost bird, which was his way of teasing me for not being present enough in his life' (VanderMeer 2014a, 109). Her narrative becomes a way of filling this absence, the reader becoming a substitute partner while she searches for the one she has lost. Her absence in their marriage was marked by an attention to data, a fixation on analysis, 'existing apart' while able 'to appear social' when out with her husband and their friends (VanderMeer 2014a, 109). This constant fixation on working things out – to process the data in ways that correspond to her sense of reality – drives her away from him, while all her medic husband wants is 'to be of use' to others: a first responder or a triage nurse (VanderMeer 2014a, 57). This was his reason for going on the eleventh expedition. When his clone reappears, he comes back to their kitchen, next to the refrigerator, drinking milk out of the carton, still in his expedition clothes; later, it is established that the clones come back to places that were particularly meaningful or important to their originals. The husband fixes on the part of the house that facilitates nourishment; in contrast, when Ghost Bird appears, it is in an abandoned parking lot where the biologist used to go on solitary walks, 'a patch of urban wilderness', keeping it secret from her husband (157).

The first book of the Southern Reach trilogy is a portrait of a marriage dissolving, told through the analogy of a person returning after a time away, transformed in ways that neither party can fully grasp or explain. This analogy extends across genetic and social descriptions: the husband's genetic code has returned, with some of the original's memories, but not all of them. The distance between them loops around the silences in their marriage before his expedition (secrets), and the silences of incomprehension after it (illegibility), and this new illegibility cannot be confirmed by genetic deduction. In terms of his DNA, he is the 'same' person, but a version that has been somehow contaminated by forgetfulness and distance. Not yet realizing that this is not really her husband, but rather his genetic copy, the biologist encourages him to remember how he left Area X and got back to their house. He cannot give her answers: 'There was an odd calm about him, punctured only by moments of remote panic when, in asking him what had happened, he recognised that his amnesia was unnatural' (VanderMeer 2014a, 56). This description moves across biological and social: it implies that some kind of contamination has effected a shift in personality, a rewriting of code ('punctured only by moments'), and an obliteration of memory. The strange formulation, 'remote panic', feels unrecognizable – what kind of panic can be perceived while remaining far off? – and a fusion of psychological state and spatial configuration. The character is clearly vulnerable, but in ways that cannot quite be delineated or diagnosed. His psychic world, at this point, turns only between 'odd calm' and 'remote panic', neither of which can give the biologist data for deductions.

This distance reverberates between them across time. 'He now contained within him the distance he'd accused me of,' an oscillation of affect between partners, distance as entity or character or even topography, one expressive while the other fades away, doomed to miss each other (VanderMeer 2014a, 56):

> After a time, I couldn't take it any longer. I took off his clothes, made him shower, then led him into the bedroom and made love to him with me on top. I was trying to reclaim remnants of the man I remembered, the one who, so unlike me, was outgoing and impetuous and always wanted to be of use. The man who had been a passionate recreational sailor, and for two weeks out of the year went with friends to the coast to go boating. I could find none of that in him now. (VanderMeer 2014a, 57)

This passage is about dominance, time and a desperate, violent procedure of trying to jog someone's memory. It is driven by the biologist's claiming of time in a series of starkly acquisitive and forceful actions, where all actions are carried out by the speaking I. The husband is made into an object; the pronoun 'he' does not appear, stripped out of her memories. The passage turns on the contrast between this 'he' and a spectral personality – someone characterized by being generally 'outgoing and impetuous' who 'always wanted to be of use': a description frozen in time, a snapshot of a person perpetually in motion. The person she finds now is reduced to a 'him' to whom things are done.

This is character building in the ruins of a relationship, the reconstruction of a person through someone else's memory of them, who can exist only as an object in contrast to them ('so unlike me'), whose passion and care take up the biologist's horizon of nostalgia. In the meantime, the present enforces the evacuation of those attributes through some kind of invisible contamination of the person who was. Nature appears as a site of leisure, a place to be used for socializing and outdoor pursuits. The word 'recreational' has a double meaning here, indicating both an activity done in spare time, as well as a transformation, or making anew. The husband was making trips to the coasts whose purpose was explicitly transformational, suggesting an inevitability to this final scene when he returns one last time from the coast back to their house, now changed into something else.

In postgenomic terms, the idea of character that remains stable across a lifetime – or which develops according to a relatively stable programme determined at birth – diminishes with the possibility that character is subject to 'the *chanciness* of consequences' (Beer, 202). Character development is one of the last defences of the liberal order, the place where certainties of an individuated self can be placed, those certainties premised on uneven constitutions of human difference. Rather than showing the annihilating logic of this fiction in the era of the genome, VanderMeer moves the fixation into a different set of concerns, more radical in their approach to ecology than those of genomic dystopias. This shift from character to ecology corresponds to Michel Serres's question at the beginning of *The Natural Contract*: 'Does anyone ever say *where* the master and slave fight it out?' (1995, 3; italics mine). Dialectics of self-determination cannot take place in a conceptual vacuum. In his readings of VanderMeer's weird fiction, Benjamin J. Robertson has theorized this as 'abdifference':

> The 'ab-' in abdifference designates a movement away, a constantly renewed flight from difference and from everything particular and toward nothing in particular, a movement without trajectory within a space without markers. It is a nonattitude, a nonrelation, a means of identifying the measureless gap between the human with its knowledge practices and the weird planet without a capacity to be known. (2018, 134–5)

Living in abdifference is necessarily a state of uncertainty, but this uncertainty can be reconfigured from 'detachment from knowledge' (and the implication that something can be worked out) to the impossibility of reading the world. This returns to the question of living at and in the periphery, where – to follow Simone – flight towards 'nothing in particular' means that there is no stable or fixed horizon, no end that will fulfil the speculations of the present.

What connects Robertson and Simone's arguments is an acknowledgement of the weirdness of the incommensurability between knowledge and the messy work of living. For some, it has never been possible to know 'the globe' as such, and knowledge about its totality is repeatedly shown to be unreliable, untrustworthy or in motion. Reorienting lines of flight from the global periphery – Area X, Chernobyl, the Urban South – is to approach this impossibility and consider its implications for praxis, 'a series of rhythms that enable surprising, frustrating, sometimes confusing, sentiments and practices of residents caring for and enduring with one another' (Simone 2018, 137). VanderMeer's periphery is a site where character development cannot be relied on, and where characters that enter Area X as apparently whole and stable units gradually disintegrate and are remade into new forms across psychological and biological levels of transformation. This is not for the sake of endless self-fashioning as for Bron in *Triton*; transitional characterization at the periphery portrays, instead, sociogenetic constitutions across interrelations of economy and ecology.

Characters do not just transition between environments. Lived experiences transition between characters: the Area X-produced doubles offer different routes and courses of action to their originals. The melancholy of the biologist in the first book – the enormity of her loss propelling her into Area X – is offset by the love story in the final volume of the series, *Acceptance*. There, the narrative is guided by the (often comic) development of a new relationship between (the hopelessly out of) Control/John and Ghost Bird, as the two trek through Area X in search of the biologist. Their dynamic mirrors that of the biologist and her husband, a shared synergy of contrasts that de-individualizes the problems that drove the biologist and her husband apart. Like her original, in Area X Ghost Bird is constantly on the search for 'more data'; Control wants to get somewhere, 'as if a destination meant something', Ghost Bird notes wryly, while keeping distance between them as they make their way through an unknown territory (VanderMeer 2014c, 28). He, in contrast, notes a 'brightness' inside her, and a 'corresponding darkness inside of him' (VanderMeer 2014b, 221). This Manichean opposition is not to be trusted. It is a contrast formed by their shared experience of having to manage a crisis, and the security of Control's ad hoc characterization does not hold for long. The sense of symmetry between the couples fades into something less stable. They are not individuals placed in opposition to each other, but points that shift on a topography which seems itself to be being remade anew. At times the biologist and her husband come closer together, and at points Ghost Bird and the biologist; these proximities are influenced by and dependent on the territory of Area X. The shape constituted by these relations is, in geometrical terms, in flux, the length of the lines between them contracting and expanding.

This movement is to do with the interdependency of the characters with each other and the shifting terrain of Area X's ecosystem. In the Southern Reach's headquarters, Control learns a theory that goes some way to describing this interdependency, epigenetic in its formulation. He hears a fellow scientist – who will later go mad – say what he hears as 'the terror, the terror' (close to Kurtz's 'the horror, the horror'). It turns out that Whitby was actually saying 'the terroir, terroir', a term from oenology:

> It means the specific characteristics of a place – the geography, geology, and climate that, in concert with the vine's own genetic propensities, can create a startling, deep, original vintage . . . Terroir's direct translation is 'a sense of place', and what it means is the sum effects of a localised environment, inasmuch as they impact the qualities of a particular product. Yes, that can mean wine, but what if you applied those criteria to thinking about Area X? (VanderMeer 2014b, 131)

This is a rare moment of explanation in a narrative without much in the way of reliable analysis. The analogy is embedded in an ideology of cultivation – of harnessing the particularity of place in order to create a particularly desirable and competitive product for circulation. This sense of place is centred, implicitly, in the vantage point of the vineyard owner who curates their vines according to knowledge of their locality. The understanding that a plant's hereditary material is 'in concert with' local environments has long been an accepted truth in a multibillion dollar industry. Why not apply this to the processes of accelerated adaptation produced through localized contexts going on in Area X?

Much of *Authority* takes place with the headquarters of the Southern Reach, a complex of interrogation rooms replete with one-way glass, laboratories and offices without windows, a 'dingy bizarre building with its worn green carpet' suffused with a 'sense of diminishment', where the sun 'half-heartedly pushed through the high rectangular windows', a space of blockage, disrepair and artifice that echoes, if weakly, a dying forest (VanderMeer 2014b, 5). It is an enclosed space, full of data that do not make sense, a non-place that repeats state forms of sovereign violence in architecture designed to contain (Augé 1992). The people there all seem to be running away from something into this dimly lit half-life full of secrets and loss. In this space, seemingly impervious to infiltration and contamination, the only way that absence can be recorded is as damage, death or annihilation. The Southern Reach is a space of sealed data, where practices of conversion and analysis take place; a space, even, of cultivation, where the material of Area X might be cultured into something useful, even valuable.

The cultivation metaphor invoked in Whitby's theory of terroir ends up driving him mad. The underlying assumption is that the kinds of biological dynamics at work, at pace, in Area X are producing novel forms of life that might also be attached to particular calculations of surplus value. This is epigenetics for niche-market capitalism: "'no two wines can be exactly the same because no combination of elements can be exactly the same,'" says Whitby (VanderMeer 2014b, 131). It is a way of domesticating what appears from the hermetic chambers of the Southern Reach to be a biological monstrosity, an unprecedented event, which has resisted years of scientific analysis. Control/John is unconvinced:

> The border had come down in the early morning, on a day, a date, that no one outside of the Southern Reach remembered or commemorated. Just that one inexplicable event had killed an estimated fifteen hundred people. How did you factor ghosts into any terroir? Did they deepen the flavour, or did they make things dry, chalky, irreconcilable? (VanderMeer 2014b, 133)

The exchange between Whitby and Control/John stands in for all the other moments of attempted scientific deduction, and the way that theories from the core are impressed upon peripheral spaces, while leaving out, ignoring or downplaying anomalies – the spaces and events and happenings left unaccounted for. Whitby is trying to make Area X work in a way that would make sense the violence of its operations. Control/John's train of thought in the passage above reveals an agitation, not only around cause and effect but also towards events happening simultaneously whose lack of legibility leads to a lack of memorialization. The history of Area X is disappearing because this history cannot be made sense of. For this reason, Area X cannot be made into culture, and if it cannot be made into culture, then it threatens to make the existence of all those lost by it and through it spectral. Whitby's epigenetic explanation via a metaphor of cultivation – and its implicitly extractivist logic – implies that there is the possibility of domesticating Area X's processes, for research and for profit, and upholding a colonial–capitalist time-regime as the basis for a theory of cultivation rooted in fantasies of individual self-transformation.

Control/John resists this instrumentalization of epigenetics for extractive purposes, because he senses that something different is happening with and through the matter of Area X. If Area X is simply a case of large-scale ecological cultivation, why is there a need to seal off the Southern Reach from its influence, and what is the reason for its violence? His unspoken rejoinder to Whitby comes through metaphors of texture and time (chalk and date), rather than product and space (wine and ground). This is a regime that privileges what can be produced, and the kinds of spaces necessary for production, and which invisibilizes the processes of labour and the extractions of time that production demands.

At the end of *Authority*, Control/John realizes that even the strict protocols of the Southern Reach, with its sealed environments and body suits, cannot guarantee immunity. Looking for Whitby, Control arrives at the double doors that lead to the science division; reaching for the handle, he finds nothing to grasp onto: 'there were no doors where there had always been doors before. Only wall. And the wall was soft and breathing under the touch of his hand' (VanderMeer 2014b, 290). This is a monstrous moment: a character rushing headlong through the corridors of the place he assumes is separate from what is happening directly outside it, behind the border of Area X, in a position of surveillance – a position of control – to find this outside bearing in and sealing him off from the area of the Southern Reach, the space that is supposed to yield answers. Instead, a living substance that breathes, and whose breath seems somehow connected to his presence. This is the moment that the analogy of whatever life-force is sweeping through Area X and past its supposed border – the analogy of contamination, of human impotence, of the insufficiency of modern reductionism, of the complexity and vast mystery of life on earth and its processes – moves over the border to empirical object. The haunting has become real, the monster has arrived; the ghostly incantation – 'where lies the strangling fruit' – is among the living. He realizes, 'the Southern Reach hadn't been a redoubt but instead some kind of slow incubator ... placing trust in a word like border had been a mistake, a trap. A slow unravelling of terms unrecognised until too late' (VanderMeer 2014b, 297). They have put their trust not only in the possibility of deciphering code but also in ensuring immunity through code (the syntax of boundaries, the architecture of the Southern Reach). The idea of the border does not retain its significance – it has fallen out of the semiotic economy. All along they were infiltrated by a presence – 'some presence' – that lay undetected.

The theme of an undetected presence begins to take up equivalent space to the novels' characters. In the final book of the trilogy, *Acceptance*, not all characters are visible or embodied. The third novel considers character as a process of constitution, where the borders between influence and actor are not determined by the constraints of plot. Identities shift, and not always in the way they have been programmed to, in response to aspects of the environment that are not always explained. The beginning of *Acceptance* reimagines Area X's ghosts, affects and hauntings as aspects of the environment that influence and alter its 'real' characters.

The book begins with another complementary pair, Suzanne and Henry – one a scientist and the other 'an investigator of the uncanny' (VanderMeer 2014c, 14) – decades before the events of the first book, and before Area X has been evacuated of humans. They have come to 'analyse and survey' what Suzanne calls 'prebiotic particles', and what Henry calls 'ghost energy' in the area (15). We meet them through Saul, the lighthouse keeper, who finds the two of them and their activities – séances and documentations – 'tiresome and increasingly predictable', and their theories of 'necromantic doubling' – 'which had to do with building a room of mirrors and darkness' – incomprehensible and 'lightweight' (14, 15). He has noticed something strange in the area since he moved to the lighthouse four years prior, but is now distracted by his relationship with a local man, Charlie, and the 'afterglow' of his nights with him (17). He does not understand what Suzanne and Henry might be so intent on finding, these outsiders getting caught up in their own imaginations. After all, this landscape can trick the mind:

> He knew the history of the coast here, the way that distance and silence magnified the mundane. How into those spaces and the fog and the empty line of the beach thoughts could turn to the uncanny and begin to create a story out of nothing. (VanderMeer 2014c, 14)

In the early parts of *Acceptance*, the uncanny is a character, an object in space rather than a description of sense or perception. Here, 'the history of the coast' and 'the uncanny' are made into corresponding things placed in contrast, representations of this space that offer different experiences of it, as if two characters turning up at different times to deliver different messages – not unlike the double act of Suzanne and Henry.

Much of the series' narrative tension is generated by the conflict between reality as determined by empirical data, and what matters in a given context. Saul's rumination seems to be a pragmatic stance on how to keep sane in a place whose physical and sensory properties – spaces and fog and the empty line of beach – might prompt flights of imagination. In this sense, creating a story out of nothing is a textual joke about writing: this is, after all, a narrative about an explosion that came from 'nowhere'. The full stop that leads into an incomplete sentence marks a border between knowing and unknowing. A word like 'mundane' grounds these thoughts, attached to 'magnified' through a brief alliteration, a phrase that seeks to contain and reduce fear and uncertainty. The full stop takes the place of an absent 'and' – mundane, and how . . . – cutting these two characters off from each other (history and the uncanny). This missing 'and' finds itself in the asyndeton of the second sentence, an anxious listing of details in an alienating and vacant stretch of land, as if looking for something solid to grasp. And yet 'nothing' hangs over the final part of the sentence, corresponding to the 'nowhere' on the book's final page, 'Because you are nowhere' (337). Does Area X 'exist' in the way the world has been imagined to exist, or does it force a suspension of any certainty around reality and its manifestations? Saul's rationalization gradually gives way to a realization that he is sharing the landscape with characters that he cannot see or fully perceive.

The uncanny-as-character becomes a way for the unexpressed and silenced to take up space in *Acceptance*. In this final instalment, Area X's mystery is no longer the narrative's driving force. The narrative is constructed around hearing and seeing silent and invisible forms brought into the Area alongside their expressed and visible counterparts. Time moves differently in Area X, recalling a moment in *Chernobyl Prayer* when one woman observes changes in older women still living in the Zone who 'refuse to abandon their cottages, their families' graveyards', who have come to expect treats and gifts from aid workers passing through, and who 'have a special relationship with time and death' (CP, 271). It is not that these women have become part of their environment, or that the act of staying in a toxic site is being romanticized; rather, they are living in a slower time, making the most of small opportunities to hustle – 'they have learned to talk' and 'some have become real film stars' (271) – while also encountering dying in the gerund, an event that is ongoing, attending to their dead loved ones as if they continue to take up space among the living. It is a collocation of different forms and experiences of time, in a phenomenology of dying that extends and contracts as the context necessitates. The spectre of death cannot be held at a remove; it is part of the relationship these women have with the 'weird planet' they find their homes transported to, part of the infrastructure of their dwellings, and has become their sense of place.

The abandoned lot that offers a site of refuge for the biologist in *Annihilation* also offers a way into thinking this, returning in altered form: the island that she travels to in *Acceptance*. At this point, she has found her husband's journal, and is moving across Area X in search of him. Coming across 'something pale and grub-like and monstrous [that] flailed and moaned' in a small patch of dirt, she realizes that it is the psychologist (VanderMeer 2014c, 161). The creature is in agony, traumatized and wounded, and to the biologist, 'it looked like a mistake, a misfire by an Area X that had assimilated so much so beautifully and so seamlessly' (162). She feels no pity for the creature's pain, and wonders instead whether 'what this expedition member had brought to Area X had contributed to this final state' (163). The suggestion here is some form of biosynthesis between individual and ecology – a synthesis that has caused all sorts of other transformations of those arriving in Area X and in those outside it. This synthesis does not work for the best possible outcome. The resulting forms express what might have been hidden away or concealed. Area X has the power to read experience as code: it is the territory that knows how to decode its interlopers and to incorporate them into it, rather than the other way round.

Biomorphism extends from the words on the wall of the tower to species transforming into other species, a speculative reflection on the genetic proximity of humans to nonhuman lifeforms. Swimming to the island, the biologist finds her husband, or at least a form that resembles him, 'if not in the form in which I had known him' (VanderMeer 2014c, 167). This is the intertextual moment between the biologist of *Chernobyl Prayer* doing her fieldwork on an uninhabited island, visited daily by a mouse, and the biologist in *Annihilation*. On another island unpopulated by humans, the biologist finds evidence of another human presence, 'the blackened ash of an old fire' in a small cove, where she seeks shelter (168). An owl has been hovering near her since her arrival, 'huge, four pounds at least', and ends up 'perched opposite me across the fire, atop my backpack' (168–9). It has brought her a rabbit to eat. If the husband's place in the home had been the kitchen, the space associated with the provision of food, then this owl seems to be taking on a similar role, hunting for the biologist. The reader has already been prepared for this moment by the transformed appearance of the psychologist. The owl stays, 'always watching over me, always nearby. Always a little closer, a little tamer, but never completely tame,' dropping twigs at her feet like small gifts, constantly re-establishing contact (169). Their relationship starts to be more reciprocal as she spends more and more time on the island. Empirical proof that this is her husband never arrives, but the relationship stands in for the one that disintegrated outside Area X. It becomes a relationship of reparation, a recognition of some kind that eases the biologist's prior loss. It lasts thirty years, roughly the time they would have had left in their marriage, before the owl becomes old and dies.

Area X becomes a space of wish-fulfilment. Just as it is not clear whether or not the owl is some form of the husband, it is not certain whether these conspicuously convenient transformations of psychologist and husband are not in some way creations of the biologist's imagination, 'out of nothing'. Is the uncanny-as-character taking figments and fragments out of her memory and rearranging the reality of Area X to correspond to it? What is clear is that logic-work based on scientific reason cannot help her survive; instead, her survival becomes 'predicated on hurting myself', a way of sustaining her identity as an autonomous being (179). Part of this desire to remain separate from the surroundings comes from her desire to coexist – in a situation of contrast – with the owl, their differences pronounced and rearticulated over the course of a lifetime. Once he dies (and he has become 'he' rather than 'it' by this point), the biologist gives up the form she protected through pain and suffering, and moves into something else. This gap of thirty years, a calculable measurement of time, is the fulfilment of the fantasy that she brought with her into Area X – a fantasy of proximity, and of finally being able to reciprocate, of reunion and of living out a life. It is fulfilled on a vector, without guarantees, somewhere between what makes sense and what cannot be proved, in a quiet periphery.

In the Southern Reach trilogy, characterization is constituted by ongoing acts of mediation and compromise, rather than a definitive sense of reaching a clear horizon. This vast Area where wish-fulfilment happens 'in concert with' the annihilation of self is the primary metaphor of the series, and the question left open at the end. At its most philosophically captivating, it makes space for a plurality of tactics that might lead to all sorts of unpredictable and possibly illegible transformations, like birds that might change, mid-flight, into different species of winged creatures. Rather than taking this literally – or, more specifically – taxonomically (that is, organisms as products in space), these transformations gesture to forms of time that do not just accelerate or slow down evolutionary change, but through which a whole panoply of possible forms, silenced or emerging, might be expressed, depending on circumstances; that is, depending on chance junctures of different trajectories available at a given moment. Unlike the disappearance of the subject into algorithms, this form of characterization has more in common with those fossils at the Burgess Shale: weird, complex experiments of life that may go nowhere, but which lived, and whose living left traces, and that show us that 'contingency matters where it counts most', where 'a million scenarios' might play out, 'each perfectly sensible' (Gould 1989, 321). Making these million scenarios both possible and sensible is the peculiar task of speculative aesthetics.

VanderMeer and Alexievich's narratives of peripheral shock take place in contexts where the full picture is not available, where evidence and procedures of data collection cannot be relied on, and where various kinds of silence, absence and refusal come to stand in as characters that influence events and trajectories. These are worlds on the make, where the profound ontological insecurity of not being able to access information necessitates a radical reconsideration of what can be known, and whether reality can ever be fully constituted by breaking it down into its smallest component parts. Enduring in these texts is not a matter of manipulating the smallest possible scale, but of moving between scales – massive and molecular. Recourse to a romanticized ecological vision of human futures is not available; these are violent topographies whose power over life remains largely invisible. Unlike Smith's invisible hand, they are not directed towards 'good' outcomes, nor are they centred on individual flourishing. It is this with which metaphors of the postgenomic era now grapple.

# Disappearance, community, characterization, genre and scale

This book has attempted to think through narrative in the age of the genome by way of some of the genome's fictions, emphasizing the globalization of genomics while also attending to some of its anachronisms and failures in peripheral and marginalized contexts, across geographical and historical differences. These fictions encompass policy, science writing and biological theory as much as aesthetics, and genomics' historical attachments to both social policy and evolutionary theory mean that its proponents are also reliant on narratives of social good to make some of their claims to its universal applicability. Forms of scientific praxis adopt and adapt narrative forms to transmit their findings, but these forms are embedded in ideological infrastructures that, in turn, attach particular values to these findings – political, cultural and economic. I'll end by going through some of the big thematic questions that this book raises through the lens of genomic science – its epistemology, its history, its practices and its representations – and with some thoughts on what the postgenomic era yields for literary and cultural studies.

First, disappearance. Chapter 1 looked at the crisis of Anglo American hegemony and the end of the post-war welfare consensus in the 1970s through the lens of sociobiology and the selfish gene. I argued that Richard Dawkins's description of genes as selective agents operating at great distance, managing the 'survival machines' in which they are housed, while also competing with each other, was as much an argument against collective organization (group selection) as it was a theory about the role of genes in evolution. With the gene as the new unit of calculation in selective accounts of evolution, liberal narratives of character development tied to a public sphere begin to disappear, replaced by a consumer/innovator whose primary horizon is endless self-fashioning. This emerges in various ruptures of kinship, in which heteronormative forms of social reproduction exclude relations with racialized and queer characters. Paradoxically, it is the inclusion of otherness through a typologized eugenic hierarchy in the name of a supposed multicultural liberalism that permits novel forms of neo-Darwinian violence.

By the 1990s, as Chapter 3 argued, individuals are broken down into fragments – sequences of code, body parts, hair, skin and nails – while the memoir's first-person struggles to grapple with the assault to a sense of self derived from remembering the past. In place of this, science memoirs which emphasize utopian genomic futures free from disease become technologies of partial amnesia. Memoirs serve as monuments to an ideal subject of genomic futures, while also facilitating the disappearance of this subject into disaggregated data bodies. This sees the subject disappear from the marketplace of self-fashioning to machinic enslavement, where data is stolen and co-opted as surplus value under new forms of algorithmic governmentality. This logic of disappearance, as a principle of capitalist accumulation and technology of control, is nothing new. Chapter 4 considered uses of genetic ancestry testing for tracing lost and broken genealogies across the historical void of the Middle Passage, from the United States to West Africa, and the attending ambivalence around genomics as a de facto good among Black American communities via a history of disappeared, violated, mutilated and stolen Black lives. For all that it makes visible, genomics also engenders new forms of disappearance and silence: the disappearance of non-coded effects and experiences, of data, of history and of alternative modes of reading embodied relations.

Second, community. The genomic model of health and identity privileges a model of heteronormative reproduction that assumes the legibility of family health and ancestral history, as well as often using categories of ethnicity that correspond to colonial topographies of the globe, and imperial ethnologies (European, Asian, etc.). While initiatives like the Human Genome Diversity Project aimed to address some of these problems – as well as the lack of ethnic diversity in the data collected through the Human Genome Project – methodologies often betray problematic starting positions, and produce exploitative practices of data collection. Reading narrative in the age of the genome makes it possible to chart a shift in the way that descriptions of community and relatedness have had to be reconceived in molecular biology following the results of the HGP. This is bound to the challenges of accessing relevant data: when information runs dry, or when there is not much of it to begin with, alternative modes of narrating belonging and history emerge. These descriptions often already had precedents in peripheral and marginalized histories and cosmologies; the examples I have looked at here are speculative and fictive forms of kinship in African American history, made necessary by the rupture of family units through enslavement, forced displacement and the selling on of enslaved peoples from place to place. Information about genealogy is often insufficient or inaccessible. Extended kinship networks move across space and time, covering continent and diaspora, in ways that are not always certain or reliable, but which offer ways of holding the past where genomics fails.

Chapters 2 and 5 consider community through alternative accounts of biological change, where evolution does not happen at the level of individual, but, in Soviet biology, at a collective level and, in postgenomic narratives, as the result of complex interdependencies at the level of ecosystem, in which individuals move between habitats while also being sites of habitation for other forms of life. Neither of these accounts takes community as a unilateral or generic good. Instead, these narratives foreground infrastructures of violence, corporate and state responsibility, and industrial toxicity in their imaginings of proximity and interdependence. They make space for a more conditional and speculative interpretation of evolution, whereby the species called *Homo sapiens* – to follow Stephen Jay Gould – was only one evolutionary possibility out of a number of others, happening to emerge out of a plurality of other happenings, by chance.

Third, characterization. While narrative in the age of the genome registers the disappearance of the subject of liberal humanism into algorithms – and as such, presents a crisis for character development – I have also looked at examples where this disappearance is resisted or countered via emergent conceptions of character in the postgenomic era. For this, I offered the concept of transitional characterization, whereby characters shift past certainties of identification (of themselves, of others, of their surroundings), and considered how this makes new questions of political engagement and praxis possible in the postgenomic era. In Chapter 2, this is reflected through a shift from descriptions of exposure, in which the environment acts upon the individual, to proximity, whereby destructive forces are closer at hand than they seem, and often imperceptible. In Chapter 5, characters move from their declared function in the texts – 'biologist', 'husband', 'Control', 'lighthouse keeper' and the plethora of types of labour described by the interviewees of *Chernobyl Prayer* – through the strange peripheral topographies they find themselves in, illegible and secret, finding themselves and their practices transformed in the process.

Who is the protagonist in narratives of the genome? Chapter 3 suggests that for all the efforts of the HGP's protagonists, it was never humanity, or at least the version of humanity premised by the project. If anything, the characters that linger longest in these texts are the 'Old Ones', to borrow again from Gould and the Burgess Shale: those characters exorcized by ideologies of genealogy that privilege biological families – and families able to stay together. These are the ones that disappear out of data or into algorithms, the silences of the genomes where unexpressed potential waits, the uncanny landscapes that invent characters in the imaginations of their visitors, and lost ancestors whose voices surge into the present.

Fourth, genre. Many of the texts in this book fall under the heading of genre fiction: science fiction and fantasy, popular memoir, Black horror and oral history. This signifies two things: first, that genetic and genomic fictions have created a particular – and particularly lucrative – niche of cultural imaginaries. Second, the generic malleability afforded by genre fiction makes possible some of the narratological experiments in these texts. Not only are lots of these texts genre fiction, but they also move across genres in order to bend, twist, and tilt the metaphors of realism in their explorations of the strange possibilities of thinking life at the level of molecule, atom and gene. Genre implies borders, control, boundaries and constraints; moving across genre, using multiple strategies, becomes a way to scan the metaphorical infrastructure of narrative – its common place assumptions and semiotic economies – and of dismantling some of the analytic categories it might seem to take for granted.

Narrative in the age of the genome is a crisis of genre, because it is above all a crisis of the subject and the way this subject positions themselves in space, across time, and in relation to others and their surroundings; in short, it is a crisis of the meaning of freedom. It involves the ongoing conflict – by no means novel, and constitutive of narrative – between experiencing oneself in the world (subjectivity) and being identified by others (identity). In the various experiments some of the texts discussed here conduct with form, plot, character and place, genre becomes a site for overturning this conflict, not for the sake of utopian futures, but to rework side-lined mythologies of chance and contingency into workable and thinkable practices.

One final point about scale. Where is DNA? Visible via microscopes or in computerized representations, thinking life at the scale of the molecular privileges a rarefied and increasingly privatized sphere of biotechnological and biomedical analysis. DNA is now read and tracked at border crossings to determine entry, to prove or disprove family connections, to design precision medicine treatments, to solve crimes, to trace the aetiology of diseases, to map evolutionary history and to identify biological remains. This is world-building at the scale of micrology. Like Vincent trapped on the molecular highway in *Gattaca*, crossing the road in blind faith, existing in genomic narratives forces characters to risk all kinds of insecurity for the sake of reaching a conclusion that looks something like a good life, or a satisfactory ending. Part of the enormous and continued cultural power of the genome is the way it casts out time like a vast bright net across the stories passed down and across about human worlds past, present and future, and all their countless differences. It promises to capture everything. Its failure to do so is not a failure of technology, science or data. The limits of genomics are in the narratives that its practices have not been able to read: the ways that time does not capture consequences in advance, but proliferates chance.

# Works cited

Alexievich, S. (1997), *Chernobyl Prayer*. London: Penguin.
Allen, E., Beckwith, B., Beckwith, J., Chorover, S., Culver, D., Duncan, M., Gould, S. J., Hubbard, R., Inouye, H., Leeds, A., Lewontin, R., Mandansky, C., Miller, L., Pyeritz, R., Rosenthal, M., and Schreier, H. (August 1975), 'Against "Sociobiology"'. *The New York Review of Books*. Accessed online 20 March 2020: http://www.nybooks.com/articles/1975/11/13/against-sociobiology/
Aranova, E., Baker, K. and Oreskes, N. (2010), 'Big Science and Big Data in Biology: From the International Geophysical Year through the International Biological Program to the Long Term Ecological Research (LTER) Network, 1957-Present'. *Historical Studies in the Natural Sciences* 40.2: 183–224.
Ardrey, R. (1970), *The Social Contract*. New York: Atheneum Books.
Arendt, H. (1958), *The Human Condition*. Chicago: University of Chicago Press.
Arrighi, G. (1994), *The Long Twentieth Century: Money, Power, and the Origins of Our Time*. London: Verso.
Augé, M. (1992), *Non-Places: An Introduction to an Anthropology of Supermodernity*. London: Verso.
Bal, M. (2007), 'Over-writing as Un-writing: Descriptions, World-Making, and Novelistic Time'. In: F. Moretti (ed.), *The Novel: Volume Two*. Princeton, NJ: Princeton University Press. 571–610.
Baptist, E. E. (2014), *The Half Has Never Been Told: Slavery and the Making of American Capitalism*. New York: Basic Books.
Barad, K. (2007), *Meeting the Universe Halfway: Quantum Physics and the Entanglement of Matter and Meaning*. Durham, NC: Duke University Press.
Bataille, G. (1988 [1949]), *The Accursed Share: An Essay on General Economy*. New York: Zone Books.
Bauer, S. (2014), 'Mutations in Soviet Public Health Science: Post-Lysenko Medical Genetics, 1969–1991'. *Studies in the History and Philosophy of Biological and Biomedical Sciences* 47.1: 163–72.
Bauer, S. (2015), 'Population Genetics, Cybernetics of Difference, and Pasts in the Present: Soviet and Post-Soviet Maps on Human Variation.' *History of the Human Sciences* 28.5: 146–67.
Baylin, S. (2016), 'Jacob, Monod, the Lac Operon, and the PaJaMa Experiment – Gene Expression Circuitry Changing the Face of Cancer Research'. *Cancer Research* 76.8: 2060–2.
Beer, G. (2010 [1983]), *Darwin's Plots: Evolutionary Narrative in Darwin, George Eliot and Nineteenth Century Fiction*. Cambridge: Cambridge University Press.

Beever, J., Tønnessen, M. and Hendlin, Y. H. (2015), 'Interview on Biosemiotic Ethics with Wendy Wheeler'. *Zeitschrift für Semiotik* 37.3–4: 177–87.

Benjamin, R. (2019), *Race After Technology: Abolitionist Tools for the New Jim Code*. London: Polity.

Benjamin, W. (1968 [1935]), 'The Work of Art in the Age of Mechanical Reproduction'. In: H. Arendt (ed.), *Illuminations*. Trans. Harry Zohn. New York: Harcourt. 217–52.

Bennett, J. (2009), *Vibrant Matter: A Political Ecology of Things*. Durham, NC: Duke University Press.

Bentley, N. (2009), 'The Fourth Dimension: Kinlessness and African American Narrative'. *Critical Inquiry* 35.2: 270–92.

Bergson, H. (2003 [1907]), *Creative Evolution*. Trans. Arthur Mitchell. London: Dover.

Bodin, P. and Suslov, M. (2020), *The Post-Soviet Politics of Utopia*. London: I. B. Tauris.

Bradway, T. (2017), *Queer Experimental Literature: The Affective Politics of Bad Reading*. New York: Palgrave Macmillan.

Bressey, C., Cain, J., Das, S., Fearn, T., Fonagy, P., Garb, T., Talwar, A., Thomas, M., Vashist, N. (2020), 'Investigation into the History of Eugenics at UCL'. Accessed online 2 March 2020: https://legacies-of-eugenics.org/wp-content/uploads/2020/02/recommendations-ucl-eugenics-inquiry-more-group-university-college-london-february-2020.pdf

Brown, K. (2019), *Manual for Survival: A Chernobyl Guide to the Future*. London: Penguin.

Buck-Morss, S. (2000), *Dreamworld and Catastrophe: The Passing of Mass Utopia in East and West*. Cambridge, MA: MIT Press.

Buckley, J. H. (1994), *The Turning Key: Autobiography and the Subjective Impulse since 1800*. Cambridge, MA: Harvard University Press.

Bulychev, K. (1985), 'Another's Memory'. In: K. Bulychev, *Earth and Elsewhere*. Trans. Roger DeGaris. London: Collier Macmillan.

Burgin, X., Blackwell, A. and Burrows, D. (dirs.) (2019), *Horror Noire: A History of Black Horror*.

Bürkner, D. (2014), 'The Chernobyl Landscape and the Aesthetics of Invisibility, Photography and Culture'. *Photography and Culture* 7.1: 21–39.

Butler, J. (2009), *Frames of War: When Is Life Grievable?* London: Verso.

Carroll, R. (2012), *Rereading Heterosexuality: Feminism, Queer Theory and Contemporary Fiction*. Edinburgh: Edinburgh University Press.

Césaire, A. (2001 [1939]), *Notebook of a Return to a Native Land*. Trans. and Ed. Clayton Eshleman and Annette Smith. Middleton, CT: Wesleyan Poetry.

Chakravarti, A. (2015), 'Perspectives on Human Variation through the Lens of Diversity and Race'. *Cold Spring Harbor Perspectives in Biology* 7.9: a023358.

Chan, E. K. (2001), '(Vulgar) Identity Politics in Outer Space: Delany's Triton and the Heterotopian Narrative'. *Journal of Narrative Theory* 31.2: 180–213.

Chandler, A. (1977), *The Visible Hand: The Managerial Revolution in American Business*. Harvard, MA: Harvard University Press.

Chandler, M. (2018), 'Techno-Ethno Genealogy: An African Ancestry Narrative in the Digital Age'. *Genealogy* 2: 32–40.

Chen, M. (2011), 'Toxic Animacies, Inanimate Affections'. *GLQ: A Journal of Lesbian and Gay Studies* 17.2–3: 265–86.
Clare, E. (2017), *Brilliant Imperfection: Grappling with Cure*. Durham, NC: Duke University Press.
Csicsery-Ronay, I. (2004), 'Science Fiction and the Thaw'. *Science Fiction Studies* 31.3: 337–44.
Davidson, G. (2008), 'Sexuality and the Statistical Imaginary in Samuel R. Delany's Trouble on Triton'. In: W. Pearson, V. Hollinger and J. Gordon (eds), *Queer Universes: Sexualities in Science Fiction*. Liverpool: Liverpool University Press. 101–20.
Dawkins, R. (1990 [1976]), *The Selfish Gene*. Oxford: Oxford University Press.
Dawkins, R. (1986), *The Blind Watchmaker*. New York: Norton & Company.
DeJong Lambert, W. (2013), *The Cold War Politics of Genetic Research: An Introduction to the Lysenko Affair*. New York: Springer.
Delany, S. (1996 [1976]), *Trouble on Triton: An Ambiguous Heterotopia*. Middletown, CT: Wesleyan University Press.
Deleuze, G. (1992), 'Postscript on the Societies of Control'. *October* 59: 3–7.
Deleuze, G. and Guattari, F. (1987 [1980]), *A Thousand Plateaus: Capitalism and Schizophrenia*. Trans. Brian Massumi. Minneapolis, MN: University of Minnesota Press.
Du Bois, W. E. B. (1993), 'Liberia, the League, and the United States'. *Foreign Affairs* 11.4: 695.
Duden, B. and Samerski, S. (2008), '"Pop Genes": The Symbolic Effects of the Release of "Genes" into Ordinary Speech'. In: F. Molfino and F. Zucco (eds), *Women in Biotechnology: Creating Interfaces*. Heidelberg: Springer. 161–70.
Fanon, F. (2008 [1952]), *Black Skin, White Masks*. Trans. Charles Lam Markmann. London: Pluto.
Fanon, F. (2001 [1963]), *The Wretched of the Earth*. Trans. Richard Philcox. London: Penguin.
Fortun, M. (2008), *Promising Genomics*. Harvard, MA: MIT Press.
Fortun, M. (2016), 'What Toll Pursuit: Affective Assemblages in Genomics and Postgenomics'. In: Richardson and Stevens. 32–55.
Foucault, M. (1978), *The History of Sexuality*, Vol. I. Trans. Robert Hurley. New York: Pantheon.
Foucault, M. (2003), *Society Must Be Defended*. Trans. David Macey. New York: Picador.
Foucault, M. (2003), *Society Must Be Defended: Lectures at the Collège de France 1975–76*. New York: Picador.
Freeman, E. (2005), 'Time Binds, or, Erotohistoriography'. *Social Text* 84–85, 23.3–4: 57–68.
Fuller, S. (2011), *Humanity 2.0: What It Means to be Human, Past, Present and Future*. London: Palgrave.
Galton, F. (1869), *Hereditary Genius*. London: Macmillan Publishers.
Garay, J. P. and Gray, J. W. (2012), 'Omics and Therapy: A Basis for Precision Medicine'. *Molecular Oncology* 6: 128–39.
Gill, J. (2020), *Biofictions: Race, Genetics and the Contemporary Novel*. London: Bloomsbury.

Gilroy, P. (1993), *The Black Atlantic: Modernity and Double Consciousness*. London: Verso, 1993.

Gilroy, P. (2004), *Postcolonial Melancholia*. New York: Columbia University Press.

Gofman, J. (1992), 'Biomedical "Un-knowledge" and Nuclear Pollution: A Common Sense Proposal'. Public talk. On the occasion of the Right Livelihood Award, Stockholm, 9 December 1992.

Gorky, M., Radek, K., Bukharin, N. and Zhadanov, A. (1977), *Soviet Writers' Congress, 1934: The Debate on Socialist Realism and Modernism*. London: Lawrence and Wishart. Accessed online 20 March 2020: https://www.marxists.org/subject/art/lit_crit/sovietwritercongress/index.htm

Gould, S. J. (1988), 'Kropotkin Was No Crackpot'. *Natural History Magazine* 97.7: 12–21.

Gould, S. J. (1989), *Wonderful Life: Burgess Shale and the Nature of History*. New York: W. W. Norton & Co.

Gould, S. J. (2001), 'Humbled by the Genome's Mysteries'. *New York Times*. Accessed online 25 October 2019: https://www.nytimes.com/2001/02/19/opinion/humbled-by-the-genome-s-mysteries.html

Gould, S. J., Alper, J., Beckwith, J., Bruce, B., Crompton, R., Dusek, V., Egelman, E., Hubbard, R., Inouye, H., Lange, R., Leibowitz, L., Lewontin, R. and Salzman, F. (1979), 'The Politics of Sociobiology'. *New York Review of Books*. Accessed 20 March 2020: http://www.nybooks.com/articles/1979/05/31/the-politics-of-sociobiology/

Gould, S. J. and Lewontin, R. (1979), 'The Spandrels of San Marco and the Panglossian Paradigm: A Critique of the Adaptationist Programme'. *Proceedings of the Royal Society of London*. Series B 205.1161: 581–98.

Graham, L. (2016), *Lysenko's Ghost*. Cambridge, MA: Harvard University Press.

Greenidge, K. (2018), 'The Family History DNA Can't Reveal'. *New York Times*. Accessed online 20 March 2020: https://www.nytimes.com/2018/12/15/opinion/sunday/dna-ancestry-test.html

Griffin, G. (2009), 'Science and the Cultural Imaginary: The Case of Kazuo Ishiguro's Never Let Me Go'. *Textual Practice* 23.4: 645–63.

Gross, H., Joy, L., Lingenfelter, K. and Nolan, J. (2016), *Westworld*. HBO.

Gutman, H. (1977), *The Black Family in Slavery and Freedom, 1750–1925*. New York: Vintage.

Gyasi, Y. (2016), *Homegoing*. London: Penguin.

Habermas, J. (1989 [1962]), *The Structural Transformation of the Public Sphere: An Inquiry into a Category of Bourgeois Society*. Trans. T. Burger and F. Lawrence. London: Polity.

Hacking, I. (1990), *The Taming of Chance*. Cambridge: Cambridge University Press.

Haley, A. (1976), *Roots: The Saga of an American Family*. New York: Doubleday.

Hanson, C. (2013), *Eugenics, Literature and Culture in Postwar Britain*. London: Routledge, 2013.

Hanson, C. (2020), *Genetics and the Literary Imagination*. Oxford: Oxford University Press.

Haraway, D. (2016), *Staying With The Trouble*. Durham, NC: Duke University Press.
Hardt, M. and Negri, A. (2009), *Commonwealth*. Cambridge, MA: Belknap Press of Harvard University Press.
Harrison, M. J. (2005), 'Clone Alone'. *Guardian*. 26 February 2005. Accessed online 5 March 2020: https://www.theguardian.com/books/2005/feb/26/bookerprize2005.bookerprize
Hartman, S. (1997), *Scenes of Subjection: Terror, Slavery, and Self-Making in Nineteenth Century America*. Oxford: Oxford University Press.
Hartman, S. (2006), *Lose Your Mother: A Journey Along the Atlantic Slave Route*. New York: Farrar, Straus and Giroux.
Hobbes, T. (2017 [1651]), *Leviathan; or, The Matter, Forme and Power of a Commonwealth Ecclesiasticall and Civil*. London: Penguin.
Hoffmeyer, J. (2008), *Biosemiotics: An Examination into the Signs of Life and the Life of Signs*. Trans. Jesper Hoffmeyer and Donald Favareau. Scranton, PA: University of Scranton Press.
Hundarova, T. (2001), 'The Canon Reversed: New Ukrainian Literature of the 1990s'. *Journal of Ukrainian Studies* 26.1–2: 249–70.
Huneman, P. and Walsh, D. M. (2017), *Challenging the Modern Synthesis: Adaptation, Development, and Inheritance*. Oxford: Oxford University Press.
Huntingdon, S. (2002 [1996]), *The Clash of Civilisations and the Remaking of the World Order*. New York: Simon and Schuster.
Huxley, A. (2007 [1932]), *Brave New World*. London: Vintage.
Ireland, A. (2019), 'Alien Rhythms'. *Alienist* 6: 58–71.
Ishiguro, K. (2005), *Never Let Me Go*. London: Faber and Faber.
Ivanov, V. (2011), 'The Lessons of the Strugatskys'. *Russian Studies in Literature* 47.4: 7–30.
Jablonka, E. and Lamb, M. (2005), *Evolution in Four Dimensions: Genetic, Epigenetic, Behavioural and Symbolic Variation in the History of Life*. Boston, MA: The MIT Press.
James, E. and Morel, E. (eds) (2020), *Environment and Narrative: New Directions in Econarratology*. Columbus, OH: The Ohio State University Press.
James, J. (2016), 'The Womb of Western Theory: Trauma, Time Theft, and the Captive Maternal'. *Carceral Notebooks* 12: 253–96.
Johnson, H. (16 February 1972), 'Blackouts Will Total Nine Hours Daily'. *Guardian*.
Kay, L. (2000), *Who Wrote the Book of Life? A History of the Genetic Code*. Stanford, CA: Stanford University Press.
Keller, E. F. (1992), 'Nature, Nurture and the Human Genome Project'. In: D. J. Kevles and L. Hood (eds), *The Code of Codes: Scientific and Social Issues in the Human Genome Project*. Cambridge, MA: Harvard University Press. 281–99.
Keller, E. F. (2000), *The Century of the Gene*. Harvard, MA: Harvard University Press.
Keller, E. F. (2010), *The Mirage of a Space between Nature and Nurture*. Durham, NC: Duke University Press.
Keller, E. F. (2016), 'The Postgenomic Genome'. In: Richardson and Stevens. 9–31.
Kevles, D. J. (1985), *In the Name of Eugenics*. New York: Alfred A. Knopf.

Kirksey, S. E. and Helmreich, S. (2010), 'The Emergence of Multispecies Ethnography'. *Cultural Anthropology* 25.4: 545–76.

Kowalski, C. J. and Mrdjenovich, A. J. (2017), 'Personalized Medicine, Genomics and Enhancement: Monuments to Neoliberalism'. *Journal of Clinical and Experimental Medicine* 5.3: 75–92.

Kropotkin, P. (1902), *Mutual Aid: A Factor of Evolution*. New York: McClure Phillips and Co. Accessed online 20 March 2020: http://dwardmac.pitzer.edu/Anarchist_Archives/kropotkin/mutaidcontents.html

Lacan, J. (2001), *Écrits: A Selection*. Trans. Alan Sheridan. London: Routledge.

Lambert, M. (2017), '"Problem Families" and the Postwar Welfare State in the North West of England, 1943–74'. Doctoral thesis: Lancaster University.

Laughlin, R. (2005), *A Different Universe: Reinventing Physics from the Bottom Down*. New York: Basic Books.

Lazzarato, M. (2014), *Signs and Machines: Capitalism and the Production of Subjectivity*. Los Angeles, CA: Semiotext(e).

Leitenberg, M., Zilinskas, R. A. and Kuhn, J. H. (2012), *The Soviet Biological Weapons Program*. Cambridge, MA: Harvard University Press.

Leroux, D. (2019), *Distorted Descent: White Claims to Indigenous Identity*. Winnipeg, Manitoba: University of Manitoba Press.

Lessing, D. (1988 [1974]), *The Memoirs of a Survivor*. London: Vintage.

Levina, E. S. and Sedov, A. E. (2000), 'Molecular Biology in Soviet Russia'. *Molecular Biology* 34.3: 420–77.

Levine, P. (2010), 'Anthropology, Colonialism and Eugenics'. In: A. Bashford and P. Levine (eds), *The Oxford Handbook of the History of Eugenics*. Oxford: Oxford University Press. 46–61.

Lindee, M. S. (1994), *Suffering Made Real: American Science and the Survivors of Hiroshima*. Chicago, IL: University of Chicago Press.

Linton, M. (22 April 1988), 'The Sami and Chernobyl'. *New Statesman*. 16–18.

Lowe, L. (2015), *The Intimacies of Four Continents*. Durham, NC: Duke University Press.

Malabou, C. (2016), *Epigenesis and Rationality*. Trans. Carolyn Shread. Oxford: Wiley.

Malthus, T. R. (1807), *An Essay on the Principle of Population, or, A View of Its Past and Present Effects, Volume II, Fourth Edition*. London: J. Johnson.

Mantel, H. (22 May 2010), 'The Immortal Life of Henrietta Lacks by Rebecca Skloot'. *Guardian*. Accessed online 20 March 2020: https://www.theguardian.com/books/2010/may/22/life-henrietta-lacks-rebecca-skloot

Marchenisi, I. (2017), 'A New Literary Genre. Trauma and the Individual Perspective in Svetlana Alexievich's *Chernobyl'skaia molitva*'. *Canadian Slavonic Papers* 59.3–4: 313–29.

Margulis, L. (1991), *Symbiosis as a Source of Evolutionary Innovation: Speciation and Morphogenesis*. Boston, MA: The MIT Press.

Margulis, L. and Sagan, D. (2003), *Acquiring Genomes: A Theory of the Origin of Species*. New York: Basic Books.

Marris, E. (2005), 'Free Genome Databases Finally Defeat Celera'. *Nature* 435: 6.
Mazumdar, P. (1991), *Eugenics, Genetics and Human Failings*. London: Routledge.
Mbembe, A. (2003), 'Necropolitics'. Trans. Libby Meintjes. *Public Culture* 15.1: 11–40.
McClintock, B. (1993), 'The Significance of Responses of the Genome to Challenge'. In: Tore Frängsmyr and Jan Lindsten (eds), *Nobel Lectures, Physiology or Medicine 1981–1990*. Singapore: World Scientific. 180–99.
McKittrick, K. (2006), *Demonic Grounds: Black Women and the Cartographies of Struggle*. Minneapolis, MN: University of Minnesota Press.
McLellan, D. (ed.) (1971), *Marx's Grundisse*. St. Albans: Paladin.
Means Coleman, R. G. (2011), *Horror Noire: Blacks in American Horror Films from 1890s to Present*. London: Routledge.
Meloni, M. (2019), *Impressionable Biologies*. London: Routledge.
Mendlesohn, D. (2010), 'But Enough About Me'. *New Yorker*. 25 January 2010.
Moore, J. (2013), *Capitalism and the Web of Life: Ecology and the Accumulation of Capital*. London: Verso.
Moore, J. and Patel, R. (2018), 'Unearthing the Capitalocene: Towards a Reparations Ecology'. *Roar* 7.
Müller, R., Hanson, C., Hanson, M., Penkler, M., Samaras, G., Chiapperino, L., Dupré, J., Kenney, M., Kuzawa, C., Latimer, J., Lloyd, S., Lunkes, A., Macdonald, M., Meloni, M., Nerlich, B. Panese, F., Pickersgill, M., Richardson, S., Rüegg, J., Schmitz, S., Stelmach, A. and Villa, P. I. (2017), 'The Biosocial Genome? Interdisciplinary Perspectives on Environmental Epigenetics, Health and Society'. *Science and Society* 18.10: 1677–82.
Nelkin, D. and Lindee, M. S. (1995), *The DNA Mystique: The Gene as a Cultural Icon*. Ann Arbor, MI: University of Michigan Press.
Nelson, A. (2016), *The Social Life of DNA: Race, Reparations, and Reconciliation After the Genome*. Boston, MA: Beacon Press.
Niccols, A. (dir.) (1997), *Gattaca*.
Niewöhner, J. and Lock, M. (2018), 'Situating Local Biologies: Anthropological Perspectives on Environment/Human Entanglements'. *Biosocieties* 13: 681–97.
Noble, V. (2008), *Inside the Welfare State*. London: Routledge.
Novas, C. and Rose, N. (2005), 'Biological Citizenship'. In: Aihwa Ong and Stephen J. Collier (eds), *Global Assemblages: Technology, Politics, and Ethics as Anthropological Problems*. Oxford: Blackwell Publishing. 439–63.
Pandey, A. (2011), '"Cloning Words": Euphemism, Neologism and Dysphemism as Literary Devices in Kazuo Ishiguro's *Never Let Me Go*'. *Changing English* 18.4: 383–96.
Patterson, O. (1982), *Slavery and Social Death: A Comparative Study*. Cambridge, MA: Harvard University Press.
Pearson, W. G. (2009), 'Destiny and Destinerrance in Samuel R. Delany's *Trouble on Triton*'. *Science Fiction Studies* 36.3: 461–77.
Peele, J. (dir.) (2017), *Get Out*.
Peele, J. (dir.) (2019), *US*.

Peirce, C. S. (1931–35 [1867]), 'On A New List of Categories'. In: C. Hartshorne and P. Weiss (eds), *Collected Papers of Charles Sanders Peirce*, Vol 2. Cambridge, MA: Harvard University Press. 49–58.
Perez, M. (2013), 'Evolutionary Activism: Stephen Jay Gould, the New Left, and Sociobiology'. *Endeavour* 37.2: 104–11.
Petryna, A. (2002), *Life Exposed: Biological Citizens After Chernobyl*. Princeton, NJ: Princeton University Press.
Phillips, J. (2006), 'The 1972 Miners' Strike: Popular Agency and Industrial Politics in Britain'. *Contemporary British History* 20: 187–207.
Pihet, V. (2017), 'Speculative Narration: A Conversation with Valérie Pihet, Didier Debaise, Katrin Solhdju and Fabrizio Terranova'. *Parse Journal* 6: 65–77.
Plokhy, S. (2019), *Chenobyl: History of a Tragedy*. London: Penguin.
Poli, R. (2017), *Introduction to Complexity Studies*. London: Springer.
Prainsack, B. (2017), *Personalized Medicine: Empowered Patients in the 21st Century?* New York: New York University Press.
Rajan, K. S. (2006), *Biocapital: The Constitution of Postgenomic Life*. Durham, NC: Duke University Press.
Reardon, J. (2017), *The Postgenomic Condition*. Chicago: University of Chicago Press.
Rheinburger, H. and Müller-Wille, S. (2017), *From Genetics to Postgenomics*. Trans. Adam Bostanci. Chicago: University of Chicago Press.
Richardson, A. (2003), *Love and Eugenics in the Late Nineteenth Century: Rational Reproduction and the New Woman*. Oxford and New York: Oxford University Press.
Richardson, S. and Stevens, H. (eds) (2016), *Postgenomics: Perspectives on Biology After the Genome*. Durham, NC: Duke University Press.
Ridley, M. (1999), *Genome: An Autobiography of a Species in 23 Chapters*. London: HarperCollins.
Roberts, D. (1997), *Killing the Black Body: Race, Reproduction, and the Meaning of Liberty*. London: Vintage.
Robertson, B. J. (2018), *None of this is Normal: The Fiction of Jeff VanderMeer*. Minneapolis, MN: University of Minneapolis.
Robinson, C. (1983), *Black Marxism: The Making of the Black Radical Tradition*. Chapel Hill, NC: North Carolina University Press.
Romanek, M. (dir.) (2010), *Never Let Me Go*.
Roosth, S. and Schrader, A. (2012), 'Feminist Theory Out of Science'. *Differences* 23.3: 1–8.
Rose, H. (1994), *Love, Power and Knowledge*. Oxford: Blackwell.
Rose, H. and Rose, S. (2012), *Genes, Cells and Brains: The Promethean Promises of the New Biology*. London: Verso.
Rose, N. (2007), *The Politics of Life Itself: Biomedicine, Power, and Subjectivity in the Twenty-First Century*. Princeton, NJ: Princeton University Press.
Rose, N. (2013), 'Personalised Medicine: Promises, Problems and Perils of a New Paradigm for Healthcare'. *Procedia – Social and Behavioural Sciences* 77: 341–52.
Rouvroy, A. (2012), 'The End(s) of Critique: Data Behaviourism vs. Due Process'. In: M. Hildebrandt and K. De Vries (eds), *Privacy, Due Process and the Computational Turn*. London: Routledge. 143–68.

Rouvroy, A. and Berns, T. (2013), 'Algorithmic Governmentality and Prospects of Emancipation'. Trans. Elizabeth Libbrecht. *Réseaux* 177: 163–96.

Rudling, P. A. (2014), 'Eugenics and Racial Biology in Sweden and the USSR: Contacts Across the Baltic Sea'. *Canadian Bulletin of Medical History* 31.1: 41–75.

Rush-Cooper, N. (2019), 'Nuclear Landscape: Tourism, Embodiment and Exposure in the Chernobyl Zone'. *Cultural Geographies* 27.2: 217–35.

Rutherford, A. (2020), *How to Argue with a Racist: History, Science, Race, and Reality*. London: Weidenfeld and Nicolson.

Saini, A. (2019), *Superior: The Return of Race Science*. London: Fourth Estate.

Saini, A. (2020), 'Stereotype Threat'. *Lancet* 395.10237: 1604–5.

Sancho, M. G. (2012), *Biology, Computing, and the History of Molecular Sequencing*. London, Palgrave.

Scannapieco, M. and Jackson, S. (1996), 'Kinship Care: The African American Respose to Family Preservation'. *Social Work* 41.2: 190–6.

Schmeink, L. (2016), *Biopunk Dystopias: Genetic Engineering, Society, and Science Fiction*. Liverpool: Liverpool University Press.

Sealey-Huggins, L. (2018), 'The Climate Crisis is a Racist Crisis: Structural Racism, Inequality and Climate Change'. In: A. Johnson, R. Joseph-Salisbury and B. Kamunge (eds), *The Fire Now: Anti-racist Scholarship in Times of Explicit Racial Violence*. London: Zed Books. 99–113.

Sedgwick, E. (1990), *Epistemology of the Closet*. Berkeley, CA: University of California Press.

Sell, A. W. (2018), 'The War of Terroir: Biology as (unstable) Space in Jeff VanderMeer's Southern Reach Trilogy'. *antae* 5.1: 86–100.

Seregny, S. J. (1991), 'Peasants and politics: peasant unions during the 1905 revolution'. In: E. Mann and T. Mixter, *Peasant Economy, Culture, and Politics of European Russia*. 1800–1921, 341–77.

Serres, M. (1995), *The Natural Contract*. Trans. Elizabeth MacArthur and William Paulson. Ann Arbor, MI: University of Michigan Press.

Shapiro, S. (2018), 'Foucault, Neoliberalism, Algorithmic Governmentality, and the Loss of Liberal Culture'. In: L. Kennedy and S. Shapiro (eds), *Neoliberalism and Contemporary American Literature*. Lebanon, NH: Dartmouth College Press. 43–72.

Sharpe, C. (2016), *In the Wake: On Blackness and Being*. Durham, NC: Duke University Press.

Shelley, M. (2003 [1823]), *Frankenstein: Or, the Modern Prometheus*. London: Penguin.

Shevchenko, V. A. (1999), 'On the Genetic Risks from Exposure of Human Populations to Radiation'. In: E. B. Burlakova (ed.), *Consequences of the Chernobyl Catastrophe on Human Health*. Commack, NY: Nova Science Pubs Inc.

Simone, A. (2018), *Improvised Lives: Rhythms of Endurance in an Urban South*. London: Polity.

Skloot, R. (2010), *The Immortal Life of Henrietta Lacks*. London: Pan.

Slonczewski, J. and Levy, M. (2003), 'Science Fiction and the Life Sciences'. In: E. James and F. Mendlesohn, *The Cambridge Companion to Science Fiction*. Cambridge: Cambridge University Press. 174–85.

Smith, A. (2011 [1759]), *The Theory of Moral Sentiments*. Gutenberg Publishers.

Smith, J. M. and Price, G. R. (1973), 'The Logic of Animal Conflict'. *Nature* 246: 15–18.

Spade, D. and Willse, C. (2014), 'Sex, Gender and War in a Age of Multicultural Imperialism'. *QED: A Journal in GLBQT Worldmaking* 1.1: 5–29.

Speckhard, A. (2005), 'Psycho-Social and Physical Outcomes of Technological Disaster: Information as a Traumatic Stressor'. In: N. Berkowitz and L. Berkowitz, *A Chernobyl Reader*. Madison, WI: University of Wisconsin Press. Accessed online 21 March 2020: https://www.researchgate.net/publication/254361083_Psycho-Social_Physical_Outcomes_of_Technological_Disaster_Information_as_a_Traumatic_Stressor

Spillers, H. (1987), 'Mama's Baby, Papa's Maybe: An American Grammar Book'. *Diacritics* 17.2: 64–81.

Squier, S. M. (2003), *Liminal Lives: Imagining the Human at the Frontiers of Biomedicine*. Durham, NC: Duke University Press.

Squier, S. M. (2017), *Epigenetic Landscapes*. Durham, NC: Duke University Press.

Stack, C. B. (1974), *All Our Kin: Strategies for Survival in a Black Community*. New York: Basic Books.

Stallard, M. and de Groot, J. (2020), '"Things Are Coming Out That are Questionable, We Never Knew About": DNA and the New Family History'. *Journal of Family History* 45.3: 274–94.

Stengers, I. (2010), *Cosmopolitics I*. Trans. Roberto Bonnono. Minneapolis, MN: The University of Minnesota Press.

Stephens, S. (1987), 'Chernobyl Fallout: A Hard Rain for the Sami'. *Cultural Survival Quarterly Magazine*. Accessed online 27 June 2020: https://www.culturalsurvival.org/publications/cultural-survival-quarterly/chernobyl-fallout-hard-rain-sami

Strugatsky, A. and Strugatsky, B. (2012 [1972]), *Roadside Picnic*. Trans. Olena Bormashenko. London: Gollancz.

Sukhikh, I. (1989), 'Pravdy ne mozhet byt' slishkom mnogo: Nekotorye nabliudeniia nad zhanrom. "Literature Obozrenie: Zhurnal Khudozhestvennoi Literatury"'. *Kritiki i Bibliografii* 2: 39–41.

Sulston, J. and Ferry, G. (2002), *The Common Thread: A Story of Science, Politics, Ethics and the Human Genome*. London: Bantam.

TallBear, K. (2013), *Native American DNA: Tribal Belonging and the False Promise of Genetic Science*. Minneapolis, MN: University of Minneapolis Press.

Tarkovsky, A. (dir.) (1979), *Stalker*.

Thacker, E. (2005), *The Global Genome*. Cambridge, MA: Harvard University Press.

Thacker, E. (2013), 'Biophilosophy for the 21st Century'. In: A. Kroker and M. Kroker (eds), *Critical Digital Studies: A Reader*. Toronto: University of Toronto Press. 132–42.

VanderMeer, J. (2014a), *Annihilation*. London: Fourth Estate.

VanderMeer, J. (2014b), *Authority*. London: Fourth Estate.
VanderMeer, J. (2014c), *Acceptance*. London: Fourth Estate.
Venter, J. C. (2007), *A Life Decoded: My Genome, My Life*. London: Penguin.
Waddington, C. H. (2014 [1957]), *The Strategy of the Genes*. London: Routledge.
Wallerstein, I. (2006), *World Systems Analysis: An Introduction*. Durham, NC: Duke University Press.
Warner, M. (1991), 'Introduction: Fear of a Queer Planet'. *Social Text* 29.1: 3–17.
Watson, J. (1968), *The Double Helix: A Personal Account of the Discovery of the Structure of DNA*. New York: Atheneum Press.
Watson, J. (2003), *DNA: The Secret of Life*. London: Arrow Books.
Weheliye, A. (2014), *Habeas Victus: Racialising Assemblages, Biopolitics, and Black Feminist Theories of the Human*. Durham, NC: Duke University Press.
Wevers, R. (2019), 'Decolonial Aesthesis and the Museum: An Interview with Rolando Vázquez Melken'. *Stedelijk Studies* 8: 1–11.
Wheeler, W. (2006), *The Whole Creature: Complexity, Biosemiotics and the Evolution of Culture*. London: Lawrence and Wishart.
Wheeler, W. (2016), *Expecting the Earth: Life, Culture, Biosemiotics*. London: Lawrence and Whishart.
Wilson, E. (1975), *Sociobiology: The New Synthesis*. Cambridge, MA: Harvard University Press.
Wilson, T. W. and Grim, C. E. (1991), 'Biohistory of Slavery and Blood Pressure Differences in Blacks Today: A Hypothesis'. *Hypertension* 171: 122–8.
Worsthorne, P. (1959), 'Class and Conflict in British Foreign Policy'. *Foreign Affairs* 37.3: 419–31.
Wynter, S. (1994), '1492: A New World View'. In: V. L. Hyatt and R. M. Nettleford, *Race Discourse and the Origin of the Americas: A New World View*. Washington, DC: Smithsonian Books.
Wynter, S. (2003), 'Unsettling the Coloniality of Being/Power/Truth/Freedom: Towards the Human, After Man, Its Overrepresentation—An Argument'. *The New Centennial Review* 3.3: 257–337.
Wynter, S. (2006), 'On How We Mistook the Map for a Territory and Imprisoned Ourselves in Our Unbearable Wrongness of Being, of Désêtre'. In: L. Gordon and J. A. Gordon (eds), *Not Only The Master's Tools: African-American Studies in Theory and Practice*. Boulder, CO: Paradigm Publishers. 107–68.
Yaroshinskaya, A. (1995), *Chernobyl: The Forbidden Truth*. Trans. Michèle Kahn and Julia Sallabank. Lincoln, NE: University of Nebraska Press.
Yong, E. (2016), *I Contain Multitudes: The Microbes Within Us and a Grander View of Life*. London: Vintage.

# Index

abdifference   179, 180
abrasion   130, 131, 145
*Acceptance*   18, 172
Acker, Kathy   44
adaptation   55, 56, 58, 60, 67, 77, 116, 152, 156–61
aesthetic forms   55, 108, 124, 151
agriculture   3, 55, 59, 62
  agricultural production   56–8
Alexievich, Svetlana   18, 151
algorithmic governmentality   6, 87, 111–18, 190
altruism   28–30
ambivalence   66, 67, 109, 122, 144, 148, 190
anatomy   130, 131
ancestors   121, 136, 137, 139, 144
ancestry   120–3, 126, 131–3, 135, 148
ancestry-making   122–4
Anglicanism   36, 40
Anglo American biology   9, 11
animals   24, 103, 106, 110
*Annihilation*   18, 172
anomaly/anomalies   157–8, 182
'Another's Memory'   17, 56
anti-colonial   139, 147
architecture   12, 67, 68, 104, 110, 115, 116, 122, 131, 182, 183
Arendt, Hannah   100
Arrighi, Giovanni   84
art   6, 97, 106–8
author/authorial/authority   18, 32, 33, 38–40, 91, 162, 163, 171–3, 181, 183
*Authority*   18, 172
autobiography   13, 14, 124

Bal, Mieke   12
Baptist, Edward E.   134
Barad, Karen   155
Bataille, Georges   8
Bauer, Susanne   62
Beer, Gillian   4, 6, 173

behaviour   16, 21, 25, 28, 31–3, 103, 105, 169, 171
belonging   20, 120, 126, 133, 134, 136, 138, 140, 145, 148, 160
Benjamin, Ruha   99, 124
Benjamin, Walter   8
Bennett, Jane   155
Bentley, Nancy   131
Bergson, Henri   8
Berns, Thomas   117
Big Genomics   7
Big Science   75, 92, 152
Bildungsroman   97, 108
biobanks   7
biocapital   6
biocentrism/biocentric   88, 155
biological citizenship   165
biological families   142, 192
biological life   1, 72, 90, 153, 170
biological processes   21, 28–30, 61, 165, 170
biological warfare   12, 17, 55, 63, 64
  programmes   17, 55, 63, 64
biological weapons   56, 63, 64, 71
biologist   170–8, 180, 181, 186, 187
biomatter   3, 4, 8, 85, 93, 104, 114, 116, 118, 127, 129
biomedical un-knowledge   166
biomorphism   161, 168, 186
biopower   22
biosemiotics   151
Black horror/*horror noire*   125–30, 192
Black studies   125
*The Blind Watchmaker*   159
Bodin, Per-Arne   56, 81
*The Book of Knowledge of Ingenious Mechanical Devices*   28
border   35, 46, 67, 68, 169, 172, 174, 182, 183, 185, 192
bourgeois individualism   15
Bradway, Tyler   52
*Brave New World*   112
Buckley, Jerome Hamilton   85

Buck-Morss, Susan  65
Bulychev, Kir  17, 56, 74–81
Burbridge, Arthur  73
Burgess Shale  157, 158
Bürkner, Daniel  154
Butler, Judith  36, 37

capitalism  2, 5, 8, 9, 11, 23, 26, 27, 125, 127, 130, 166, 168
Capitalocene  16
care  11, 25, 28, 41, 53, 85, 127, 129, 139, 145, 151
Carroll, Rachel  101
*C. elegans*  91, 95
Césaire, Aimé  139
Chan, Edward  44, 49
Chandler, Alfred  84
Chandler, Mario  132
character development  102, 105, 179, 180, 189, 191
characterization  189–93
  transitional  172–88
characters  11, 12, 34, 80, 105, 106, 140, 143, 173, 178–80, 184, 185, 191
chattel slavery  133
Chen, Mel  72
Chernobyl  18, 151–6, 160, 162, 163, 165–70, 175
*Chernobyl: History of a Tragedy*  167
*Chernobyl Prayer*  18, 151, 154, 160, 162, 163, 175, 185, 186, 191
  mutation and fragmentation in 162–72
Chernobyl Syndrome  154
children  67, 73, 112, 113, 129, 134, 144, 147, 163, 165, 169
Christian/Christianity  146
chronology  14, 16, 24, 25, 57, 68, 100, 144
  chronological time  4, 38, 42, 86, 100, 111, 145, 169
  chronopolitics  48–50, 52
citizenship  88, 92, 98, 125, 153, 165
Clare, Eli  42, 47
classical genetics  159
climate change  11, 15, 148, 149, 156
cloning/clones  16, 17, 56, 57, 74–6, 78, 87, 88, 92, 94, 98, 99, 101–2, 105, 109–12, 129, 130

code  3–5, 16, 21, 67, 90, 98, 100, 115, 120, 133, 152, 178, 183
collective adaptation  58
collectives/collectivity  10, 11, 15, 40–2, 55–8, 61, 80, 81, 123, 139, 142, 162, 164
collective testimony  162
communication  36, 67, 72, 112, 174
communities  14, 16, 39, 42, 60, 63, 77, 131, 134, 137, 142, 151, 153, 167, 168, 189–93
complexity  1, 4, 14, 18, 19, 90, 92, 143, 149, 174, 183
contamination  66, 70, 153, 154, 163, 169, 172, 174, 177–9, 182, 183
contingency/contingent  49, 71, 96, 138, 158, 159, 161, 165, 173, 187, 192
continuity  120, 122, 169
control society  39
COVID-19 pandemic  10
Crick, Francis  21
criminalization  124
critiques  5, 14, 89, 101, 117, 118, 132
Csicsery-Ronay, Istvan  56
cultivation  17, 55–9, 61, 67, 69, 71, 73, 76, 81, 182, 183
  dreamworlds  55–81
  humans  60–3
  metaphor  17, 67, 182
culture  14, 19, 45, 55, 66, 70, 120, 122, 127, 153, 182

Darwin, Charles  38, 60
data behaviourism  88
Data  3, 5, 7, 8, 18, 22, 24, 26, 42, 46, 87–9, 93, 111, 112, 117, 167, 177, 190
  Big Data  7, 46, 88, 111, 161
data-body  87, 88, 112, 114, 117, 118
data collection  188, 190
Davidson, Guy  41
Dawkins, Richard  16, 28, 30, 159
death  22–4, 68, 70, 72–4, 80, 81, 98, 99, 117, 128, 185
  dying  107, 162, 181, 185
Debaise, Didier  5
deferral  99, 101–4, 110
de Groot, Jerome  126
deindustrialization  16, 21–53

Delany, Samuel 17, 23, 41–53
Deleuze, Gilles 8, 23
detective fiction 79
development 21, 24, 48, 55, 62, 63, 76, 81, 84, 93, 95, 103, 105, 117, 180
  developmentalism 41, 45, 53, 125
  developmental time 87, 100, 144, 169
diaspora 121, 125, 138, 139, 191
disappearance 189–93
disaster 25, 151, 153, 154, 162, 163, 166, 169, 170, 173, 174
displacements 16, 120, 122, 143, 156, 173
dissolution 43, 52, 74, 163
DNA 21, 84, 86, 87, 92, 94, 96–8, 112, 114, 126, 132, 137, 159, 192
*DNA: The Secret of Life* 83
double helix 21, 25, 63, 67, 89, 94, 97, 100, 111, 115, 116, 161
*The Double Helix* 97
*Dreamworld and Catastrophe* 65
dreamworlds, cultivating 55–81
Du Bois, W. E. B. 139

*E. coli* 89
ecology 150, 158, 179, 180, 186
ecosystem 151, 158, 171, 174, 181, 191
electricity 27, 175
emergence/emergent 10, 14, 17, 20, 22, 24, 34, 151, 159, 160, 165, 175, 191
empire 34, 35, 37, 63, 74, 148
enclosure 78, 111, 153, 155, 160, 161, 168
enslavement 102, 115, 125, 127, 128, 130–4, 143–5, 190, 191
environment 3, 49, 56, 57, 60, 62, 67, 73, 76, 80, 149, 150, 157, 174, 184
epigenetics 19, 69, 149, 150, 156, 159, 160, 182, 183
era of genomics 3, 63, 98
erasure 100, 125
*Essay on the Principle of Population* 37
ethics 93–9
ethnonationalism/ethnonational 11, 15, 84, 123
eugenics/eugenic ideology 9–11, 17, 37, 40, 61, 69, 112, 119
evidence 6, 7, 48, 114–17, 120, 121, 123, 124, 133, 154, 162, 164

evolution 32, 33, 59, 61, 62, 77, 157–61, 189, 191
evolutionary history 1, 16, 22, 95, 192
evolutionary theory 22, 23
evolutionary time 67, 68
exchange 2, 3, 45, 53, 63, 64, 98, 106, 128, 136, 160
exclusion 24, 36, 37, 116, 125, 131, 139, 156, 164, 165, 175
experimentation and experiments 8, 12, 17, 58, 61–3, 71, 75, 129, 151, 156
exposure 18, 71, 73, 77, 108, 152, 154, 161, 169, 191
expression 1, 41, 44, 47, 48, 52, 53, 106, 110, 113
expropriation 132, 133
extraction 14, 15, 23, 67, 73, 100, 105, 127–9, 154, 155, 160

family 35, 37, 45, 68, 85, 124, 126, 127, 130–3, 143, 145–7, 169, 171
family history 97, 124, 126, 132, 136, 143, 146, 169
family origins 124
family tree 143, 147, 169
Fanon, Frantz 139
fantasy 69, 105, 106, 108, 130, 136, 183, 187, 192
film noir 111
fingerprint/fingerprinting 97
flexibility 158
Fordism/Fordist production 43, 113
Fortun, Mike 5, 15, 91, 123
Foucault, Michel 23, 26, 101
fossils 95, 157, 158, 187
*Frankenstein* 78
Freeman, Elizabeth 48
Fuller, Steve 10

Galton, Francis 37, 38
game theory 25
*Gattaca* 17, 84
  and algorithmic governmentality 111–18
gender 10, 31, 44, 46, 49–51, 111, 113
gender reassignment 44
gene 26–34
genealogical time 169, 170
genealogy 118, 119, 121, 122, 125–7, 131–4, 142, 143, 146, 148, 191

genetic ancestry testing/tests 120–4, 126, 132, 134, 136–7, 140, 142
genetic basis 31–3, 74
genetic disease 6, 86, 112
genetic editing 3, 20
genetics 9, 16, 17, 25, 26, 46, 47, 55, 62, 64, 86, 90, 115, 125–7
genetic structure 167, 170
genetic technologies 124, 126
genogeography 74
  'Another's Memory' 74–81
genome sequencing 7, 90, 135
genomic data 8, 170
genomic information 2, 3, 90, 151
genomics 2–7, 11, 15, 19, 20, 84, 86, 88, 90, 94, 96, 119, 123, 189, 190
genomic technologies 95, 118, 125
genre 12, 15, 79, 125–7, 130, 131, 152, 154, 162, 163, 189–93
*Get Out* 125
Ghost Bird 176, 177, 180, 181
ghosts 130, 140, 144, 182, 184
Gill, Josie 102
Gilroy, Paul 14, 120
globalization 19, 84, 134, 189
Global North 19, 156
Global South 5, 11, 19, 31, 160
Godzilla 168
Gofman, John 166
Gorky, Maxim 60
Gould, Stephen Jay 9, 141, 157
governance 21, 23, 26, 29, 30, 32, 33, 37, 112, 113, 149, 152, 156
grammar 3, 4, 49, 88, 109, 110, 171
Greenidge, Kaitlyn 121
Griffin, Gabriele 109
Grim, Clarence 119
Guattari, Félix 8
Gutman, Herbert 133
Gyasi, Yaa 18, 120, 143–8

Habermas, Jürgen 85
habitation 51, 160, 171, 191
*Haemophilus influenzae* 95
Hailsham 99–103, 105
Haley, Alex 126
Hanson, Clare 4, 33
Haraway, Donna 155
Hardt, Michael 29
Harlem Renaissance 124

Harrison, M. John 109
Hartman, Saidiya 18, 120, 135–43
HeLa cells 128–30
Helmreich, Stefan 163
Helstrom, Bron 41
*Hereditary Genius* 38
heteronormativity 41, 101, 102
Hiroshima 152, 167
historical objectivity 52
historiographies 134, 144
Hobbes, Thomas 59
Hoffmeyer, Jesper 150, 151
Hollerith, Herman 28
home 31, 34, 64, 68, 113, 117, 123, 135–8, 144, 147
*Homegoing* 18, 120, 143–8
*Homo sapiens* 158, 191
human beings 2, 3, 85, 113
human bodies 24, 98, 128, 136, 150, 168
human genome 1, 6, 83, 89, 93, 96, 111, 159
human genome diversity 121, 190
Human Genome Diversity Project 190
Human Genome Project 17, 18, 83, 86–94, 96, 97, 119
  metaphors of 89–93
humanity 10, 14, 17, 20, 50, 57, 68, 71, 119, 122, 155, 160, 191
human life 11, 19, 68, 91, 99, 109, 144, 164
Hundarova, Tamara 154, 168
Huntington, Samuel 51
Huxley, Aldous 112

illegibility 8, 18, 154, 159, 163, 175, 176, 178
*The Immortal Life of Henrietta Lacks* 127
improvisation 122, 156
industrial action 30
industrialization 57, 65, 79
influence 19, 61–3, 67–9, 93, 134, 149, 150, 152, 153, 161, 184
information 1–3, 6, 7, 23, 24, 44–6, 48, 63, 64, 86, 164
infrastructure 9, 57, 63, 64, 69, 75, 98, 115, 146, 151, 161, 167, 168, 173, 185
inheritance 24, 25, 32, 57, 62, 140, 142, 145, 149, 156, 158, 159, 165

International Biological Programme   76
internationalism   121, 125, 133
*Intimsphäre*   131
investment   6, 14, 15, 20, 64, 87, 95, 126, 137, 149, 158
invisibility   154
Ishiguro, Kazuo   17, 84
Ivanov, Viacheslav   65

Jablonka, Eve   159
Jacob, Francois   89
James, Joy   127
Jim Crow   115, 147
Junk DNA   1, 95, 159

Keller, Evelyn Fox   6, 7, 22, 86
Keynesian economics   21
Kin   28, 57, 131, 134, 136, 138, 142
kinlessness   130–5
kinship   17, 18, 120–2, 125, 126, 130–4, 139, 140, 143
Kirksey, S. Eben   163
knowledge   4, 101, 105, 129, 146, 147, 161, 165, 168, 180, 181
Kropotkin, Pëtr   59, 60

laboratory/laboratories   17, 64, 66, 75, 78, 83–5, 87, 89–91, 94–7, 113–15, 117, 128, 129, 149
labour   8, 26, 27, 31, 58–60, 72, 77–80, 100–3
Lacan, Jacques   3
Lacks, Henrietta   127–30
lactose operon   89
*laissez-faire* liberalism   32
Lamarck, Jean-Baptiste   62
Lamb, Marion   159
Lambert, Michael   37
landscape   24, 57, 77, 80, 98, 116, 171, 172, 176, 184, 185
Laughlin, Robert   159
Lazzarato, Maurizio   111
legal/legality   5, 14, 30, 88, 94, 121, 123, 132
Lessing, Doris   16, 23, 34
Levina, E. S.   64
Levine, Philippa   37
Levins, Richard   9
Levy, Michael   12
Lewontin, Richard   9, 157

lexical dissonance   109, 110
liberal humanism   8, 12, 22, 99–101, 120, 124, 140, 142, 145
liberalism   21, 23, 29, 32, 33, 38, 93, 102, 119, 131, 190
*A Life Decoded: My Genome, My Life*   83
lifeforms   153, 154, 172, 173
*Liminal Lives*   12
Lindee, M. Susan   13, 166
lineage   16, 18, 24, 25, 118, 120, 123, 124, 131, 133, 136, 138, 140, 142, 143
living processes   8, 30, 150
locality   153, 181
Lock, Margaret   150
'The Logic of Animal Conflict'   24
*Lose Your Mother: A Journey Along the Atlantic Slave Route*   18, 120, 135–43
loss   79, 88, 122, 133, 139, 142, 156, 164, 180, 182, 187
Lowe, Lisa   22, 120, 161
Lysenko, Trofim   55, 56, 61, 62
Lysenkoism   55

McGahey, Michael   27
machinic enslavement   111, 115, 190
McKittrick, Katherine   121
Malabou, Catherine   19, 150
Malthus, Thomas   22, 31, 37
Malthusianism   58, 59
mapping   26, 66, 121, 156
Marchesini, Irina   162
Margulis, Lynn   2, 150
marriage   176–8, 187
Marx, Karl   8
mathematically-enabled knowability   26
Mazumdar, Pauline   11
Mbembe, Achille   23
Means Coleman, Robin   125
Melken, Rolando Vázquez   13
Meloni, Maurizio   149
memoir   17, 83, 85, 87, 89–91, 95–7, 99, 103, 105, 109, 138
   laboratory and   83–118
*The Memoirs of a Survivor*   16–17, 23, 34
   overpopulation and whiteness in   34–41
memory   25, 73, 74, 78–81, 87, 88, 123, 124, 168, 169, 172, 178
The Middle Passage   126, 190

miscegenation 115
mismanagement 153, 165, 166
The Modern Synthesis 24
molecular biology 6–8, 21, 55, 56, 86, 91, 92, 127, 128, 149, 150, 158, 159
Monod, Jacques 89
Moore, Jason 16, 155, 166
Müller, Ruth 149
Müller-Wille, Staffan 88
multicultural imperialism 50, 51
multiplicity 8, 10, 21, 149, 163
mutations 63, 67, 90, 158, 159, 162, 167–8
mutual aid 17, 57–61, 171
*Mutual Aid: A Factor of Evolution* 59
mythic time 170

Nagasaki 152, 167
narratives 5–7, 11, 12, 18, 20, 33, 34, 42, 44, 48, 60, 67, 80, 104, 108, 109, 119–22, 124, 132, 143, 154, 173, 189, 191–3
narrative space 48, 173
natural selection 22, 24, 25, 28, 32, 58, 61, 62, 119, 123, 157, 158, 161
necropolitics/necropolitical 23, 26, 34, 130
negotiations 2, 5, 25, 31, 37, 93, 94, 125
Negri, Antonio 29
*Négritude* 124, 139
Nelkin, Dorothy 13
Nelson, Alondra 123, 126, 132
neoliberalism 6, 21, 33, 91, 93, 100, 102, 138
*Never Let Me Go* 17, 84
  end of development and 99–111
new feminist materialism 155
New Soviet Person 55, 61
Niccols, Andrew 17, 84
Niewöhner, Jörg 150
Novas, Carlos 98

overpopulation 11, 23, 30, 33–41, 60
ownership 58, 95, 96, 100

pair/pairs 4, 38, 88, 94, 98, 105, 110, 116, 117, 184
Pan-Africanism/Pan-African 121, 124–5, 134, 138, 139, 142, 148

Pandey, Anjali 109, 110
Patel, Raj 16
Patterson, Orlando 133
patent/patenting 2, 60, 92, 94, 96, 97
Pearson, Wendy Gay 44, 45
Peele, Jordan 125
Peirce, Charles Sanders 8
peripheral imaginaries 160, 161, 164
periphery/peripheral 17, 18, 31, 108, 113, 115, 129, 130, 151, 153, 154, 156, 160–2, 164, 166, 167, 170, 172, 180, 188–91
personality 130, 131, 178, 179
personhood 14, 135, 140
Petryna, Adriana 165
phenotype/phenotypic 31, 32, 49, 69, 70, 84, 147, 149
Phillips, Jim 27
plantation 18, 144, 145
plasticity 50, 149
Plokhy, Serhii 154, 167
postgenomic era 2, 18, 149, 152, 159, 188, 189, 191
postgenomic narratives 191
postgenomic/postgenomic condition 2, 9, 18, 149, 151–6, 159, 170, 188, 189, 191
postgenomics 9, 18, 19, 119, 151, 156, 158
posthumanism 155
postsocialism/postsocialist 63
postwar industrial science 152
precarity 68, 164, 165
precision genomics 7
precision medicine 10, 87, 92, 170, 192
Price, George 24
profit 93–9
proof 6, 58, 120, 123, 133, 186
property 58, 60, 85, 90, 93, 95, 100, 124, 131, 132, 134, 140, 171–3
proximity 52, 70–3, 146, 147, 149, 152, 153, 174, 177, 186, 187, 191

queer/queerness 17, 41, 51, 52, 189

rabbit hole 157
race science 147
racialization 5
racism 163
radiation 62, 152–4, 163, 165–9

radioactive/radioactivity   153, 154, 156, 165, 166
Rajan, Kaushik Sunder   3
Rawls, John   31
realism   12, 108, 192
Reardon, Jenny   2, 8, 126
reduction/reductionism   2, 4, 8, 9, 19, 22, 46, 50, 75, 106, 107, 150–2, 157, 159, 183
reference genome   6, 92, 94
relevance   19, 49, 60, 61, 78, 81, 86, 135, 150, 159, 169
reparation/reparative   121, 123, 124, 130–5, 148, 186
repetition   11, 108–10, 122, 134, 140, 144, 155
reproduction   8, 24–6, 75, 76, 78, 97, 130, 158, 160, 189, 190
resources/resource   11, 14, 15, 22–3, 29, 31, 34, 36, 37, 40, 55, 58, 60, 78, 84, 99, 145, 160, 161, 165, 168
Rheinburger, Hans-Jörg   88
Richardson, Angelique   11
Ridley, Matt   13
*Roadside Picnic*   17, 56, 63–74
Roberts, Dorothy   123, 130, 133
Robertson, Benjamin J.   179
romance   130–5
Roosth, Sophia   20
*Roots*   126
roots seekers   120
Rose, Hilary   7, 86
Rose, Nikolas   11, 98
Rose, Steven   7
Rouvroy, Antoinette   87, 88, 117
Rush-Cooper, Nick   154
Russian biology   17, 57, 58, 61, 62
Rutherford, Adam   93

Sagan, Dorion   2
Saini, Angela   10
Sancho, Miguel García   86, 92
scale of micrology   192
Schmeink, Lars   6
Schrader, Astrid   20
science fiction   79, 129, 162, 192
Sealey-Huggins, Leon   11

secrecy   63, 153, 154, 164, 175, 176
Sedgwick, Eve   101
Sedov, A. E.   64
self-fashioning   17, 53, 87, 117, 180, 189, 190
selfish gene   21–53
*The Selfish Gene*   16, 115
selfishness   28–31, 33, 108
Sell, Aran Ward   174
semi-periphery   18, 31, 153
sequencing/sequence   1–3, 6, 83, 86–90, 92–6, 98, 110–11, 115, 117, 157–9
settler colonialism   11, 125
Shapiro, Stephen   26
Sharpe, Christina   122
Shelley, Mary   78
Simone, AbdouMaliq   16, 145, 164
Skloot, Rebecca   127
Slonczewsky, Joan   12
Smith, John Maynard   24
social capital   147
*The Social Contract*   29
social life   9, 14, 132, 143, 160
*The Social Life of DNA*   132
social mobility   101, 102
social organization   19, 23–6, 31, 32, 34, 35, 39, 41, 53, 142
*Sociobiology*   31
sociobiology/sociobiological   9, 15, 16, 25, 29, 31–4, 45, 46, 50, 53, 127, 134, 157, 189
sociogeny/sociogenetic   156, 180
soil   55, 142, 163, 164
Southern Reach trilogy   172–88
sovereignty   14, 59, 84, 85, 152, 160–3, 165, 173
Soviet biology   19, 55, 56, 58, 61, 62, 67, 73, 76, 83, 191
Soviet Thaw   56, 63
Spade, Dean   50
spandrel   157
species   14, 24, 28, 29, 43, 44, 59, 148, 149, 155, 156, 158, 160, 161, 186
Speckhard, Anne   164
speculative ancestry   119–48
speculative fiction (sf)   12, 17
Spencer, Herbert   59

Spillers, Hortense   5, 128, 136
Squier, Susan Merrill   12
Stack, Carol   133
Stallard, Matthew   126
Stephens, Sharon   153
strike   26–34
Strugatsky, Arkady   17, 56
Strugatsky, Boris   17, 56
substitution   3, 30, 53, 98, 105, 106
Sukhikh, Igor'   162
Sulston, John   95, 96
surrealism   106, 108
surrogacy   105
surveillance   23, 26, 33, 34, 41, 50, 124, 183
survival   28–31, 33, 35, 60, 128, 129, 142, 151–3, 160, 162
survival machines   28–31, 33, 189
survival of the fittest   11
Suslov, Mikhail   56, 81
Synko, Vasyl   167
systems biology   4

TallBear, Kim   121
Tarkovsky, Andrei   67
Terranova, Fabrizio   5
terroir   181, 182
testimony   162, 170
Thacker, Eugene   3, 15
time of enslavement   144, 145
time-zones   51, 164, 170
toxic infrastructure   149–88
toxicity/toxins   63, 72, 148, 149, 151, 156, 159, 191
The Transatlantic Slave Trade   18, 118, 122, 129
transition   22, 23, 38, 41, 42, 46, 49–51, 53, 71, 98, 100, 180
transitional characterization   172–88
transport   34, 44, 74, 89, 97, 98, 139, 149

trauma   38, 119, 120, 162–4, 170
*Trouble on Triton*   17, 23
   brackets and choice   41–53
Tuskegee   126, 128

uncanny   71, 184, 185, 187, 192
uncertainty   3, 7, 21, 50, 52, 66, 67, 70, 164, 166, 174, 175, 180
US   125

vaccine   128
VanderMeer, Jeff   18, 67, 151, 173
Venter, J. Craig   83
vernacular   131
vernalisation   62
Vitruvian Man   88, 93–9
vulnerability   115, 127, 154

Waddington, Conrad Hal   76, 77
Wallerstein, Immanuel   19
Warner, Michael   51
Watson, James   21, 83, 97
Weheliye, Alexander   14, 99
weird fiction   179
welfare   10, 16, 22, 23, 25, 29, 36, 37, 40, 91, 93–9, 101, 165
Wheeler, Wendy   19, 150, 151
whiteness   34–41
Willse, Craig   50
Wilson, Edward O.   31
Wilson, Thomas   119
witness/witnessing   140, 162
*Wonderful Life*   157
workforce   76, 77, 113
world-system   18, 83, 93, 150, 153, 156
Wynter, Sylvia   22, 155

X-Files, The   112

Yaroshinskaya, Alla   166
Yong, Ed   2

www.ingramcontent.com/pod-product-compliance
Lightning Source LLC
Chambersburg PA
CBHW072233290426
44111CB00012B/2073